The Time in Tavel

Brewster Chamberlin

For Andrea —
O that old slap the baguette
on the book trick!
with love,
Brewster

Key West, 22.IV.10

BY THE SAME AUTHOR

A Piece of Paris. The Grand XIVth. Illustrations by
Gregory Masurovsky, photographs by Philippe Simon.
(1996)

*Paris Now and Then. Memoirs, Opinions, and a
Companion to the City of Light for the Literate Traveler*
(2002, rev. ed. 2004)

*Mediterranean Sketches. Fictions, Memories and
Metafictions* (2005)

Love's Poison and Other Poems, 2000-2005 (Limited
illustrated edition 2005)

Mario Sanchez: Once Upon a Way of Life (with Nance
Frank 2006)

A Chronology of the Life and Times of Lawrence Durrell
(2007)

*Situation Reports from the Emotional Equipoise.
Collected Poems 1959-2006.* (2007)

Radovic's Dilemma. A Mediterranean Thriller (2009)

THE TIME IN TAVEL

An Informal Illustrated Memoir of a Sojourn in Provence

by

Brewster Chamberlin

Il faut manger simplement et sainement.
-- Henri le Kroner, chef and resident
sage at the Hostellerie de Tavel

Everything is a question of time and
its defeat.
--Journal entry February 16, 1983

The Vineyard Press
Port Jefferson NY
2009

ISBN: 1-930067-74-7

First Edition

The Vineyard Press. Ltd.
106 Vineyard Place
Port Jefferson, NY 11777

Front cover: At the Abbaye de Sénanque, 1983,
photograph by Andrea Anderson
Back cover: At Le Provençal in Coral Gables, Florida,
2008, photograph by France Guillon
Unless otherwise noted all the photographs in this book
are by the author or Lynn-Marie Smith.

For our friends in the Midi

Denis and Dominique Constancias
of Montfavet (Vaucluse)

Edith and Natacha Fidler
And in memory of their husband and father Eugène
of Roussillon (Vaucluse)

Richard and Nicole Stiel
of Uzès (Gard)

Sylvette and Jean-Marie Berruyer
And in memory of their mother and mother-in-law
Marie-Louise Mourre
of Tavel and Villeneuve-lès-Avignon (Gard)

Sylvie Devaux-Sigayret
of the barge in the Rhône River and later Perpignon

Provence is a taste or more correctly a passion which once contracted cannot be cured.

James Pope-Hennessy: *Aspects of Provence* (1952)

It was a great pleasure to feel one's self in Provence again–the land where the silver grey earth is impregnated with the light of the sky.

Henry James: *A Little Tour in France* (1883)

Tavel? Tavel is a small village on a slope of land in the middle of the garrigues and vineyards the center of which is medieval, mon, medieval. They need some speed bumps there, mon, truly.

Patrice Glomokao in The Edge Bar, Avignon, 1953

There is something about the light that makes the sky of the Midi look higher, much higher than it does in the north.

Georges Braque

L'aïgo-boulido sauvo la vido.

Old Provençal proverb

Table of Contents

Il n'a pas inventé le fil à couper le
Beurre.

Old proverb translated in an
ancient dictionary as "He
will never set the Thames on
fire"!

Avant-propos

It seems to me to make more sense to organize these
memories both chronologically and, within the general
sequence of time passing, by subject, at least when
beginning to put them together. Later in the composition
the arrangement might be deranged into some other
structure, one with many digressions. After all, one of
the books read during the time in Tavel was *Tristram
Shandy* (and as far as one knows the book remains in the
box sitting in the old wine press room in the villa called
La Rose des Vents).

Fortunately my brother Dean kept the long letters I
sent him describing our life during our sojourn in the
Midi and who, some years ago when I first thought of
writing this memoir, sent me copies. These I have used
in conjunction with the journal I assiduously kept at the
time, thinking vaguely even then that I might some day
write about living there. I have also been able to read
some of the letters I wrote to friends and have spoken to
some of the people who visited us to pick bits and pieces
from their memories. My gratitude goes to all of them.

The temptation to simply print the letters and the journal entries with appropriate explanatory footnotes also raised its beguiling head and smiled seductively. But one of my alter egos who constrains my literary excesses, Eden, the Jamaican Perfect Bartender at The Edge Bar in Key West, growled in response to this idea, "No, no, no! There be awfully too many lacunae, mon, lacunae to annoy your readers. Give it to them straight, clear, chiseled lapidary phrases that anyone can understand, mon, and then they will buy your book, and *love you!*" Eden often exaggerates things beyond their proper proportions, but he is occasionally acutely correct in his judgments, and this was one of those times. Nonetheless, and despite his protests, I have included sections from both the letters and the old tattered, wine-soaked journals and notebooks that have traveled with us ever since the fates forced us to leave the Midi over 25 years ago.

Along those lines of thought, an entry from the journal on February 23, 1983, would be apropos here. "Can one 'learn' to write a journal which will be of some interest to oneself ten years hence, or must it be genetically determined? Surely Gide's Journals wouldn't have been published if his landlady had written them. But his concierge wouldn't have been able to write about dinner with Joyce or the hot afternoon with that young and willing Arab boy in Tangiers. (On the other hand, one can never tell about concierges – they too were young!)"

For fairly obvious reasons I have changed the names of some of the people who appear in the pages that follow. Some of the characters are typical of the region but are at least in part fictional. Others are all too real and I hope they are not offended. How can it be otherwise?

Once again I am pleased to thank my friend Richard Pine, director emeritus of the Durrell School of Corfu, for his close reading of the text, thus saving it from those devilish infelicities that inevitably creep in. Any of them that have snuck in the back gate are my responsibility alone.

And again I am grateful to the novelist and scholar Robert DeMaria, The Vineyard Press' founder and director, for taking on this memoir and seeing it through the press.

I gratefully and warmly thank Denis Constancias for his help in reconstructing the history of the Centre d'Étude Linguistique d'Avignon and other matters about the city.

Reconnection with friends one has not seen or heard from in 25 years is a heart-moving event. That the writing of this memoir has brought us once again in touch with Jean and Blair Williams is a small miracle for which Lynn-Marie and I are deeply grateful.

And it is to Lynn-Marie that I owe the deepest debit of gratitude. Her name does not appear on the title page but perhaps should; she has contributed greatly to the completion of this book: it literally could not have been completed without her participation.

Key West, August 2009

Prelude

Discussions and Decisions

It all began with a certain creeping metaphysical unease with my life, and the election in November 1980 of the movie actor Ronald Reagan to the presidency of the great American Republic. The unease had to do with a lack of time and energy to write the second volume of a novel about Berlin in the 20th century and the prospect of unemployment; the election eventually cost Lynn-Marie (LM) her job at the National Endowment for the Humanities (NEH).

I had spent the previous five years working for the Institut für Zeitgeschichte, the Munich-based Institute for Contemporary History, which along with the West German Federal Archives (Bundesarchiv) and other German state archives and historical institutes had negotiated an agreement with the US National Archives and Records Administration (NARS)[1] to catalogue the records of the Office of Military Government for Germany (United States), known by its acronym OMGUS[2], and microfilm the most important of them to make the documents available in Germany so young

---

[1] The institution is now called the National Archives and Records Administration (NARA), the bulk of the holdings are currently in the College Park, Maryland, facility.

[2] Over the course of the project, those who worked on it became known as "OMGEESE", the singular of which, of course, was "OMGOOSE".

1

scholars there dealing with the 1945-49 period did not have to make the expensive trip to Washington to study the files. My job was to direct the project for the German side working with the NARS project director, the late John Mendelsohn, whom I had known since graduate school in the late 1960s. When that cataloguing project ended I spent a year doing similar work for the West Berlin State Archives (Landesarchiv) with my friend Jürgen Wetzel who later became the director of that admirable institution, in the records of the US Army's occupation government in that divided city so well populated with fictional and real shadowy types connected in one way or another with espionage and the Cold War.

In 1977, LM had arrived in Washington from her position as founding executive director of the Minnesota Humanities Commission to work for two years at NEH. She was not there very long before she determined that she preferred the life and work in the Nation's Capital to that of St. Paul, Minnesota, where she had spent the first 30 years of her life. We met through my long-term friend from graduate school, Steve Goodell, who also then worked at NEH, at the end of October 1978 on the evening of the day my divorce from my first wife became final. In May 1980 we spent two weeks traveling in France (a night in Avignon allowed us a brief glimpse of the city; the hotel room was decorated in the New Orleans bordello style popular in France) and northeastern Spain, after which we realized the Fates had meant us for each other and we've been together ever since.

By the end of the spring in 1982 I had finished the Berlin job and the Reagan sweep-out brush had reached NEH in the form of the gambling addict and pontificator of conservative morality, William Bennett, whom the White House appointed chairman of the institution with the mandate to dismantle populist and other non-elitist programs, including LM's projects, and fund only those programs congenial to the ideological rightwing. (Ironically, Bennett had received considerable funding from LM's division while he directed the National Humanities Center in North Carolina.) In essence they fired her, though they clothed the dismissal in the camouflage of cutting back funds for her programs but telling her she could remain at a much lower grade and salary for an undefined but clearly not lengthy period of time. Of course she resigned.

Many years before I became a quasi-academic I entertained the thought of spending my life writing novels, poems, short stories and travelogues (the latter along the lines of Robert Byron's great *The Road to Oxiana*). I worked diligently as a young man in pursuit of this vocation, writing much unpublishable prose and many bad poems (though in retrospect some of them show a certain lilt of grace and pungency of wit; these are printed in my *Situation Reports on the Emotional Equipoise: Collected Poems 1959-2006*). Part of the dream involved living in Paris or alternatively in the South of France, where those whose work I admired such as André Gide, Lawrence Durrell (whose work I had begun reading in 1959), Scott Fitzgerald, Hemingway, René Schickele, Frédéric Mistral, Thomas Mann and his

3

anti-nazi colleagues (including brother Heinrich, Lion Feuchtwanger, Franz Werfel, Bertholt Brecht, et al., on their way to exile in California), had lived for shorter or longer periods. It is not clear to me what I expected of the landscape, the culture or the language and the people who lived there, but living with LM in Washington, especially after driving with her through Provence in 1980, I would often pine loudly with a sigh about how great it would be to actually live there and create masterpieces of English-language literature, and perhaps even take up painting. After all, Matisse, Picasso, Léger and countless others had found inspiration in the bright sunshine and whirling blast of the wind called "*le mistral*" – well, as John Lewis said to Roger Vadim one afternoon in Venice, "*Sait-on jamais*" – one never knows. In any case, I talked quite a bit about the idea, perhaps to the point of boring my listeners.

By the spring of 1982, LM was no stranger to my ramblings on the subject, which increased in number and duration as the situation at NEH continued to deteriorate and the prospects for my becoming employed did not encourage hope. These discussions usually took place during and after a well-watered dinner on the second story balcony of our rental house on South Carolina Avenue in the southeastern quadrant of the nation's capital.

Before too long, after LM quite properly demanded we either stop yakking on about it or do it, we began to seriously consider how such a drastic move might be undertaken. This required a great deal of discussion, introspective analysis and the exchange of dreams and desires.

Soon we no longer questioned the feasibility, the sensibility, the veritable sanity of the move. After all, the fates had surely prepared us for this, we were destined to be there, of this we had no doubt. By the end of June we had begun to make definite preparations for the move. LM resigned from NEH, and I, having no job to resign from, mentally resigned from Reagan's America. After we had settled in at Tavel, I wrote a short dialogue that exemplifies my thinking vis à vis emigrating to another culture.

– Where would you live if you had the choice?

– You mean how would I live?

– It's the same thing, isn't it?

– For a cultural cosmopolitan such as myself who would rather live in an alien culture in which one can switch off the banal and the offensive more easily than in one's own, yet still accept the challenges of the new, for such a person there is but one choice: winter in Paris and summer somewhere on the Mediterranean coast. Failing that, live near the Med in Provence all year round with trips to Paris and the coast as necessary. Everything is so close there: Italy, Greece, Spain ... and history in that region goes back before the Romans. It's a fine place to live, I would think.

– You won't miss your country?

– No I take it with me wherever I am,
those parts of it I cherish or find stimulating. I
just don't care to live there.

This was undoubtedly how I thought at the time, no
matter how pompous and silly the piece sounds now.

On other occasions that summer, in Bethany Beach,
Delaware, we sat in the second story corner window at
the creaking old Addy Sea Inn overlooking the ocean and
the beach of sand and rock, our minds chasing our
emotions as we pondered the how and the when. On a
more practical level we had four sessions of French
lessons from a native speaker in Germantown, the
juxtaposition did not go unnoticed. Obtaining visas for a
residence of more than three months required mounds of
paperwork including bank statements to show we had
sufficient resources to ensure we would not be forced to
become wards of the French state (until the authorities
could deport us as undesirables). We already possessed
those most important items for travelers: valid passports;
for, as the French scholar Louis Grillet has noted, "Death
is the only journey made today without passports."

For me one of the more intrinsically necessary
aspects of preparing for the journey was to read a certain
amount of the appropriate literature. Richard Aldington's
Introduction to Mistral, a book that keeps the promise
made in its title regarding the great poet of Provence;
Amy Oakley's informative travelogue, *The Heart of
Provence*, first published in 1936 and still worth reading;
Elizabeth David's thick, mouth-watering *French*

Provincial Cooking; the relevant works of MFK Fisher; the published correspondence between Aldington (who lived in the Midi for more than 25 years) and Lawrence Durrell (who moved there in 1957 and remained until he died in 1990); and the section on Provence in Durrell's *Spirit of Place*. Clearly I prepared myself well, if somewhat eccentrically, for the adventure.

We met with a couple who were friends of a former girlfriend of Steve Goodell's; the young woman's mother, Mrs. Margaret Potter, a former Foreign Service officer, owned a house called Le Marquis in the foothills outside the town of Apt, approximately an hour's drive along RN 100 east of Avignon, which she was willing to rent for a month or more to trustworthy friends of friends. (The market town of Apt is situated in the Vaucluse department on the eastern side of the Rhône River, the Gard department is to the west of the river. The French departments are similar to the American states but without nearly as much power and independence. The geography becomes important, as the Reader will discover.)

The young couple handled the negotiations, we agreed on a price and they briefed us about the region. Unfortunately, we never did meet Mrs. Potter herself. In early July, we returned to the Addy Sea Inn for a week of rest and quiet, where I finished the first draft of the first volume of a multi-volume novel about Berlin in 1945-46, the second volume of which I planned to write in France (see Chapter IX below). The Greek military attaché bought our piano and with two assistants shouldered the heavy instrument down the stairs to the street and into the bed of a truck with diplomatic license plates, leaving us saddened but happy nonetheless: this was a sure sign that we were not living in a dream bubble that could burst at any moment.

The final month of hectic preparations, a hurried round of farewell parties and last visitors to that large airy house on Capitol Hill filled our days. The most poignant of these occurred when my brother Dean, the Archpoet of Exeter as he is known in some circles, who loves France and her culture with a passionate interest, came for a brief visit. He helped us pack, lectured us about certain French *moeurs*, and how to pronounce various important and useful phrases in the language, such as: "*Valéry est le plus grand poet français depuis Verlaine.*" We gave him our Georges Brassens record.

And so it came to pass that we found ourselves there, closer to the primal elements than ever before, situated at the core of the good life, in the center of the very nature of things, the natural life without the artificial constraints of urban civilization, though we did eventually purchase a small television set.

And we learned to lie in the bleached sun and survive the mistral's hollow roar. We viewed life not through rose-colored spectacles, no, the rosé in our wine glasses sufficed.

Chapter I

Getting There and Settling In: A Month of Different Experiences

On September 1, after briefly corresponding with Lawrence Durrell about living in Provence (he noted that it was far too industrialized and overrun with tourists but that one could still find quiet niches there), we flew to Frankfurt and took the train to Munich to stay in the house of our friends from the OMGUS Project days, Wolfgang and Ute Benz, for a month while they and their young children were in Greece on a holiday. The ride south through the rolling German countryside we made in the restaurant car, perhaps the last of its type, eating a fine meal and drinking a dry Rhine wine, wondering what the future would bring. Both of us had been in Europe before: LM had been a summer exchange student in Turkey at the age of 16, had traveled throughout Europe twice with college friends and had spent part of a sabbatical in Barcelona studying Spanish before she moved to Washington. From 1961 to 1966 I lived and worked in Heidelberg where I met and married my first wife, Angela; during the year 1970-71 the Fulbright Commission supported my dissertation research in Germany and we spent ten days on the Costa Brava in Spain. After receiving my Ph.D. in the summer of 1972, I returned to Europe where Angela and I lived on or near various US military bases in Germany and Italy while I taught European and American history for the University of Maryland. In 1975 I, foolishly, thought it time to find a tenured position at a university where I would spend the rest of my working life in the groves of academe – so we returned to Washington. As already noted, LM and I traveled in France and Spain in 1980 and the following year we traveled by motor car in Greece (where we visited the Benz family at the end of the Volos peninsula) and spent a couple of days in Istanbul. So we were hardly novices at living in other cultures, but this was rather different and we really had little idea of what awaited us.

We spent several pleasant weeks in the Benz house visiting the city's many politico-cultural sights, seeing old friends from the OMGUS Project, making short trips to Vienna and Salzburg – and we purchased Ute Benz's old Peugeot (known affectionately as La petite Mo after our friend Moira Egan), which immediately broke down in city traffic, an omen of things to come. Our Institute for Contemporary History friend, Christoph Weisz, came to our rescue and somehow the car got fixed sufficiently to carry on.

Whilst in Vienna the hitherto unknown Leonard Bernstein incident occurred. Shortly thereafter I wrote it up as an occasional piece and sent it to *The New Yorker*, thinking, mistakenly, that this type of story would fit nicely into that magazine's style. Later as indicated at the end of the story, I edited it lightly to remove several infelicities of style. Here it is for the first time in print.

It had rained on and off in the morning and the sky remained overcast and gray except when the sun occasionally squeezed through with a bit of warmth. All in all it was a typical late September day in Vienna. Unfortunately we arrived too late to arrange opera tickets and our concierge did not maintain the traditional connections of his profession. Promising ourselves to plan our next visit with more care, we viewed the magnificent paintings in the Hofburg and Belvedere Castle and strolled about the center of the city.

Late in the afternoon the inevitable Sachertorte drew us to the hotel of that name across the street from the opera house just off the Kärtnerstrasse. With a couple of hours to spare before dinner we prepared ourselves to sample that overrated chunk of chocolate cake and overpriced coffee at the hotel's sidewalk café.

In a number of senses it was worth it: we rested our tired legs, read the ubiquitous and necessary *International Herald Tribune*, wrote postcards and actually enjoyed the cake and coffee. But the highpoint of the afternoon, although determined by the geography in which we found ourselves, was created by the appearance of a world renowned personality whose presence riveted both passers-by and café-sitters with a natural magnetism that pre-dates even television.

Shortly after establishing ourselves at the table a lengthy black Mercedes double-parked before the hotel entrance. The tieless, but otherwise appropriately dressed, chauffeur removed himself from behind the wheel and chatted casually with the doorman. This latter, stocky individual attired in the typical uniform of his trade did not take it amiss that the long limousine blocked the entrance to the busy hostelry. (Perhaps the doorman is also world-famous, but has not, to my knowledge, as yet published his memoirs: "Doors I Have Held.") He did, however, dominate the street, enforcing his own code of parking regulations with the sovereignty of a ruling monarch, which in a manner of speaking he was. Thus, with his tolerance the Mercedes continued to block the entrance, a possible indication of the importance of its passenger.

At this point we noticed two well-dressed Viennese ladies of a certain age standing on the sidewalk a couple of meters from our table absorbed in a discussion about the possible identity of that personage. I paid only sporadic attention to the two matrons until it became clear that they were at their station for the duration: until the personality belonging to the Mercedes (which seemed to increase in length the longer it remained there) appeared, they would neglect their appointed rounds to discover who could cause the Hotel Sacher's doorman to allow traffic to be blocked on an important central European thoroughfare.

This phenomenon piqued my interest. No bellowing mob of photographers infested the street (this was, after all, Vienna, the capital of the former Habsburg Empire: it had seen everything), but these two housewives (or so they seemed to be with their small plastic bags of groceries, though of course they could easily have been maids to the wealthy and well-

12

connected), who surely had an hour or so of cooking before them, stolidly remained magnetized by the possibility of something about to happen. Henry Kissinger on yet another whirlwind tour? Jeanne Moreau in town to make a film? A Saudi oil minister deciding next summer's gasoline prices? Johnny Hallyday? Or perhaps the Chancellor of the Austrian Republic? Someone, in any case, they had no doubt seen on the television. But they had no idea who it was, and this did not seem to matter.

So much was clear. I read the paper, drank the coffee and kept the corner of my eye free to record the activities of these rather elegant *Hausfrauen*, if that is in fact what they were. Finally, the suspense became too much for them (and for us too it must be added) and the least shy of the two walked over to the chauffeur, still conversing desultorily with the doorman, and asked outright who would be climbing into the limo. The answer did not seem to surprise her nor her companion to whom she imparted the information within my hearing: "Leonid Bernstein." Nevertheless, they made no move to leave. After all, Vienna remains one of the music capitals of the world; they did not view Bernstein's presence here as unusual: yet they stayed, a characteristic of the city I found both amusing and admirable: had it been Rod Stewart or John Travolta they would have resumed their daily rounds without a moment's hesitation, or so one would like to think.

What did they know about Leonid Bernstein (or, as we immediately thought of him: Lenny – such is the informality of the American mind and the familiarity of

13

this cultural institution)? That he often directed the Viennese orchestras, most recently perhaps in a television series performing the symphonies of Mahler or Beethoven? That he and his wife had been brutalized in an essay on radical chic by an architecture critic at the end of the 1960s? Had Austrian television broadcast his fine music appreciation series? Had they seen *West Side Story* (probably) or *Mass* (probably not)? Perhaps they owned some of his recordings? Whatever the answer, they waited.[3]

They waited for another 30 minutes, shifting their substantial weight from one foot to another, chatting and watching the long Mercedes, the headlights of which each had its own small electric wiper blade to remove dirt and crushed insects: a sign of decadence or functional luxury depending upon one's point of view. We also waited: the idea of seeing the man in the flesh, even briefly, was not without its attraction and we had the time. I sat facing away from the hotel's doorway, but by watching the women's reactions I could tell what went on behind me.

There is often the perception of movement before an event takes place. The moment before the conductor arrives at the podium is telegraphed by an extra-sensory feeling of anticipation which runs through the auditorium and silences most of the audience. So it is with the appearance of a star

---

[3] This true story was written in 1983 describing an event that took place in September the previous year. Mr. Bernstein's bisexuality was not generally known in Europe at that time; among the general public it may still not be.

personality in public: one senses movement at the appointed place and communicates this to others.

The women reacted to the sudden flurry of activity around the Sacher's revolving door by stiffening their bodies and their attention, intently focusing on the space before the limousine. The following progression of small events could, I suppose, have been predicted, but this did not lessen the quickening of the pulse as I turned around. The chauffeur and the Sacher doorman, without losing a fraction of their nonchalance, swiftly opened the automobile's doors and the former placed himself in his professional position and started the motor. The entrance (or exit) had been heralded.

Preceded by a young man with a briefcase and a large bottle of Ballantine's Scotch whisky, which he placed beside the seated chauffeur, a small group of people emerged onto the street alongside the limousine in the midst of which, animated by farewells, came Lenny, unmistakably *the* Leonard Bernstein, silver hair always the correct length, filter cigarette eternally between his fingers always the correct length. (One might be forgiven for thinking this a prop item if one had not seen him smoke the damned thing in interviews, nor is this description to be taken as facetious or burlesque, but as admiration: surely I have more time for such things than he but I cannot seem to keep my hair at the same length, and my cigarettes are continually burning down to my fingers.)

From the center of the hectic farewell embraces, kisses and fanny pattings, bits of phrases floated to our table over the noise of the rush-hour traffic.

15

"Yes, I'll call ..."
"Don't forget to ..."
"... no ... okay ... not without first ..."
"Wiedersehen ..."
"Ciao baby ..."
"Alright ... yes ..."

And, with two young people accompanying him, dressed in blue jeans, cordovan loafers and an old brown suede jacket, one of the true wonders of the postwar musical universe gracefully climbed into the Mercedes and waved once more to his farewell party as the chauffeur steered the limo off into the Viennese dusk. Oddly, I was left with the question: does Leonard Bernstein's chauffeur ever get stuck in a traffic jam?

If the two women on the sidewalk were left with any questions, I have no way of knowing. In fact, they left with a pronounced aura of satisfaction about them: they had seen their star of the week in a city with enough stars to fill the weeks of the year. Indeed, it must be admitted, I shared a certain degree of that satisfaction: I had seen the Maestro in the flesh. No transcendent epiphany, to be sure, but as we paid the enormous bill and went off to dinner we found ourselves a little lighter in spirit than earlier that afternoon. Certain individuals such as Lenny bring their own illumination with them, like heroes with their own décor, and we are all better illuminated for having been in their presence.

Tavel, 1983 – Key West, 2007

On September 29 we left Munich early in the morning, by which time the excitement of our adventure had become so intense that, once we bid farewell to our friends, we abandoned our plans for traversing northern Italy and decided to travel through Switzerland as fast as possible in order to reach our destination as early as possible. Contrary to our usual custom, we drove on the highways and superhighways to shorten the journey. After three weeks in Germany and Austria, speed suddenly seemed essential and we pushed the aging blue Peugeot to its limit through the winding Swiss mountain roads.

We moved so quickly that at times clarity of thought abandoned us to minor annoyances along the way: should we have realized that the only currency exchange booths at our crossing point were on the German side where we did not stop? Surely we should have realized that rush hour is not the time to drive around a city the size of Bern. But should we have remembered that Vevey is an expensive luxury spa inappropriate for two unemployeds planning to live for a year or more on a limited amount of savings? Actually, we took a room at one of the more moderately expensive hotels because we had no desire to schlep all our goods from the car into the hotel and considered they would be safer in the parking lot of an expensive establishment than in one, perhaps just as comfortable, on the seedy side. In fact, of course, Vevey has no seedy side.

We did not know that any of the liquid refreshments taken from the miniature refrigerator in the room would appear on the *Rechnung*, in this case *l'addition* because this was the French speaking sector of the country, the next morning, so in all of our ignorant innocence (odd in a couple such as we) we opened a tube of Scotch whisky and toasted our luck at finding a room at all after 9 o'clock at night in what appeared to be rural Switzerland in the off season. Late that evening I made a note about the thin plastic toilet seats in expensive hotels not being amenable to the most comfortable usage of same, but that the Bach on the radio helped the digestion. I also noted,

A hotel without writing paper
Even in Vevey is no hotel at all
Like a pen without ink or nib –
You can't live in it enjoyably.

My only excuse is that we were tired and excited and not quite ourselves, though I should perhaps use the singular here.

After a non-descript meal in an allegedly Italian restaurant recommended as "good" by one of the hotel receptionists, we walked along the shore of Lac Leman (so named in English presumably because the large city of Geneva is located on its eastern or western end) and watched the lights of Montreux across the dark water. We thought of the eccentric Englishmen and women whose shades haunted the area and the misanthropic Russian-American hotel lover who never attended the jazz festival in his last city of residence: the ghosts of the Byron-Shelley crew did not whisper to us in the cool late September night air, but I could envision the grimace of amused skepticism that Nabokov might have

18

condescended to give us from his hotel-fortress's balcony as Puck's lines ran through his head: Lord what fools these mortals be! But the various signs and commemorative plaques left no doubt as to the Englishness of the town, at least in the past when Britannia ruled the waves and much else. Who, for example, was Edmund Ludlow who lived, so the plaque on the façade tells us, at the Hôtel du Lac for many years until he died in 1693?

No matter! No matter! Even the cool drizzle that accompanied our perambulations along the lakeside could not diminish our enthusiasm and wildly spinning thoughts that held us willingly captive. The dream was about to become reality and we hoped we were prepared for it. Two Thomapyrin pills (German aspirin) and another sip of cognac ensured a form of sleep during a night that otherwise would have been spent tossing and turning, impatient for the daylight.

The following day, September 30, we would cross the border into France for the first time in two years, now not as tourists but as residents. If the western world had not long since given up swooning as an expression of anxious joy I would have that night in Vevey.

So the next day we raced south and west around and through Annecy, Aix-les-Bains, Chambéry, through the village of Bourg-de-Péage listening to Steely Dan, Willy Nelson and Thelonious Monk on a small battery-driven boom box purchased in Munich. We rode into Valence where we discovered we had very little French currency and received our first lesson in the necessity to time one's errands to coincide with French working hours, not the last time we would be taught the same lesson. Between noon and 2:00 or 2:30 (14 or 14:30 as the Europeans calculate time), banks and numerous other service establishments close for lunch, a civilized custom for employees, no doubt, but annoying to traveling Americans unaccustomed to such amenities. It would be some time before we learned to coordinate our movements with the local *moeurs* and we often ended up shaking our heads over a small expresso in a bistro or café while waiting for a shop to open. In Valence, while thus waiting, we ate what became our standard lunch, variations of which we took with us whilst meandering around the countryside during the next year: a bottle of wine, usually red which requires no refrigeration, a bottle of Badoit mineral water (with just a touch of gas), chicken or chorizo or cheese with various condiments on a long, crusty baguette baked earlier that morning.

We arrived in Apt that evening where we consulted our Michelin red guide (without which we never traveled in France) and sought out the least expensive hotel listed for the town. *Complet,* no room at that inn. There are not many hotels in Apt at any price, but the Michelin recommended the small Hôtel Ste. Anne, named after the nearby church, on the tiny nondescript Place Balet across from the arroyo through which the Calavon River at one time flowed. We never learned what happened to the river, only that water no longer even trickled along its bed. This constituted one of the many mysteries of the region we did not resolve, but if we know everything we become afflicted with boredom, the great sickness of the 20th century. The pleasant concierge provided us with a large room equipped with a closed-off fireplace and a small balcony overlooking the garden. We would stay one or three nights; we were not sure at that point if we could arrange to receive the keys to the house in the hills outside the town from the *notaire* because we arrived three days ahead of schedule. The concierge accepted this condition with a smile and the news that the petit dejeuner would be served from 7 to 9 and we could leave the car in the square if we found a parking space. This helpful woman, who spoke her language with care and at a slow pace so we could better comprehend it, was the first of a lengthy list of people we met in comparable situations who belied the image of abrupt, hostile French and their condescending inhospitality.

Before dinner we walked around the center of the town to get our bearings in a place where we would be staying for a month. The fact that the evening meal would be our first in Provence determined that it would take on at least a symbolic weight as an omen of things to come out of proportion to any realistic, objective assessment of its importance. If the first repast thrilled us, made us smile with good will and repletion, the prognosis for our stay in France would be eminently positive. Not only armies march on their stomachs. We did not wish to rush the matter or make a precipitous decision, which meant a lengthy stroll through that part of the town closest to the hotel and a careful study of posted menus with as detailed a reconnaissance of the various establishments as possible through curtained windows and open doors. The circumstances also demanded full consultation and exchange of opinions lubricated by the tangy, anis-flavored aperitif of the region: pastis, which we recommend in lieu of the Anglo-American taste killers known as cocktails. A pastis (or two but no more) before a meal has the desirable quality of enhancing one's appetite and activating one's taste mechanism rather than dulling both as is the case with whisky, vodka or that horrid juniper-flavored liquid known as gin. If the taste of anis, similar to liquorish, is offensive, a glass of dry faintly chilled white wine can be safely substituted, but when in the Midi: pastis.

In brief, we decided to take a risk: in the short narrow lane called the rue Septier we gazed through a pair of dingy open windows into a kitchen that the Washington board of health surely would have closed down on sight. A sweating figure with an immense belly, a mass of unkempt black hair and a Nietzschean mustache stood over a series of pots and pans peering into each in turn as if he had difficulty in comprehending their contents. A burning cigarette between the fingers of one hand and a pair of glasses hanging from his neck by a piece of string, he stirred and prodded the bubbling mass of pungent wonders with a long wooden spoon, occasionally bending further over the stove to taste his wares. We salivated mightily and felt the smells of Greece in our nostrils. The round mustachioed head looked up at us, smiled grandly and gestured vaguely with his spoon spotting his already lavishly stained apron, then returned to his labors. Did I imagine I heard him humming as he worked?

The well-stained apron of this rotund *chef de cuisine* was the only lavish aspect of the restaurant. A few steps further on we viewed the ground floor dining room in which five tables of various sizes took up all the available space. Non-descript and eclectic rather than shabby, the room contained nothing that matched anything else in it, no set of anything embellished the worn appointments: every chipped place, chair, table (uncovered and scrubbed), utensil and glass represented a unique example of its form and function. The only item of any uniformity in the place was the collection of baguettes standing in a large paper sack against the back wall under the supply of unlabeled bottles of red and white wines.

At one table sat a middle-aged man in tie and white shirt who, we decided spontaneously, served as a clerk in the nearby Hôtel de Ville, deep in the solitary concentration of a bachelor at dinner. At another table *une femme d'un certain âge*, well-dressed and plump, sat with what we took to be her daughter, less well-dressed but equally as plump, deep in conversation about some mutually disagreeable subject. A group of long-haired youths in tee shirts simultaneously deep in animated conversation and concentration on their plates hovered around the third table. A tailored but uniformly clothed middle-aged couple sat at the fourth table talking in evident enjoyment to a third person we could not see from our vantage point. The fifth table, set for two, was free. A young, thin, wild-haired figure with beads, gold chains and flowing open-necked shirt moved quickly but without panic to wait upon the customers, puffing on a cigarette as he broke off large lengths of baguette which he place with some vehemence but without a basket on the tables, talking all the while. The heavy cooking odors filling the lane caused a slight hysteria in my stomach.

The faded sign above the door read: "Taverne du Septier". We needed look no further, we had found our restaurant for the first meal in Provence.

The waiter, who also cooked on occasion, was an art critic on the side and had written a profusely illustrated book on female fannies and the popular imagination in Provence, a copy of which rests with other of our goods in the Tavel house garage where it has been for 25 years, undisturbed we hope and, alas, since then unread. We continued to eat there occasionally during our time in Apt, more about which can be read below under the rubric "baguette on the book".

The schedule called for us to move into Mrs. Potter's house on October 4, and we arrived in Apt on September 30, our excitement driving us beyond the confines of time bound constraints. Thinking ourselves pretty clever we sought to employ a ruse and showed up at the *notaire*'s office innocently asking for the key and directions. Naïve, of course, but also smiled on by the goddess in charge of luck, Mme. Fortuna, who arranged for the fellow to be friendly, expecting us and quite willing to fork over the key and provide the directions. (A *notaire* is someone who hovers professionally between a lawyer and an estate agent.) About four kilometers from the town we turned into a vaguely paved lane winding up into the hills, then on a long stretch of rutted dirt road to, finally, there above us, the old stone house named Le Marquis. It was, perhaps still is, a solidly constructed rambling edifice of two stories and two living quarters built into the hillside with a grand view over the valley toward the town; the living room in our part of the house is a large spacious open area of two floors, the tiny kitchen and dining area and a loft-like space on what would have been the second floor; the bedrooms and single toilet and bathroom on the first floor. The plumbing probably was constructed in the Middle Ages and the toilet flushed just fine if one did not flush after each pee. Central heating was not a prominent feature of the house but it did contain a large fireplace and a handy-dandy portable electric heater which turned out to be a favorite item on cold nights, when the electricity did not pop off for longer and shorter periods of time.

The house overlooked the Calavon River Valley, though the river hardly deserved that name at that point, the bed running through Apt was as dry as a spinster's honey pot, and the view was gorgeous.

Heating the place proved something of a problem, one that bedeviled us throughout our time in the Midi. The stone walls of the Apt house made the interior chilly but oddly not damp as autumn closed in on us, and the electric heater helped while burning the small pieces of olive tree wood we collected on the mountainside contributed to warming the space but had to be constantly replaced because they burned so quickly. We were glad to have packed thermal underwear and occasionally wore woolen socks at night.

Indeed we became much more conscious of the weather than we had been in Washington: it played an increasingly important and large role in our lives, perhaps in part due to our not having a regular, and regulated, schedule within which to parcel out our quotidian time; we had more time to think about it, and during the cold months with no or inadequate central heating one did think about it every day. And it continued to conduct itself in a more erratic manner than we had been accustomed to.

For example, consider the mistral, the roaring wind that screams down the narrow Rhône River valley from the French Massif Central and the Swiss mountains at unexpected moments that can become days, sending the temperature plunging and occasionally thrashing the rain about the landscape like a demented Lash LaRue with his black snake whip. This unpredictable wind storm is called by different names in other places: *sirocco* in Sicily, *Föhn* in Bavaria, *moria* elsewhere, but they all mean the same thing and, some say, madness can be achieved when the winds whomp and whish for too long. The farmers in the region call it *"mange fange"* (mud eater) because it usually dries up the muddy pools the rains bring that serve as breeding grounds for mosquitoes and other nasty creatures humans prefer to avoid.

On the other hand, me, I generally welcomed the phenomenon because, while it had its negative aspects, it washed the sky clear and drove the air pollution south over the Mediterranean Sea, and frankly I enjoyed the sounds it made as it careened around the corners outside the house. The sound reaffirmed that we indeed had moved from a well-known environment to one filled with questions, unknown rules, a vaguely comprehended language and a climate that both bedeviled and enriched our lives. For many, however, they found the time of the mistral to be a burden and an unfortunate experience. The French "*mistral*" comes from the word "*mistrau*" which means "master" in Provençal. It is said that Alphonse Daudet counted some 30 different winds from the windmill he lived in briefly in Fontvieille, but he may have exaggerated a bit for the sake of drama. Drama there is in a mistral: the wind bends the silvery olive trees, the pines and plane trees to extreme positions but they do not break; one's motor car often sways dangerously on the roads through the open fields; walking even in a town the size of Avignon can be awkward as one pushes against the flow of a force of wind so strong as to stop forward motion; the tall pines planted as wind breaks along the vineyards suffer extraordinary punishment but continue to do their job – it is a remarkable experience to be alive in the middle of a mistral. The Romans made "a dreaded god" of this fearsome wind, the strength and duration of which has not changed since those times: it is said the mistral blows in units of three, six or nine days, but our experience taught us that it could blow for 30 minutes then suddenly stop, or for two or four days without letup.

The first weeks of our living in the exposed Apt house did not lack the wind, but it was feeble compared to what we later went through. The mistral howled around the mountain and the house like a wailing, mad Greek woman bereft of children and husband and farm. For six days there the wind blew, the rain and temperature fell and we shivered; then for two days we basked and lolled about in the sun on the terrace.

Waking up on those sunny mornings with the Luberon mountains across the valley at our feet was an exhilarating thrill that made rising and breakfast so much more fun. However, this weather unpredictability continued for the entire time we lived in the Midi.

We very much enjoyed our stay at Mrs. Potter's house and communicated with the permanent tenants (Claude, Jeannot and their daughter, three dogs and a cat called Gaston), who lived in the building's ground floor section, with some difficulty since they had only a minimum of English and our French was still in the non-existent to primitive stage. This circumstance led to what they considered to be an amusing and harmless incident, confirming our ignorance of local custom. The day after we arrived we slept late and started out shortly after noon to drive to one of the two supermarkets (*supermarché*) in Apt. On the way to the car we met the tenant couple and somehow made known what we were up to. This confession led to a gale of French which barely concealed the laughter in their voices, which we only understood when we reached the store to discover it was closed for lunch until 3:00 p.m.. As noted above, the French will not do without their lunch period, a sacred ritual bordering on the religiously upheld. Indeed most of the stores, except the bars and cafés, closed over the lunch hour (or two), the tradition continuing for several years until the lure of expanded profits won the struggle with traditional working hours. Eventually we learned to time our excursions rather more carefully in tune with local mores and habits. In some places even the museums closed for lunch. The French tradition of closing and opening store hours had not then been broken by the Americanization of France. This led one to think that the French shopkeepers did not have the same intense interest in making money as their American counterparts who would not think of closing at lunch time when so many potential customers were on the streets. Nowadays, everything stays open all day, except the smaller stores in the villages that continue the ritual.

Nonetheless, examples of the apparent French indifference to the profit motive continued to amaze us then, though things have changed since. In October the following year, just weeks before we sadly left the country, we walked to the Tavel village market where we attempted to purchase four sheets of raviolis for dinner. The woman in the wagon asked us if the pasta would serve just the two of us. When we replied positively, she removed two sheets, saying two would be sufficient for the two of us, thus losing half the sale. We paid, and we all smiled and wished each other "*une bonne journée*".

Another exceedingly pleasant and useful aspect of Mrs. Potter's house was a small but well appointed library within reach from the solid wooden refectory table on which we served our meals. While still in the house, at the end of October that year, I wrote an appreciation of her library, which would fit nicely here.

A FEW WORDS OF APPRECIATION FOR MRS. MARGARET POTTER'S LIBRARY IN APT

We had no idea what the house would be like and that made it even better when we arrived. High above the

Calavon Valley with a magnificent view of that part of
Provence, the old stone house several kilometers from
the market town of Apt offers many things to the guest,
of which the most important is a small but splendid
library. What a pleasure it was to spend that October in
the company of so many old friends and to have made
at least one new one! The few volumes of prose (a
severely limited working library) and poetry (Auden,
Cavafy, Seferis) we had been able to carry with us from
Washington would not have sufficed for the month.
Avignon, an hour to the west on national road 100, had
no decent supply of English language books and we did
not discover the Paradox in Aix-en-Provence until
November.

Of course the motto is: learn French. But in the
first month of an extended residence in France, with the
necessities of finding a place to live, the bureaucratic
bother of the *cartes de séjour* and automobile registration,
and exploring all the fabled sites one has read so much
about (those sifted from Aldington's *Introduction to
Mistral* alone demand weeks) – with all that and more,
how much of the language can one learn except the
minimum required to request information about rents
and utilities and to puzzle out the local newspapers?
Thus the warm surge of pleasure to discover the
bookshelves in the house called "Le Marquis" full of
old and comforting friends: Nabokov, Hemingway,
Julia Child, Nietzsche, an old well-worn copy of *The Joy
of Cooking*, Huxley, Edmund Wilson, the acerbic Alice
Toklas with her cookbook full of recipes requiring
dexterous improvisation and hours of time; and the
enjoyment of reading *Village in the Vaucluse* again after
30

so many years, this time, however, after exploring Roussillon, that village, the day before! And the new discovery: Le Roy Ladurie's *Montaillou*, a book that contains enough drama for a novel – for which one has already made notes. Any academic who describes a historical figure as "a sort of compulsive Maigret" and "a very devil of an Inquisition" must be read and enjoyed.

October nights in the Midi can be cold, especially when the price of heating oil is so high as to prohibit turning on the central heating until the desperate days of December. Gathering wood for the fire assumes an unusual importance, at least for a city-bred fortyish academic turned novelist. But once the fire had nudged the chill from the room and supper was over, one stretched across the table to the bookshelf and selected a volume: perhaps to reacquaint oneself with Bruce Lockhart's idiosyncratic memoirs of revolutionary Russia, or a thriller about a plot to assassinate the leaders of the Manhattan Project. These alone gave warmth and comfort on such chilly nights.

And the sun-brightened southern mornings on the terrace looking through *Les Châteaux Historiques Vauclusiens*, planning to visit this one or that, and finally finding Apt's own Château de Ville and discover it is still lived in!

Indeed, the very presence of those well-thumbed volumes on the shelf made one feel at home. Melville, Graves, old red Guides Michelin, dictionaries, Thurber, Koestler – and those books on Provence in French one looked through in an attempt to get *at* the area more intensely than possible with the usual guides (or even

31

Amy Oakley's fine *The Heart of Provence*) drew one toward the conclusion that it is time for an up-to-date volume in English on the history of Provence. Should one attempt it? It would be fun, but no, alas there will be no opportunity for a history of Provence for English readers with insufficient French. (One does, however, muse desultorily on the possibility of a novel about Petrarch and the mysterious Laura.)

Even the arrival of some boxes of our own books did not dim the enjoyment of simply gazing at the shelves, removing a random volume to sample the contents or stand for minutes on end, rooted in concentration on a particularly well-done or evocative passage. The possible provenance of the book in hand often tempted one to speculate: was this bought in Geneva in the 1930s? Rome? Athens? We knew Mrs. Potter had been a career foreign service officer and had spent many years in Europe. The romance of an era one had not lived through oneself crept out of the older volumes on the shelf drawing one closer still.

One resented the demands of daily life, which took one away from the library (but how could anyone miss the Saturday morning market in Apt?). Finally, in the last few days of our stay in Le Marquis, a shadow of sadness slipped across the joy of having at last found an apartment in the village of Tavel across the Rhône River from the former city of the popes. We will miss the intense drive up the stony pathway from the road to the house, the dogs' sudden howling for no apparent reason, the terrace with its splendid view of the autumn hued landscape, the fireplace, the erratic water supply – but most of all, the library, so eclectic, so full of the familiar and the unknown! Our one compensation is the hope of visiting the house again when its owner is present next summer so we can offer our deepest gratitude in person.

Apt, 31.X.1982

Envoi: Key West, 28.VII.2005:

Alas, the visit was not to be and we never again saw the house on the hill where we spent the first month of our grand sojourn in the Midi.

•

The month overflowed with various activities and visitors. Mrs. Potter had generously provided her renters with not only the wonderfully diverse library, but also with a smoothly functioning old manual portable Smith-Corona typewriter. True, for some mysterious reason, we had brought our ancient electric typewriter with us, but for some other mysterious reason, after a few minutes the necessary current transformer refused to function properly and outlet plug adapter was thus rendered useless for the moment. The old manual drew me to it like blue serge attracts lint. The machine offered a great deal of satisfaction as I batted out the first several pages of a story about a certain Julio Cortez and his laughter, the first paragraph of which I was able to write on our electric machine before having to switch to Mrs. Potter's. Alas, I never finished the story.

Our first month in the Midi proved to be exemplary in that the type of activities that engaged us were set then and varied little during the remainder of our life there: work, trips around the region with and without visitors enlivened our stay at the Potter house. Our first guests from America arrived soon after we settled in. From Washington came Nancy Worssam (one of LM's colleagues at NEH) and Bill Seach who spent several days with us that included our first trip to Marseille to eat bouillabaisse at the old port.

Another of LM's colleagues at NEH, Andrea Anderson, came toward the end of the month and went with us to Arles and other sites of note. It was at this point that we first encountered the "baguette slapped on the book" syndrome. But a prefatory note must be inserted here before we continue. Before Andrea arrived in Apt, LM and I had been eating a late, well-watered dinner one night with the radio playing the usual assortment of radically unrelated musical selections when the oddest sound halted our ebullient conversation and astounded us with something approaching awe: an old black singer, obviously of the Leadbelly generation, croaking a blues dirge about having to go to New Jersey with empty pockets and empty belly and all sorts of scabrous diseases. Amazed and not quite catching all the phrases and words, all we could do was nod and mutter, "Goddamn, goddamn" in emotional admiration. The disk jockey, if there was one, did not identify the singer or the name of the song, different music followed directly and off onto another, less emotionally wrenching path.

Now, the "slap the baguette on a book" procedure is executed as follows: One begins by locating the restaurant called Taverne du Septier, hidden away down a narrow lane in old Apt and, ignoring the tables on the ground floor, climbs the rather unpleasantly dark and dirty stairs to the dining room on the first (European) floor. There are five tables, one of which is occupied by a young couple obviously more concerned with their relationship than the food they eat mechanically as they gaze deeply into each other's eyes, and fidget, and sigh, but quietly as is appropriate in a small public room. Their voices would in any case have been hard to hear above the sound of that same old conversation-halting black singer we'd heard on the radio groaning about this woman's man called Henry and what a wastrel he is, wasting money on the horses and generally doing no good. The end of the song, as she cries out *"Henreee! Henreee!"*, cannot be heard without the listener choking up with tears. What stuff to be playing as background to a meal in a restaurant!

This was too much. Andrea, as taken with the phenomenon as we were, moved to unusual socially forward action, jumped up and ran downstairs loudly demanding *"Qui est le chanteur*?!" Shortly she climbed back up the stairs with a look of astonishment on her face holding a cassette container emblazoned with a photograph of a thin haggard white man by the name of Tom Waits on the album entitled "Bounced Checks." The tape is a compilation of songs from various Waits' albums and it has remained a constant companion of ours ever since. But do not attempt to find it for sale in the USA because it apparently was never released there. Our battered copy is still with us, a reminder of the somewhat seedy and dimly lit restaurant that, of course, no longer exists. The story also reminds me of the first time I heard Johnnie Ray's record of the song "Cry" in late 1951: I was convinced I was listening to a black woman blues singer. One's ears occasionally deceive one, but not for long.

The waiter, the unshaven friendly fellow who also owned the place and served as cook when the chef could not drag himself away from the fiery local Schnapps, called "*marc*,"[4] took our order for a bottle of local red wine, the savoring of which would be of assistance to us as we perused the hand-scribbled menu, so short it could have been written on a medium-size postage stamp. He promptly returned with the wine and the ubiquitous baguette which he gently slammed onto the copy of our Michelin red guide that rested on the unclothed table next to inevitable salt and pepper shakers. The fact that smoke from the cigarette stuck in the side of his mouth curled up into his eyes forcing him to squint through his rimless glasses did not then disturb us as it would today: LM and I smoked a great deal then so the scene was more amusing than annoying. Thus the origin of the baguette slapped on the book story, now become legend in certain circles. The food, by the way, as on previous occasions, was excellently cooked, tasty and filling and not at all expensive; the baguette freshly baked that afternoon. This was, after all, France, not America where finding a real baguette is almost impossible except where the few

---

[4] This highly distilled spirit comes in many forms and variations of taste but remains a dangerous drink to consume too much of. It is however very good against the penetrating chill of a Provençal winter, in moderate quantities, of course.

and far between real French bakeries are located. A real baguette has a life of no more than eight hours and is best eaten within three or four hours of being baked, which is why French bakers, at least then, baked at three to four in the morning and again at three in the afternoon. A real baguette has a snappy crust and a soft airy inside and is never made with sourdough. It is eaten with gusto three times a day and well accompanies just about anything and everything.

The business of the baguette in France was and is fascinating. People of all classes walk around with the long loaves sticking out of their briefcases, bicycle and moped racks, under their arms and wherever else they find space for the ubiquitous staff of life. In eateries other than the Taverne in Apt the presentation may be more refined but it is still the same baguette. The baguette is the great leveler in France. Even the young thugs in the poverty-ridden volatile Paris suburbs chew on a baguette when they are not burning cars and buildings.

Ode to a Baguette

O ubiquitous length of air and flour
You rule the morning like a bird of passage,
As aesthetically pleasing as you are tasty.
You contribute to the community as no other
Drawing all to the focus of daily life – the
      bakery,
To josh the old folk, enliven the lonely and
Give the weary world that eternal image:

Old man, beret, bicycle and you strapped
    behind.

23 February 1983

In France, the citizens know the world continues to
revolve on its daily axis and all is at least sufficiently
well in the universe as long as they can obtain their
quotidian baguette at the bakery in the morning. They
realize something is terribly amiss only when the matinal
baguette is not available.

Within two weeks of moving to Apt we met a family
that over the years became close to us and which we
never failed to visit whenever we landed in the Avignon
area: Edith and Eugène Fidler who lived in a small house
cum studio in Roussillon, the village made famous under
another name by Laurence Wylie in his sociological
study of the place in the mid-1950s, *Village in the
Vaucluse*. Eugène's family originally came from Russia
whence they escaped from the rabid anti-Semitism virus
there before the First World War. During the Second
World War he lived with his first wife, also Jewish, in
Mougins on the Côte d'Azur working as a ceramicist and
in the underground resistance movement against the
Germans and their French collaborators. At some point
they found it necessary to go into hiding when the
Gestapo and their French collaborators closed in and they
needed a place to hide. His friend the painter Henri
Hayden found them that place in Roussillon and the

38

Gestapo and their French collaborators closed in and they needed a place to hide. His friend the painter Henri Hayden found them that place in Roussillon and the mayor of Mougins provided the couple with fake identity papers under the name of Fournier.[5]

While there he met another *résistant*, the Irishman Samuel Beckett, who gave him several English lessons to help pass the time. After the war Eugène and his wife returned to Mougins where they divorced and he spent several months in Paris before returning south to the small town of Vallauris in the early 1950s.

Edith and her family, originally from the Azores, left the Portugal of the dictator Salazar and emigrated to London where she studied English, then to Paris whence she moved to Vallauris to study ceramics. There she met Picasso, whose presence and creation of ceramic art had revitalized the town's main industry. She also met Eugène in the winter of 1952-53; shortly thereafter they married. In 1960 they visited Roussillon with their daughter Natalie (who chose the name Natacha to sign her work as a ceramicist and painter). Edith fell in love with Provence and they decided to buy a piece of land on the outskirts of the village where they established a home with a pottery studio and sales room. Both of them created functional and aesthetically pleasing plates, platters, cups, pitchers and other fired art works, and

---

[5] In his biography of Samual Beckett, James Knowlson errs in having Edith with Eugène in Roussillon during the German occupation; they did not meet until several years after the war. (*Damed to Fame. The Life of Samuel Beckett*. New York: Simon & Schuster, 1996, 302.)

Eugène mastered the arts of collage and oil painting and created many strikingly beautiful works in those genres.

Through my friends Marsha and Eberhard von Dürckheim, who met the Fidlers when Marsha served as US Consul General in Marseille for several years, we contacted them and spent several happy hours at the studio in Roussillon with Andrea during her visit that October. Then for some reason, the relationship lapsed and we did not call them again until we planned a farewell visit the following October, a visit that did not take place because I became quite ill (at the thought of leaving, to be sure, but also a violent influenza took its toll). Since then we have more than made up for the missed opportunity, but those stories belong to another book. Eugène died of cancer at home in Roussillon on September 30, 1990 at the age of 80. Edith and Natacha, who is now the mother of a 23-year old daughter, carry on at the studio, creating gorgeous works of pottery for both use and looking at; we have many of them in our house, in addition to several of Eugène's colorful lineoprints.

•

There are two annual events (in May and October) at the small village of Stes-Maries-de-la-Mer on the coast of the Mediterranean at the edge of the Camargue: the blessing of the sea in the presence of the Maries in a small boat stored for the remainder of the year under the ceiling of the fortified village church. According to one of the legends of Provence, about the year 40 CE the

Maximus; Mary Salome, mother of James Major and John; and the blind man Cedonius. The Maries' Negro servant, Sarah, left behind on the shore, wept so loudly that Mary Salome threw her cloak onto the water for Sarah to walk on and join the others in the boat. The vessel, somehow guided by an invisible hand or eye, landed on the shore where the Stes-Maries-de-la-Mer village is now located. Here the passengers separated after constructing a simple oratory to the Virgin on the sandy shore: Martha traveled to Tarascon south of Avignon on the Rhône River, Mary Magdalene moved on to preach throughout Provence ending her days in a cave at Ste-Baume, and the two Maries remained with Sarah in the Camargue and were eventually buried under the oratory. The fates of the blind man, St. Maximus and Lazarus the legend leaves shrouded in the age-old mists that hover over the swamps throughout the region.

Be that as it may, the oratory and the village that grew up around it soon became a pilgrims' destination that attracted not only penitent Christians but also large numbers of Europe's Gypsies who developed a particular veneration of and affinity for the black servant Sarah. Before the modern period, the simple oratory underwent several considerable changes ending in the 9th century incorporated into the town's protective ramparts as a fortified church under the watchful eye of the Archbishop of Arles. During the construction a band of pagan Saracens descended on the village and carried off the unlucky Archbishop and held him for ransom. The infidels demanded 150 silver livres, 150 slaves, 150 swords and 150 mantles, which, it must be admitted, the authorities raised in a short period of time, but not fast enough. While in captivity the prelate died of unknown causes, perhaps due to the pagan diet and lack of basic sanitary facilities. However, not to be done out of their booty, the Saracens returned to the Camargue with the body of the Archbishop which they installed on a richly appointed throne with all due respect and swiftly departed with the ransom before the Arlesians discovered their Archbishop had himself departed this life. "Never trust a Saracen" became the informal motto of Arles. Meanwhile the construction of the fortified church came to a successful conclusion and the fortifications were reinforced over the succeeding centuries. The church buried the remains of the Maries and Sarah under the chancel during the Barbarian invasions where they rested undisturbed until in 1448 the King of Provence, *le bon roi René*, had the saints exhumed and the relics enshrined in the church with great ceremony.

On May 24 and 25 the Gypsies come to celebrate Mary mother of James and Sarah in 48 hours of religious veneration and revelry, dancing, singing, parading with the saints from the church to the shore and into the sea accompanied by the Camargue *gardiens* (cowboys) where the priests and bishops bless the sea, the people and the fishes before the saints are returned to their places in the church. The people these days include busloads of tourists, overweight with cameras and fast foods, who are welcomed by the shop owners and the Gypsies who read their fortunes, sell them trinkets and occasionally redistribute their wealth. The tourists, cowboys and the clergy are also present on the closest

Sunday to October 22 when pilgrims once came to celebrate Mary Salome with a similar event.

In May of 1980, LM and I drove from Paris to the south on our own two-week holiday pilgrimage to see how well we traveled together before making a commitment to living together. Our destination at the time was Barcelona, but we decided to take our time and see something of the French Mediterranean coast before crossing the Pyrenees into Spain.[6] We spent a night in Avignon at the Hôtel Regina, on the rue de la République a block off the main square, the Place de l'Horloge, with its New Orleans bordello décor, where we read in the Michelin green guide about the celebrations in the Stes-Maries and decided to stop there for the night and witness the event. However well traveled we may have been, a certain naïveté continued to cling to our spontaneous plans.

We steered the rented motor car with Portuguese license plates into the northern reaches of the Camargue, the great alluvial plain (367 square miles) at the Rhone delta, through which once flowed sufficient sand, mud and the detritus of the annual flooding to cover Paris in a blanket of silt 10.5 inches thick, had it flowed through that city. The state constructed a seawall and river dikes

---

[6] In fact, we did not stay in that marvelous city: when we arrived the rain poured in dark gushings and we'd neglected to make a hotel reservation (never again!). LM recalled staying years earlier in a small coastal town called Sitges, about 20 kilometers southwest of Barcelona, and so we drove in the slashing rain to that then quiet place and found a room with a balcony facing the sea in the same hotel LM had stayed in previously managed by a Portuguese "letch" (as the young women used to say) who claimed to remember her perfectly. Whether or not he did turned out to be irrelevant and we enjoyed several days of good food, drink and sunshine before taking the overnight train back to Paris.

in the 19th century which have partially curtailed the loss of earth to the sea, but not completely: the town of Aigues-Mortes, whence in 1248 Louis IX (later made a Saint for his efforts on behalf of Christendom and his treasury) embarked in an armada on a crusade to combat the infidels in Palestine, is today five kilometers inland. The Camargue supports some agriculture and salt farming but is best known for its cattle-raising, some of which are supplied to bull fight organizers, and the ranches' cowboys called "*gardiens*" herding the cattle on horseback, poking the beasts with the traditional long-poled trident, their wide-brimmed felt hats protecting them from rain and sun, though one suspects that these have become more tourist attractions today given the technological advances in cattle-raising.

As we moved deeper into the flat, largely unpopulated landscape, dotted here and there with a ranch house called "*mas*" (with the "s" pronounced in the region), we noticed an increasing density of traffic on the only road to the sea. Indeed, traffic soon came to a standstill and moved only occasionally in jerks and stops before coming completely still. With several kilometers remaining before we even reached the outskirts of the town, we came to our senses and realized that, if the traffic was so heavy this far from our destination, we would encounter severe difficulties in finding a room, not to speak of a place to park the car. In brief, with much effort and cursing the Fates who oversee the tourist industry we turned the car around and headed north and west to see what we might substitute for the Gypsy fête at the Stes-Maries-de-la-mer. We spent the rest of the day and into the darkening evening unsuccessfully searching for a place to rest our weary heads, including frustrating stops in Montpellier and Grau-du-Roi (where we at least ate a small slice of pizza each for energy). Finally, exhausted, frustrated and hungry, we rolled into the coastal town of Sète, parked the car illegally on the canal, walked into the Grand Hotel where a room overlooking the canal was available (prices at this point played no role at all). By 10:00 p.m. we were ensconced on the terrace of a restaurant sipping a pastis ordering a splendid seafood meal in an aura of relaxed well-being bordering on a marijuana-induced high. But we did not forget the Gypsies and the village on the sea with the fortified church.

Now, in October two years later, we were determined to achieve that which we had missed then. We called ahead and made reservations at a hotel across the street from the low seawall and beach, having assured ourselves that blustery, rainy and chilly October would preclude the presence of unduly large numbers of tourists. The satisfaction of making a correct prediction is similar to that of the pothead's spiral into the outer space of the mind, and is completely legal.

I have written elsewhere about our visits to the Stes-Maries, so the note I made in the journal at the time may suffice here.[7]

24.X.82. The Saintes Maries de la mer at the end of October in the soft rain and gray skies is still worth

---

[7] "Blessing the Sea at the Saintes-Maries-de-la-Mer" in *Mediterranean Sketches* (Vineyard Press, 2005).

visiting, esp. for the Fête involving the blessing of the sea (even if one misses the mass in the church and has to put up with the inevitable busloads of pink and gray tourists in their raincoats and cameras). The procession itself has surely degenerated since the origin of the phenomenon. The priests have bull horns and the *gardiens* have seen better days. Even with all the jostling and clicking of cameras there is a certain dignity in the procession until it reaches the boat on the beach, set up an hour before with the assistance of a McCormick tractor, whereupon, once the *gardiens* and their horses (gray all like the others) are standing shivering in the drizzle in the waves of the sea, a few sentences are spoken by the chief priest into the bullhorn, a few phrases (possibly in Provençal) are sung by the other priests and acolytes and, presto, the whole entourage turns around, riders using their horses to push the crowds back, and heads across the beach to the street and back to the church. The service in the church lasts one hour, the procession almost the same time. (I somehow doubt these cowboys would understand Waylon Jennings' "This Outlaw Bit has Done Got Outta Hand".) In the innocuous but chilling overcast day the pilgrimage seems oddly unreal, as if it were done for TV rather than for any intrinsic, traditional reason. Perhaps the tourist spectacle element of it has ineluctably altered the proceedings to the point of atrophy. It no longer *means* anything except the spectacle itself. When this is done in the spring in fine weather it must be a circus. Still, looking out of the hotel window onto the deserted beach and the washed out colors of the sky and the sea remains

46

somehow satisfying; like the opening of English thrillers from the 30's – Brighton beach in the mist as Macheath slips around the corner with his smile and invisible knife after having violated the underage widow while a corpse floats cold and lonely under the pilings of the rotting dock. Somehow gray chill and shivering does not seem appropriate for the Mediterranean coast of France, but we're no longer tourists in this land. The Sunday issue of the local newspaper has a full page article on Georges Brassens. Only in France could this happen. Or …?

No doubt the town lives from the income provided by the masses of tourists that infest the place during the celebrations and in the summer; it is after all a seatown with a beach and stores selling trinkets. As early as the mid-1950s sensitive admirers of France and its cultures such as Richard Aldington (in his book *An Introduction to Mistral*) complained about the tourists and *cinéastes* who made the event a travesty. There are far more of them today than then.

Not mentioned in the journal but implacably fixed on the screen of my memory is another lesson learned in the Stes-Maries that October: vigilance when reading menus is the pre-requisite for staying out of the poor house. The invoice printed below remains a sharp reminder of that experience. If I may plagiarize and paraphrase my own work:[8] The restaurant Le Brûleur de Loups sat comfortably warmed below our hotel and we settled in

---

[8] *Paris Now and Then* (Vineyard Press, rev. ed. 2004), 46-47.

for seafood delight we believed on the basis of no previous knowledge would be not just good but excellent. As we sipped a pastis, feeling good in our skins, I noticed the fresh lobster appeared to be very reasonably priced. The waiter raised our anticipation to a higher level of intensity by hauling out one of the beasts from the aquarium to allow us to visually imagine the treat awaiting only our order.

And a glorious meal it was, one of those life-enhancing culinary experiences that occur all too rarely in one's life. But what price glory? The price I read on the menu reflected the cost of the lobster per 100 grams – the full animal, shell and all, weighed close to 600 grams! We barely had enough cash to cover the cost of the trip and at the time possessed no credit cards. Our new motto, obviously, was "read menus with sufficient attention to details."

●

Whilst all this happened, we seriously searched for a permanent place to spend the time we would have in France.

During Andrea's visit toward the end of the month, we continued to look at possible rental houses around Avignon which we chose over Aix-en-Provence as the place where we would live for as long as the money held out. We chose Avignon over Aix because we found the former smaller and more compact, at least inside the ramparts that encircle the old city, and more comfortable to walk around. In his informative and gracefully written, if occasionally inaccurate, book *Aspects of Provence* (1952), James Pope-Hennessy has this to say about the differences between Avignon and Aix:

> Avignon is in every way the antithesis to Aix-en-Provence. Aix is a sad and secret city. It is a composition of shadowy streets and moss-grown fountains, of old ladies dressed in black on long, late Sunday afternoons, of high, cold, echoing cafés only noisy in the university term. People in Aix walk quickly, but with discretion, while Avignon (like New Orleans) is one of those cities in which people look you in the eyes. In Avignon there are days on which everyone seems young and all the young seem beautiful.

The gap between 1952 and 1982 is only 30 years, a mere generation, but the numbers do not tell anywhere near the full story which must consider the deleterious effects of mass tourism and the polluting of the environment. It is unlikely any sensitive witness to the times would today, or in 1982, describe the two cities in such terms. We, in any case, found Avignon to be friendlier, more *doable* that Aix. There are other points of view, one of which is contained in the exemplary memoir of the place by M.F.K. Fisher entitled *Map of Another Town. A Memoir of Provence* (1964), a model of how such memoirs should be written.

One matter did not enter into our considerations when we chose Avignon: tourists. Since the end of the 1950s one cannot avoid the grumbling, tumbling, mumbling, stumbling tourists in their masses cluttering up the landscape by the busloads, pandering to the ubiquitous greed of local, small and big-time entrepreneurs who will destroy both viable historic traditions and customs as quickly as they destroy the land with bulldozers and cranes to construct yet another cement block full of ticky tack spaces, all the same measurements and ugliness. One would like Pope-Hennessy to have been prescient when he wrote in the book already cited, "In spite of certain magnificent churches and some world-famous Roman remains, Provence will never be as overrun with tourists as, say, Tuscany. Patently it has less to offer." But in this regard he could not have been more wrong.

Even without considering the unfortunate problem of tourists, the places around Avignon we looked at were too dark and damp, or too expensive, or in an inconvenient location. As the end of the month approached, and our anxiety and trepidation increased, we stumbled upon a small ad in the weekly, *84*, an advertisement publication for the Vaucluse (84 is the number of the Vaucluse department), announcing a furnished apartment for rent in the village of Tavel, some 15 kilometers northwest of Avignon in the Gard department across the Rhône River. The advert provided a telephone number, true enough, but of what use could that be to those who cannot speak the language of the person on the other end of the line?

Recalling that in Germany at least there existed in railroad stations what is called a *Zimmernachweis*, a hotel information bureau that not only offers data about accommodations but will make reservations for those whose linguistic accomplishments do not include German, we drove as quickly as we could to Avignon and the old railroad station at the foot of the rue de la Republique and cours Jaurès. There a friendly woman who spoke good English agreed to call the number in the ad and get directions to the village should the house still be for rent. It was, she made appointment and armed with the directions (once in the village, turn right at the hardware store – *quincaillerie*), we drove with Andrea as dusk began to fall to meet the owner of the property, Mme Marie-Louise Mourre, an elderly Taveloise who spoke no English (but was a great fan of the *Dallas* television show, dubbed in French, which had convinced her that Texans spent the entire day cheating on their spouses and business partners, and drinking bourbon). The combined French knowledge of the three Americans was not terribly wide, or deep, but we all persevered.

The property certainly seemed worth our desparate perseverance, even in the deepening crepuscule of the evening in October when night comes early to the South. We did indeed make a right hand turn into the mildly steep rue Mireille and found the gated house and grounds about 100 meters up the road on the right. We later discovered that the address we were to use was:

Chez Mme Mourre
rue du Seigneur
30126 Tavel

The discrepancy is explained by the fact that Mme Mourre, a fourth generation Táveloise, had moved in her early married life from a smaller house in the rue du Seigneur to the present one on the eastern edge of the village, but the couple were reluctant to give up their original address, which she proudly informed us was a noble one, and so it was. The village officials, not wishing to bring the wrath of the formidable woman and her husband down on their heads, allowed the unusual circumstance to stand. The mailman would have known where they lived in any case; the village is that small, with barely 1300 inhabitants including those in the village's horrible suburb further up the hill. Apparently it is not uncommon for villages constructed in the Middle Ages to have grown suburbs in the 20th century. The only thing that recommends Tavel's Provençal Levittown called Vallongue is the view of the village from an unusual angle on one side and the *autoroute* to Narbonne on the other. The awful collection of sterile villas in the "Provence style" no doubt appealed to those who grew up in the old cold, stone, unelectrified, unheated buildings of the village; to them I suppose it was (and is?) paradise, not to speak of status.

Mme Mourre had an albino cat named Bébé and a hysterical terrier called Finette, both of whom we would come to know all too well, in addition to an Italian *femme de ménage* called Micheline who came to clean two or three times a week.

The section of the house bordering on the street contained a small, one-bedroom apartment at ground level with an unheated toilet inserted a meter or so from

52

the front door. As noted, Mme Mourre was a formidable woman; I am not at all sure I could have made regular use of that facility during the rather cold winters that can chill the region, despite the fact that I had lived for three years in a cold-water flat with an unheated toilet up a flight of stairs in Heidelberg.

Abutting Mme Mourre's apartment were two large spaces originally containing the various paraphernalia required of a working vineyard which she and her husband had operated until his death some years earlier. Above these spaces they had constructed an apartment consisting of a bathroom (with a sink, a sitting tub and a handheld shower head on two meters of flexible rubber), a separate toilet (quite a civilized invention), three small bedrooms, a kitchen and a living room, both of the latter afforded access to the large terrace overlooking the valley and the wine cooperative to the southeast. The garden with its fig tree, fountain and space for growing vegetables lay at the foot of the property. A series of large and small windows allowed sunlight and breeze into two of the bedrooms, the kitchen and the living room. The Mourres called the complex La Rose de Vents, spelled out on the façade facing the courtyard.

All this we discovered more or less by accident. French law governing owner-tenant relations is complex and to a large extent protects the tenant as much or more as the owner. Given this situation owners are hesitant to do anything that might jeopardize their legal relations with their tenants. All of which is to say that Mme Mourre, ever over-cautious about such matters, informed us we could not enter the apartment because the present renters still occupied the premises, though our potential *propriétaire* (landlord – *proprio*, in the vernacular) allowed us (her potential *locataires* – tenants) to mount the stairs and look in the windows and enjoy the darkening vista of vineyards and small houses with ocher-tiled roofs from the extra large terrace. While the three of us shyly peeked in the windows to the living room and made our way around the walkway, the young lady of the tenant couple with no hesitation opened the kitchen door and beckoned us inside to view the apartment, which we did leaving as quickly as we thought polite, surprised at the number of rooms.

All this would cost a monthly 2000 francs (approximately $285 at the time) rent plus utilities. Despite the lack of language facilities, somehow we explained our reasons for being there, a bit about ourselves, and reached an understanding regarding what we would like and what it would cost. Mme Mourre allowed as how she would decide which of the petitioners clamoring for the house would get the nod, so to speak, by the end of the month, which we were fast approaching with panic beginning to gnaw at our bellies. We said as best we could that we hoped she would smile with the brightness of the Provençal sun upon us and we took our leave, thinking that the fact of our being Americans might be of sufficient interest to her to sway her in our direction. In the meantime we continued the frustrating search.

Among other steps we took toward resolving the housing problem was the placement of a small advert in the same weekly, *84*, which read,

Ecrivain américain cherche à louer
Villa ou appart meublé 2 chbres min
Env Avignon. Tél. (90) 74.11.21. Ecr.
84 D 847

All of two people responded; one didn't show up for
the appointment, the other very friendly couple gave us
cognac and Gauloise and showed us a small house in the
middle of the village of Velleron near L'Isle-sur-la-
Sorgue: three bedrooms, a WC and separate bath
upstairs, kitchen and living room with fireplace
downstairs, directly across from the *mairie* and the
village square. The rooms we found minuscule and dark,
in addition to which the house lacked central heating, a
telephone, a balcony and a garden. We had not made this
move to live in the situation described by the French
phrase for crepuscule, *"Entre le chien et le loup."* We
wanted the Van Gogh luminous light of Provence,
nothing less (or darker) would do – we hoped. After all,
did not Stephen Spender note somewhere something
about "the sun of serious intent in the south where the
day's business is to be light." And we had already been
spoiled by the house in Tavel with all the things we
looked for, including a telephone. Another small
apartment in a Saint Rémy house possessed a fine garden
but was otherwise not appropriate for us.

Our anxiety increased, though we attempted to
repress it, and we tossed and turned at night without
restful sleep. Finally, on November 1, at 6:15 p.m., Mme
Mourre telephoned us at the Potter house to say we could

sleep soundly that night: she had decided, after discussing the matter with her children, to reject the other 19 applicants and rent the apartment to us. Witty lady, Mme Mourre. We could move into the place on the third of November. We wrote to the couple in Velleron offering our thanks but no thanks.

One speaks of a flood of relief, and so it is as we experienced it that night. True, we didn't really know the condition of the furniture or the kitchen, though we had briefly walked through part of the place. We also had no idea what the winter would be like, surely no snow in the sunny South of France, and how cold could it possibly be when the rest of the year baked under the Mediterranean sun? What we did know is that we would have a Provençal roof over our American heads, and that for the nonce was entirely sufficient.

And as far as the Apt house mouse was concerned, Mme Mourre's telephone call came not a moment too soon. He'd been there from the beginning and I did my best to trap him, but clearly I was and most probably still am not good at mice, and I could not figure out how the mousetrap worked. Generally he made no demands and maintained his invisibility with only minor noises after we'd retired for the night. Toward the end of the month I found it necessary to conduct an interesting one-way conversation with the mouse; when we finished communicating I thought he'd promised to leave the potatoes alone and stay out of sight until we went to bed; whatever he could get out of the garbage was his. Couldn't take much to fill that minuscule stomach; he was a very small if persistent mouse. The day before we moved to Tavel the ballsy little devil, who had been hesitantly with us for several days, suddenly became rather too rambunctious with too much courage, perhaps driven by hunger. At mid-morning he (we always somehow assumed it was a male in those comfortable pre-politically correct days whereas today we are bludgeoned by the PC-police into using such cumbersome locutions as, in this case, "he-she-or-it") began stumbling around behind the fridge making a lot of noise. We thought that he probably missed the baguette we had unthinkingly left out a couple of nights previously, which he of course assumed was meant for he himself and he ate the crust off half of it before we awakened to the deed the next morning.

So Tavel it would be, a village about which we knew little beyond its reputation for growing and vintnering fine rosé wine.

Chapter II

Early Days Chez Mme Mourre

A week before we moved to Tavel, LM began attending a beginner's French language class at the University in Avignon where she met the partially demented young German, Roswitha, who became our first acquaintance in the Midi. Her French boy friend, Jean-Louis, with whom she lived on a hill on the western side of the river in Les Angles, was in the process of completing his medical studies and had just announced to her that he was gay, throwing her into something of a tizzy. He made regular trips to Marseille to work on a course in sub-aquatic medicine, or so he told everyone; Roswitha said he went to a gay sauna. She arranged an appointment with an acupuncturist in Aix; we wondered if this would be of any help to them, but we never found out. A short, slender figure with bright red hair, she seemed not quite made for the real world in which some nasty things occasionally happen. She clearly had little idea how to deal with the situation with which Jean-Louis presented her and she tended to run about, not quite amok, but with little direction. Nonetheless, she was generous with her time and provided us with much useful information about living in the region. Her French, while far from perfect, was far better than ours, and her English good enough, though occasionally she and I spoke German when her

English broke down. One felt sympathy for the young woman, but would rather not have heard the details about her troubled relationship with the apparently incorrigible Jean-Louis. We continued to see her from time to time throughout our stay; she moved into her own small apartment after it became clear Jean-Louis' future did not have room for her. We last saw her in late September when she came to dinner with some other friends. The last we heard, she had opened a hair salon in Avignon, but that was many years ago.

While still in Apt, after breakfast on the small terrace overlooking the valley, LM drove a few times the hour each way back and forth along the two lane so-called national road in the Peugeot clunker. We eventually came to know that road intimately before the authorities chopped it up in the late 1990s, installing a series of round-abouts to control the traffic that did not require such constructions bur rather a closer attention to the road that most drivers apparently were willing to give. *Bouf*! Since the class started early, when it started, LM had to leave in the dark in order to reach the university, down the rocky driveway to the street. Fortunately when we moved to Tavel the trip was much shorter and less hazardous. While she studied with due diligence, I began making notes for the second volume of the Berlin novel and started however hesitantly to write out by hand pages of the rather meandering notes of the dying, ancient professor of history who had survived the war and was struggling in the bombed out city to make sense of his life and his nation's history.

Avignon, the fabled City of the Popes during what is known as the Babylonian Captivity (1309-1377) when French popes ruled the Roman church from this French city. A Provençal proverb has it that "he who takes leave of Avignon takes leave of his senses." One needn't be so extreme in one's view of the matter but the city does captivate many of us who came to know it even in its late 20th century incarnation as a mass tourism destination: there remain certain corners and small squares and lanes where few tourists venture and where one can still become infused with the spirit and physical atmosphere of the place throughout its long and varied history.

Lawrence Durrell, who lived in the Midi for the last 33 years of his life, wrote a considerable number of words about the city in prose (*The Avignon Quintet*) and poetry. Here is an example of the latter.

Avignon
Come, meet me in some dead café –
A puff of cognac or a sip of smoke
Will grant a more prolific light,
Say there is nothing to revoke.

A veteran with no arm will press
A phantom sorrow in his sleeve;
The aching stump may well insist
On memories it cannot relieve.

Late cats, the city's thumbscrews twist.
Night falls in its profuse derision,
Brings candle-power to younger lives,

Cancels in me the primal vision.

Come, random with me in the rain,
In ghastly harness like a dream,
In rainwashed streets of saddened dark
Where nothing moves that does not seem.

I like the "late cats", of which there are many in the region, and if the city's metaphoric thumbscrews twist the poor creatures, one can imagine the squalls of screeching pain in the night. I also like the use of the word "random" as a verb for walk: the French for a walk or a ramble is *"randonnée"*, so the wordplay works well. But the poem is rather too dark on the whole and doesn't convey the possibility of one becoming overcome with a swoon of vertigo at the pleasures of simply being part of life there. Even in what the city officials call "off season", winter is also the time to be there when the trees and streets are bare.

In his *Notes d'un Voyage dans le Midi de la France* (1835) Prosper Mérimée, the author of the original text of "Carmen" among much else, wrote that "Avignon gives the impression of a garrison town (or has the look of a garrison town). All the large buildings are designed in military style, and its palaces, as well as its churches, look like so many fortresses ... everything points to a tradition of rebellion and civil war." Mérimée wrote not long after the Revolution and the Napoléonic Wars, the depredations of which caused havoc to the city's architecture, but if one looks at the Palace of the Popes one cannot help but agree with his judgment, for the very good reason that the Avignon popes, over a period of 30 years, caused the structures to be built higgledy-piggledy as a fortified palatial residence and church with cloisters.

There are countless stories of the corruption and decadence of the religious officials, their courtiers and the common people during the reign of the French popes in Avignon; the sobriquet "Babylonian captivity" is well deserved. The poet and former priest, Francesco Petrarch (1304-1374), who lived there then, wrote several of these to a friend and, without dismembering the integument of this chapter, here is one of his general views of the matter (in the Morris Bishop translation).

> Avignon is the home of infidelity. The future life is regarded as an empty fable, and hell likewise. The resurrection of the body, the world's promised end, Christ's coming to sit in judgment, are treated as old wives' tales. License to sin is taken as liberal open-mindedness. The city is the habitation of demons. Prostitutes swarm on the papal beds. Aged striplings, white-haired, wide-gowned, foul-minded, abandon themselves to every lust. Satan urges them with every stimulant for failing powers.
>
> Husbands of ravished women are driven from their homes to keep them quiet, they are forced to take back wives pregnant by the courtiers, and then, after child birth, to return them to their unholy unions. Everyone knows this, but few dare speak, or they are deterred by shame.

That does somehow recall Sodom and Gomorrah, with a touch of the Marquis de Sade, and one wonders how close to the truth the description really is. Clearly and deeply offended by what he saw, Petrarch in fact removed himself from the sinful city as often as he could to the clean air and pastoral environment of the Fontaine-de-Vaucluse where he contemplated life, wrote poems and thought about his beloved Laura (more about her in Chapter V), where he did not have to see the increasingly stupendous construction as an increasingly pompous and self-reflective palace.

The vast yellow-beige buildings did not escape the ravages of the Revolution when anything associated with the Old Regime, such as the Catholic Church, suffered severe damage if not destruction by a populace delirious with pent-up frustration violently released at its former oppressors. If they did not kill the royalty (though several died at the guillotine), the nobility (the sword) and the priesthood (the robe) the enraged peasantry and working class could vent their explosive temperaments on the property of the various aristocracies. The disparagement of church property did not end with the bourgeois takeover of the Revolution: Napoléon stabled his army's horses in the Palace of the Popes and the soldiers had no hesitation in using the rooms there as toilets. One can easily imagine the stench this added to the already foul-smelling city where bathing was considered an unnecessarily dangerous and unhealthy thing to undertake.

During his 1882 visit to the city, as it had on two earlier occasions, the Palace made a deep, but negative impression on the American-British novelist Henry James, though he admitted that this third encounter with the gigantic pile he associated with an umbrella because it rained most of the time he spent there. He thought it "The dreariest of all historical buildings ... The place is as intricate as it is vast and as desolate as it is dirty." He does, however, note that the vast structure of buildings and courtyards had suffered abuses and despoilments throughout its existence, including use as a barracks for line regiments, as it was when he then made his way through its passages "... and the main characteristics of a barrack – and extreme nudity and a very queer smell – prevail throughout its endless compartments." There is a school of thought that believes Henry James was of a particularly overly finicky constitution, whose olfactory and other senses took offence at the slightest hint of the vulgar and common. A reading of his travel works should dispel that notion when one recalls the conditions under which he traveled in the age without air-conditioning, modern transportation opportunities, and no flush toilets. He was indeed a rather hearty, and cleverly observant traveler.

The Papal Palace suffered additional pillage and destruction during the German occupation of the city (1942-44). Along the walls of the smaller chapel, soldiers cut out the heads of the frescoes and sold them to unscrupulous art dealers. In the vestiary that contained a statue of Charles IV, the Wehrmacht members decorated him with a swastika then placed a bottle in his hand which they proceeded to knock off by throwing large stones at it. The French curator attempted to stop the game but the soldiers laughed and shoved him out of the room. The trembling official found an officer and explained to him that Charles IV was in fact the King of Bohemia, a German, not a Frenchman, whereafter the officer ensured that the statute reverted from target to memorial once again. When we took visitors to see the Palace they found little evidence of the depredations; realizing the value of the great edifice looming over the Place de la Palace as a tourist destination, national and local officials had restored the grand conglomeration to a clean and well-lit environment so beloved by tour groups of many nationalities.

There was, and is, more to Avignon than the big ticket tourist venues and we learned to know them rather quickly, but more about them anon.

•

On November 3, we moved into Mme Mourre's house, intimately and dangerously close to the source of the *premier rosé du monde*. The Taveloises limit their claim for the wine to France, as the bright neon sign on the roof of the cooperative proudly proclaims, but we've learned it *is* the best in the world, at least the top quality vintages. The Papal Court in Avignon consumed considerable amounts of it during the period of the Popes in their palace there. Louis XIV and Philippe le Bel both praised and drank the wine, which became known then as the wine of kings and the king of wines. In 1936, the wine police awarded Tavel the first AOC (Appellation d'Origine Contrôlée) designation for a rosé in France. In order to be a Tavel wine it must be a rosé. Given the inordinately large role wine plays in our life having the Tavel cooperative just down the road from our house made certain aspects of that life relatively easier. And given the limited budget at our disposal we warmly welcomed the, for us, novel idea of purchasing wine *en gros*. During the first several days there we bought from the local vineyards that had caves in the village, but over the long haul this would impinge far too deleteriously on our budget. At the cooperative, for a few francs we invested in an 11-liter plastic container which the fine people there would fill as needed. The filling process was also new to us: since in those days we drank the least expensive blend of rosés from various small vineyards in the region (something we can no longer tolerate because apparently our taste buds have matured and reject the cheap plonk formerly savored with gusto), when we trudged into the sales room the attendant took our container to a pump, unceremoniously stuck the nozzle into the container and pumped eleven liters of the stuff, the same action and the same hose and nozzle as that in the local gas station's gas pump. Thirty-five francs for 11 liters was a reasonable price for fairly good but not excellent wine. Once we got the wine home we decanted it into bottles we'd saved from previous purchases of other wines at the supermarket or vineyards in the Vaucluse.

And so we rarely ran out of that titillating nectar, except on occasion in the summer time when it sat too long in the container (shortage of bottles) or in the closet where we stored the bottles. The refrigerator in the apartment was European, not American, in size, which means a third of the capacity found in most American fridges, and thus could not simultaneously contain more than one or two bottles of wine requiring cooling. The European concept of refrigeration requirements has changed in recent decades, that is to say it has grown larger and their cooling apparatuses have increased in size accordingly. But in those days the habit of supermarket buying for a week or more and storing the goods appropriately at home had not yet filtered completely through the socio-economic consciousness of the general population. One shopped as needed for the day or at most two days, thus did not require extensive refrigeration. Indeed, I well recall living in Heidelberg without any refrigeration capacity except the space between the windows and the shutters which could only be used in the winter. Today, with the Americanization of European societies, as much as they either refuse to admit it or loudly and constantly bemoan it, all this has changed to a large degree. To be sure, one can still find small family owned grocery stores, bakeries and butcher shops in the villages and towns in France, but the shopping malls now spread their ugly but functional structures across the landscape like the dreck from a broken oil pipeline.

Be that as it may, we became loyal and frequent customers at the Tavel wine cooperative. Indeed we had heard about Tavel rosé before we discussed moving to the Midi. In early 1981, the professors Ian MacNiven and Harry T. Moore published, and I immediately read, the correspondence between Richard Aldington and

Lawrence Durrell in which the latter enthuses about the qualities of the Tavel wine. Not to be outdone I enthused about it a bit myself as soon as we moved into Le Marquis in Apt. A citation or two from letters I wrote to my brother Dean will give the Reader some idea of the excitement with which we greeted the godly nectar.

> ... I feel compelled to write if only to tell you that if nothing else, Durrell is right about the Tavel; it is marvelous ... (This Tavel is *bloody* good, and dinner lies yet ahead ...) By the good leg of Christ, this place must be what is meant by joy. Imagine yourself looking for miles over a valley in Provence from the terrace of an old stone house with a bottle of Tavel and a copy of *Joy of Cooking* ... The bottle of Tavel is empty and dinner must be started ...

The infatuation with the wine commenced early in our stay: I wrote the letter on the first of October, the day we moved into the Apt house. The dinner would be our first home-cooked meal in France: fillets of veal, salad, a baguette and of course the wine. The infatuation has never lost its intense fascination, though we do not drink much of it here on this sub-tropical island: too rare and expensive.

The Tavel cooperative required we take with us a "*congé du registre*" form in case the customs police ("*flic de duane*" in the vernacular) pounce on us as we wended our way home, less than a kilometer away. Highly unlikely, but form is form, and form must be followed.

These days we no longer receive such a form. It is all very mysterious, very French.

One is at times reminded that Christianity is a Mediterranean religion that brought with it to the north "the grapes and vine-branches indispensable to its mysteries." (Thus Marc Bloch in his scholarly study *French Rural History.*) Indeed, historically wine production in Europe responded to not only the demand for a pleasurable libation but also to the requirements of the liturgy: without wine there would be no mass, no communion, an unthinkable situation in Roman Catholic countries.

In 1734, an obscure, and for us anonymous, royal official wrote in the capitation register, "The inhabitants of Tavel do not have any commerce or industry. But do have a major resource with the sale of their highly desirable wine of quality." One cannot help but wonder how much of the wine the clerk tasted before writing about it. Long before this the Phoenicians and the Romans introduced vines into the Rhône River valley and over the centuries the landowners in and around Tavel planted both cereals and vines to produce their increasingly well-known rosé. By the 16th century the peasants in the neighborhood had abandoned any cultivation of cereals and planted vines in the craggy, rock-strewn earth of the fields outside the village. At the end of the 18th and the beginning of the 19th centuries, as the wealth and number of the bourgeoisie expanded so did their taste for quality wines, including the Tavel rosé. The landowners and vintners of the village prospered until the phylloxera epidemic of 1870 destroyed the vineyards. Determined not to lose the well-earned reputation for producing the best rosé in France, and to replenish their bank accounts they regrouped and replanted and harvested anew the source of their livelihoods. One of the first pressure groups in French agriculture was established in Tavel in 1902 and in 1928, after a lengthy, rough and tumble, legal battle, the vintners achieved a legal definition of the Tavel appellation growing region. Finally, in 1936 they obtained the AOC classification: other areas of the world now produce rosé wines, but only those grown in Tavel can proclaim their origin in the fields around the village. And none of them equals the best of the Tavel growths.

And speaking (writing actually, and you The Reader are reading) of wine, I cannot allow the opportunity to pass unused to cite a short piece cut from a newspaper (in English so it probably appeared in the IHT) and pasted in the journal on April 2, 1983.

> Some years ago, so the story goes, Philippe de Rothschild, the owner of Château Mouton-Rothschild in Bordeaux, was entertaining a notably aggressive wine writer–we'll call him George–at the château. A steward appeared for instructions on lunch. "What shall we drink?" Baron Philippe said, more to himself than to anyone else.
>
> The scribe was ready. "You know," he said, "it's been years since I tasted the 1874."
>
> Without missing a beat, Baron Philippe patted his guest's arm, smiled sadly and said, "It's not a luncheon wine, George. It's not a luncheon wine."

Needless to say, since then the phrase "It's not a luncheon wine, George" has become a staple in my (I won't speak for LM here) bag of vocabularies to be pulled out at appropriate, and some no doubt not appropriate, moments.

●

Settling in to a new residence can be an unsettling experience, particularly when the décor and appointments are not one's own, but this time the process went smoothly, such was our joy and relief at finally having a place to call our own. We immediately discovered several disadvantages in the apartment, which our excitement at being there allowed us to accept with a modicum of equipoise and a bit of a dent in the bank account. For one thing the heating oil tank lacked oil. Mme Mourre called the oil delivery firm to arrange to have it filled. This took several days. Additionally the bedrooms contained no electric outlets; the kitchen and living room sported one each, and not a reading lamp could be found in the place. In fact, the only light shed after dark came from the dim overhead fixtures for which some of the bulbs were missing. Fortunately the village hardware store is just down the street, and the shopping center south of Avignon sells extension cords and lamps.

To add to the richness of the settling-in activities, Mother Nature threw a welcome party for us. *"Bienvenue à Tavel!"*

The party began with dinner the evening of November 6 at the Auberge de Tavel, to which we treated ourselves. The wind had picked up considerably but no more than the customary mistral to which we had more or less accustomed ourselves in the short time we'd been in the Midi, despite the power outages. One of the good things about the Auberge was the fact that it took us all of one and a half minutes to walk to it. The restaurant is rustic in décor but comfortable with high-beamed ceilings and whitewashed stone walls covered with mediocre oil paintings of local sites, a small bar and a garden where meals are served in season. The food, of course, constituted the more important attraction and we did not deny ourselves in this regard.

Given the supper we ate the following night, it may be of interest to relate in some but not too much detail our meal at the Auberge. We each chose the 85 franc menu, which with a bottle and a half of Tavel rosé (what else?) and two espressos brought the total to 290 francs, about $40.00 at the current exchange rate. This was too expensive for us to indulge in too often, but we thought then and do so now, where can one eat so well for that amount? A rich duck paté and flan of salmon in curry sauce, followed by *sole aux Châteauneuf-du-Pape* (the first time I'd ever eaten fish done in a red wine sauce), a luscious lamb stew, then a cheese course and an obscenely rich chocolate cake. Not at all bad for the start of our welcome festivities.

To say we suffered the next day for the richness of the dinner would be safe to say, if one defined "suffer" as many trips to the WC and a mild amount of discomfort in the lower abdomen. Nonetheless, we learned yet another lesson to guide our gustatory experiences, not always, to be sure, but often enough: order one first course to be shared, two entrées (also to be shared), a few morsels of cheese and no dessert fits our capacities quite nicely.

The consumption of a couple of glasses of cognac at home before going to bed abetted such a sound and deep sleep that we were not aware of the weather until rather early the following morning at 3:00 a.m., when the savagery of the tempest shocked us with its intensity. This was no usual mistral. And what one thought was the mistral in Apt turned out to be nothing more than a gentle sway of breeze in the olive trees.

The raging wind that stormed and howled at monster hurricane speed through the region that day astounded us with fright. When the doors to the terrace began to shake and bow inward, popping out of their closing joints, we panicked thinking the glass would shatter into a thousand pieces and cut the interior to shreds. We hurriedly closed the metal shutters and left one glass paned door open in the living room and kitchen to relieve the pressure on the doors and allow less resistance to the wind. This made the place breezy and chilly, not to say cold, a discomfort added to by our complete ignorance as to what one should do in such instances and an indisposition caused by the meal the night before. The electricity went off at regular intervals and we told each other this could not possibly go on much longer, but of course it did. We had not considered the fact that our apartment and terrace sat on the one of the highest most open parts of the village, affording a fine view, to be sure, but also providing the focal point for the wind to concentrate its force and power.

With some trepidation about leaving the place unattended we drove off to the Utopia repertory film theater in Avignon to see the early evening showing of Werner Herzog's wild and crazy *Fitzcarraldo* (German with French subtitles), hoping the car would not be blown off the road. Klaus Kinsky, at his most over-the-top, scenery chewing best, played the role of the demented Fitzcarraldo, giving a fine imitation of Richard Widmark's infamous giggle as he shoved the old lady in the wheelchair down the flight of stairs. For two hours we forgot the storm and gave ourselves to the cinema. Afterward, hesitating to drive back to the wind-torn environs of Tavel, feeling secure in the relatively calm streets on the city, we marched into the then French equivalent of McDonalds called Quick on the main thoroughfare and ate burgers and fries and drank Kronenberg beer on the second floor in the window watching bits of flotsam and jetsam fly about the street and citizens give up trying to protect themselves with umbrellas that snapped and turned inside out in the space of a second or two. We felt just fine for those moments.

Welcome to Provence.

We reached the house safely but slept poorly: the electricity went awry again in the middle of the night and things began to fly about in the air: tree branches, the well-known ochre Provençal roof tiles, light animals, wigs, and the like. At some point in the depths of the early morning's swirling blackness the metal chimney for our heating system snapped off at the base. The cracking sound sent us into a paroxysm of panic until I ventured outside on the walkway around the apartment to determine its origin. The broken pipe leaned forlornly against the terrace railing; clearly it had not been cemented into place by a professional cementer. Not being one myself, I did what I could to jam it back into its place without much faith that it would hold in that wind until morning when we might be able to find a real cementer to ensure its secure placement against winds of any speed and force.

Several days later an ancient, age-bent at the waist with uncombed white hair and beard, a true exemplar of the adjective "grizzled", showed up with an equally ancient scuffed leather tool bag. In one of the garages we found a small wooden ladder that had long since lost whatever colored paint it once wore, onto which the ancient climbed to examine the damage. Gutturally mumbling to us incomprehensible phrases in what seemed to be the local Provençal dialect, and not waiting for any response from us, which he could not have received in any case, he plunged a gnarled hand (another exemplary appendage) into the faded brown-beige sack. Out came various implements from the world of house repairs, none of them of recent manufacture: hammer, screwdriver, screws, nails, smaller and larger pieces of bent metal; no cement or water or sand, but half an old baguette which must have been a talisman of sorts. To this day we are not entirely sure exactly what he hammered and screwed into place, but we never had any further trouble with the chimney pipe. Slowly he climbed down to the walkway, stuffed his implements into the sack, smiled ever so briefly as if he'd long forgotten how to arrange his facial muscles for the act, mumbled what seemed to be an attempt to say "goodbye" in English. Mme Mourre would pay him whatever his going rate was, but, mumbling our warm thanks, we gave him 20 francs for his time and effort, which he accepted with the dignity that comes with the knowledge that one is due what one is due, most especially in an emergency when one is the only alternative to discomfort or disaster. One can, in a pinch, as it were, get along without a professional cementer.

The electricity had gone out during the night, which meant, if it continued too long, everything in our minuscule *frigo* would spoil. But at least we had heat because ours came from the oil tank, which apparently powered itself (what did or do I know about such complexities?), while village electricity generated Mme Mourre's warmth. That morning at 9:00 o'clock I stood in the short line at the bakery awaiting my turn to purchase a half loaf of bread: the baguettes had long since sold out as the villagers ensured their supplies of this staff of life for the day. The baker, in a white tee shirt, wooden clogs and a large white apron covering his lack of trousers, reached out of his kitchen in which wood and fire, not electricity, charged his oven, and switched on the lights. Everyone smiled, "*Ahh ... comme toujours, alors.*"

By the time I reached our house with the warm half-loaf the power had popped off again and the baker was baking another supply of baguettes and soon all would be well with the village world. But, oh my, hadn't it been something? Thirty, 50, perhaps 100 years since the last such tempest, *bouf!* Actually it was the smaller number of years, according to the trustworthy local newspaper, which we carefully read each day to ascertain what really went on in the world. We experienced many roaring mistrals over the following 12 months, but nothing like this storm.

Narbonne-Plage flooded, large trees ripped from the ground in Sète, trains two hours late throughout the Midi, a school collapsed in Millau, windgusts of up to 170 kilometers per hour, flying objects, the Rhône spilled over its banks, parts of the Ile de la Barthelasse (that "considerable island" as Henry James called it, in the middle of the river beneath the crenellated towers of the Palace of the Popes) flooded ...

But life did move on.

Thanksgiving, there's a good example. Moira and Jim telephoned on that day, an American invention not recognized in France, despite Art Buchwald's best efforts to explain the phenomenon; LM was of course in class in Avignon. Jim rather flippantly exclaimed, "What do you mean, they don't have Thanksgiving on the last Thursday in November? The French don't like turkey?" I assured him that they do indeed like *"dinde"* and eat it quite often, but not necessarily on what Americans consider a holiday. Three hours later they called back and talked at length with LM about many things, among them the information that our friends Martin and Kate Sullivan were considering bringing their six-month old daughter Abigail for a visit in January or February, in the middle of a harsh Provençal winter. We would warmly greet them, of course, but they might find the weather rather less welcoming.

The following Saturday morning we drove to Nîmes in the rain to visit a small combination book shop and English-language school operated by a youngish English couple, June and George Lumsden, where I purchased Paul Theroux's *The Mosquito Coast* and Gertrude Stein's *The Autobiography of Alice B. Toklas*. The school had been in operation for five years but the shop had only been opened since February and held a limited collection of Penguins and the Faber paperback editions of Lawrence Durrell, but not his latest, *Constance*, or the slender *Smile in the Mind's Eye* (published by Wildwood), both of which I would have bought. June asked me to leave my name and telephone number in case any of the few other English-language writers scattered throughout the region wanted to chat about this and that and writing. For a while we thought this might lead to an interesting acquaintance or two, but it never did. We did however experience a pleasant scene at the post office when we mailed an envelope to Moira and Jim decorated with six or seven lovely colorful stamps gently placed on it by the post mistress who murmured as she pasted them in place, "*Jolies timbres.*" And so they were.

After returning from Nîmes, we drank a *marc* and smoked a cigarette against the cold and began preparations for our own Thanksgiving supper despite the fact that this was the following Saturday. The ringing of the telephone interrupted these culinary gestures: the Sullivans called to announce that, yes, they would be there at the end of February and would have with them Marty's 11-year old niece, Erin, to help care for the infant and simultaneously live through a European, or at least a French experience that would contribute toward making her "a well-rounded person of culture", if not wealth. We greeted this news warmly but warned them to bring jackets and sweaters.

We returned to the kitchen and the supper. A massive leg-thigh piece of a turkey plus three *escalopes* of white meat required roasting, potatoes required mashing, gravy to be made, but the can of Leseur peas brought with us from Washington for this purpose required only to be opened and heated. Not having a bird into which we could stuff the chestnut stuffing (improvised based on the *Joy of Cooking*), we rolled some of it up in the *tranches* of white meat for roasting and cooked the rest in a covered sauce pan on top of the stove above the lowest possible heat. Everything tasted so good we overate and had to imbibe an additional *marc* to help the digestion accompanied by some fairly moderate sounds on the *France-Musique* radio station. A fine, happy supper, Thanksgiving or not.

•

In early December LM had enough of the eccentric manner in which the university operated its French for foreigners' classes. She studied diligently, did her homework and made progress, but she never knew until she arrived whether or not the class would be held or cancelled for reasons never clearly explained. So she and several of her classmates looked around for another option and came upon the Centre d'Études Linguistiques d'Avignon (CELA)[9] located in one of the buildings in the pedestrian zone off the Place de l'Horloge. There she met a young teacher, Denis Constancias, with whom we remain friends to this day, fellow students Mary (or Maria, cannot recall her family name, alas) an English-Greek woman working in Dubai on a sabbatical to learn French, Karin Joram a young German girl learning French preparatory to the study of medicine, and Jean Williams, who with her husband Blair and two youngest children were spending his sabbatical from Concordia University (Montreal) in France living on the Ile de la Barthelasse at the Ferme Jamet, where over many subsequent years LM and I spent much time on our almost annual pilgrimages to the Midi, but more about these friends in a later chapter.

Learning a new language after the age of 12 is not a simple matter, but with persistence and a great deal of mental effort one can achieve a level of expertise to be able to conduct an intelligent conversation. (LM's examples of the early difficulties she encountered she described to Dean in a letter as "Now if I can quit calling goat cheese horse cheese – *chevre* and *cheval* are similar, *non*? – I should be okay.") One important, indeed vital

---

[9] The institution has gone through several incarnations since then and is currently called Cercle d'Echanges Interculturels et Linguistiques Avignon (CEILA). In June of 2006 we slipped into the garden of the building in which it is located where a public event was taking place; when the director saw LM he stopped the proceedings with a whoop of surprise and laughter and introduced her to the assembled audience as one of the first and best students CELA had taught at the beginning of its history. Everyone applauded.

aspect of the learning process is the possibility of constant and regular practice; that is the ability to speak to someone in the language every day. LM quickly discovered she could not do this with her fellow students who continued to talk amongst themselves in their common language regardless of their nationalities: English. (There were exceptions, to be sure, such as the young Italian banker, Mateo, on leave to learn French who had no English to which he would admit so one had to talk to him in primitive French with an occasional Italian word thrown in if one knew one. He was surprised that I knew of the poet Giacomo Leopardi, though I could not recite any of his verses the way Mateo reeled off great chunks of them.)

To our great good fortune, Mme Mourre soon served as LM's interlocutor and mentor in the language. Our grandmotherly landlady spoke no English and lived an essentially lonely life since the death of her husband several years previous to our arrival in her house. Consequently she liked to talk with people, but her poor physical condition precluded easy walks about the village to stop here and there in this shop or another to chat. And apparently she had few friends left in the village. This latter phenomenon rather surprised us because we assumed that most native villagers passed the time of day with each other. This was a naïve assumption as any one who has any experience in living in a village or small town knows. We thought the reason for her relative isolation might have been a certain amount of class consciousness; that is Mme Mourre and her husband could have been viewed by many other villagers as belonging to a slightly higher social level as the owners of a successful vineyard, thus a brief hello when passing in the street may have been acceptable but gossiping about fellow villagers was not on. Perhaps her husband employed villagers in his business and was therefore viewed as a boss, hardly a social equal. Village life can be sharply hierarchical, though less so now than 50 or 60 years ago, as Laurence Wylie makes so wonderfully clear in his classic study of postwar life in *Village in the Vaucluse*. We never did find an acceptable solution to the question, and later over the years as we ate many meals with Mme Mourre's daughter, Sylvette Berruyer and her husband Jean-Marie and their two children, we never did ask them about the matter.

One day soon after LM began classes at CELA, which often took place during the afternoon, Mme Mourre stopped her before she mounted the stairs to our apartment and began a brief conversation about the weather, the traditional topic to open a dialogue between strangers. The conversation did not last very long, perhaps five minutes, but it initiated an almost daily series of such talks that grew in duration and complexity as LM's abilities expanded. By the autumn of the following year these lessons in language and local culture (including gossip) had grown to an hour or so, without which LM insists she would not have mastered nearly as much of the language as she finally accomplished. "*Madam Leen*", as Mme Mourre always referred to LM (for her I remained "*Monsieur Brewst*", along with other older French people she could not quite pronounce the "er" sound in English so simply dropped it)[10], learned a great deal from her conversations with our generous *propriétaire*.

She was not the only mentor of language in the village. Early on we chose one of the two bakeries as our own because we liked the quality of the baguettes better than those baked by the other. Why a small village such as Tavel should have two bakeries is easily and rationally answered: a bakery just like any other village business must have a weekly day of rest and relaxation, *n'est-ce pas*? Therefore there must be two of them so one is always open and customers can be assured of a fresh baguette or two twice a day. Both of course baked through the early Sunday mornings in order that the surrounding citizens could purchase their Sunday tartes, cakes and other sweets, without which no Sunday midday dinner would be complete. On Sunday mornings we allowed ourselves a *pain au chocolat* each, along with the fresh baguette.

Soon after I began to appear with regularity at *our* bakery, the baker's wife who served as cashier and gossip-purveyor decided to contribute to my education in her language, which she could speak with or without a distinct Provençal accent, not like the owner of one of the two grocery stores across the street whose heavily accented French I could never penetrate. This she accomplished by withholding my baguette each morning until I learned to pronounce a new word she provided and assure her that I understood its meaning. Once I had

---

[10] We have found that the Haitians in Key West possess the same characteristic; to them I am "Mr. Brewst" and LM is "Miss Lynn."

83

successfully passed the test for the morning she smiled, took my money and wished me the most pleasant of days: *à demain*. Two weeks before we left the village, the baker's wife said that it was sad that we could not stay, that we had become part of the village and she and her husband would miss us.

We did stop back to see her over a couple of years after we began to stay in the region on holidays, but then for some reason we no longer did. The last time we visited Tavel in June of 2008 to buy wine and eat in a restaurant that did not exist when we lived there, the bakery was closed for the annual vacation, so we don't know whether the same family owns it or not. The chances are they do not, but we would prefer not to know this.

And the other baker, not *our* baker of course, figures in a gossip story related by Mme Mourre during one of her sessions with LM. Some years ago the operator of the Petit Casino grocery store[11] had an affair with the wife of the baker across the small square, the bakery we used when our regular one further up the main street through the village was closed on Wednesdays and for vacation. The cuckolded Casino owner's wife thereupon cut all the blossoms off the baker's wife's flowers and left nasty messages on bits of paper at the bakery. Shortly thereafter the Casino owner began an affair with his wife's sister and they left town together. Allegedly

---

[11] The national supermarket chain called Casino licensed smaller and larger stores in the region, the smaller ones (petite) in villages, the medium size ones in towns such as Avignon (grand) and even larger ones in the malls that sprang up in the 1970s devastating the landscape with blatant ugliness.

the baker never suspected a thing, but in a small village like Tavel this is hard to credit. Finally the sister became tired of the Casino owner who in the meantime had taken ill with a debilitating disease. He came home, presumably with his tail between his legs, so to speak, where his wife nursed him for a long time. Actually, these people were all so unattractive it is hard to give credence to the story, but Mme Mourre insisted it was true.

In mid-summer, *our* baker lost two fingers in an accident and closed the shop for six weeks, a major catastrophe for us and the village: we all lost the best baguette in the village and I lost six weeks of language lessons. The first day of the unexpected closure I could find no bread at the other bakery or the alimentation (grocery store, which sold mass produced industrial baguette wrapped in a thin piece of cellophane), so Mme Mourre gave us two croissants for breakfast. When the other bakery closed down for vacation, we had no choice but to eat the uncrispy cellophane stuff which the grocer kindly saved for us each day. When our baker returned to baking, the missing digits did not negatively affect his abilities and we once again enjoyed the traditional staff of French life.

Mme Mourre, normally rather self-effacing and shy, conducted herself with the aplomb that sometimes comes with age, sometimes with effort; since we did not know her as a young or middle-aged woman, we comfortably believed hers came with age and experience. She remained typically French in her concern about the legal rules governing proprietor-tenant relations: she never came into our apartment except once to see our Christmas tree, and allowed us to persuade her but once to come up to the terrace so we could take her picture.

Whenever the postal delivery person left something for us in the mailbox, Mme Mourre would come to the foot of the stairs to our apartment and inform me in a mild but insistent voice, *"Monsieur Brewst! Le facteur était là!"* and I would scamper down the stairs to the courtyard where she would hand me the mail and exchange a few pleasantries about the weather (*"Il fait beau aujourd'hui"*) or some equally mundane matter such as the erratic performance of the furnace; she remained well-aware of my limitations of language. During the winter and on days of inclement weather she would telephone with the same message invoking the same behavior on my part. We smiled a lot at each other and nodded, the recourse of those who cannot completely make themselves understood to one another. She possessed the patience of Job (without the carbuncles and scourges, I hope) when talking with me.

I admired our stalwart *proprio* for a number of reasons including her mental agility and her willingness to be helpful in matters of the property when something did not function correctly, but also because she appeared to us to be so very French; by which I mean at her age she carried on as if she were still 20 in that she applied a heavy coating of rouge to her cheeks and a swatch of red to her lips, activities which were not entirely out of place, of course, but striking to me at least. French women are popularly noted for their attention to their appearance: the famous little scarf, for example, which is not a myth at all but, in those days, a reality regardless of age. Mme Mourre served as an exemplar of this admirable characteristic.

Her normal equipoise did, however, break down from time to time and always for the same reason: the hysterical terrier Finette, one of the most obnoxious examples of its kind we have ever had the misfortune to live with or near. We never learned why Mme Mourre put up with this demented beast, but we concluded that someone in her family had given it to her to ease her loneliness after her husband's death and she thought it unkind and socially unacceptable to have the thing done away with. Alas. At first we smiled at the dog's appearance on our terrace on days of clement weather when we opened the double doors and she strolled into the apartment to check out these newcomers. At first, but not later.

This mutt, charged with an incredible amount of kinetic energy, violently reacted to the smallest noise or movement within its ken. It would race up and down the courtyard at the speed of a TGV without a driver, hurl itself against the stone post holding up one side of the green gate and claw its way up the post propelled by its forward trajectory almost to the top where the propulsion ceased and it fell back to the ground, only to speed to the back of the courtyard and repeat the same action over and over until even its demonic energy flagged, or the cause for the actions had moved on past the gate and it crept away to its flannel bedding in a separate tiny room by the boiler off the courtyard to regain the strength to onc again explode at the slightest sound or movement in the street or at the end of the garden.

One morning during the winter, in addition to the usual barnyard noises and Finette's yapping, we heard the sound of hammering and discovered a young man constructing a stronger appendage to hold the green gate tighter against the dog's smashing attempts to get at anything and everything that passed by in the lane from indifferent tractors to sadistic cats which sat just beyond the gate to torment the little beast with their galling presence – so near and yet so far. This drove the dog mad and to even wilder and louder attempts to scale the walls of frustration. One wonders what she would have done had she succeeded in escaping, especially when the cause was an automobile or a tractor. If Finette had been a boxer or a Rottweiler we would have had a killer in the yard. As it was, she was merely loud and paranoid.

Had all of this occurred in silence, one might have accepted it as an unfortunate but harmless eccentricity that disturbed only the animal or human walking by the house outside the green gate and the small terror itself. This, however, was far from the case. Indeed the accompanying thin, shrill, constant hysterical yapping might have driven a less phlegmatic personage than Mme Mourre round the bend. It damn near did that to us. This mindless rending of the air and landscape could go on for 10 or 15 minutes without let up, giving rise to thoughts of a wide variety of means to cause it to cease, all of which involved severe damage to the vocal chords of that racing, screaming, clawing, leaping ball of fur and flesh that tormented our mental balance several times a day.

In the final analysis: cut the mutt's throat, but of course we're much too civilized for that act, besides which we would have immediately been the number one suspects in the case. And of course I do not wish to exaggerate the matter, but I find it difficult not to, though I should add that this raucous behavior did not occur every *single* day and perhaps on some days only *once*, maybe. The memory remains appalling in its clarity.

In fact, the closest we came to violence occurred after the gray cats became part of our lives in the village. Finette had already reached a form of accommodation with the albino cat, Bébé, and the other two, one named Bambino, which Mme Mourre fed regularly, and that roamed the courtyard, garden, roof and environs: with rare exceptions the dog did not seem to bother them. When two entirely different gray cats began sitting at our kitchen door to the terrace things changed radically. Until that time Finette rarely showed up on the terrace and even less often wandered into the apartment during clement weather when the doors and windows stood agape in the mild sunshine. After the advent of the gray cats the hound began to run up the stairs and around to the terrace where we, perhaps inappropriately, had set out two plates of food and a water dish at lunch and dinner when the strays appeared for a meal. How Finette knew at what time they were present on the property is a mystery, to me at least, but suddenly she raced onto the terrace yapping in her usual hysterical shrill voice and made as if to pounce upon the frightened hungry smaller beasts. Usually one of us heard the yapping and stomped out to the terrace in time to smack the dog with a folded

Herald Tribune or *Paris-Match*, or land a swift kick on the beast's rump and send her scurrying back down the stairs until the next time. We acted unmercifully, it is true, and most of our kicks missed the target but made the point.

The only quid pro quo vis-à-vis the dog I can recall occurred when friends brought their two rather un-housebroken children to visit during the summer: somehow they found the garden hose and terrorized the water-avoidant Finette screaming even louder and more insistently than the mutt. Finally we took the hose away from them and they calmed down. That was the only time Mme Mourre showed any annoyance with us, and we completely understood and agreed with her.

One mistral maddened day in the spring I planned to importune the gods to raise the temperature with an offering of Finette's entrails on the terrace facing the south. The wind-crazed hound had cornered a village cat underneath a large bush below our living room window in the courtyard. With a constant stream of hysterical yelps the frantic terrier darted in and out of the bush creating a godawful barrage of noise. The cat, however, was not to be buffaloed, so to speak, and when Finette's piercing howls suddenly rose by several decibels I knew without getting up from my chair that the puss had struck back. And, taking advantage of the brief lull in the attack, it immediately made a break into the nether reaches of the garden followed by the dog whose howling had now achieved a banshee level overwhelming even the mistral's roar. Beside herself with emotions unknown to me, the little monster leaped in the air, ran about in circles, jumped up the garage wall, screaming at a painfully intense pitch common to all spoiled little nippers, until the cat somehow eluded its tormenter. At least I thought so because from my chair I heard odd cat hissing noises from below, but Finette did not respond. We never discovered the real end of the story.

We were not alone in reacting negatively to the hound's crazed behavior. From Mme Mourre's *femme de ménage*, the darkhaired Italian Micheline, emanated a hostility more intense than ours because of longer duration. Indeed the sight of Micheline hugging one of the kitties to her generous bosom and lashing out with her well-shod leg at the frenetic leaping beast both amused and frightened us: had she connected the animal with more than a grazing kick the thing would have flown into the air and, yowling in pain, have landed outside the green gate in the street with, we sincerely hoped, a broken neck. Unfortunately Micheline's kicks never landed with sufficient force to achieve this result.

We did occasionally substitute for Mme Mourre's dog care when her age and aching legs refused to move her out of her apartment: during the infamous snow storm in mid-February we took over the responsibility of putting the hound in her room at night and letting her out the following morning so Mme Mourre could feed her. If the cold alone could not quieten the quotidian dynamics of propulsion, yelping madly, scrambling up the gate post, falling down and repetition, what chance did the snow have in accomplishing this humanitarian task? It may have curtailed slightly the occurrences, but even that is questionable. For some now obscure reason during the winter LM took the dog on a leash for a walk out into the countryside to relieve us all of the hysterical screeching. She does not recall this as an unpleasant experience, but once was enough.

Occasionally, the dog did somehow escape the confines of the courtyard and disappeared into the village and vineyards, causing Mme Mourre to lose her emotional equilibrium, the only times we saw this happen. Whenever we heard her keening the dog's name over and over again into the whomp of the mistral like a grieving Greek widow we knew the thing had gotten out. Mme Mourre's lamenting that the dog would never return of course did nothing to find the mutt, but one or another of the villagers, accustomed to the phenomenon, usually caught the thing somewhere in the streets or lanes and brought it back, alas. Several times LM and I volunteered to scour the village by-ways and once or twice unfortunately found the beast and brought her home. To my embarrassment I must admit that once or twice I heard Mme Mourre pleading with the hound to return and did not offer to help, hoping the dog had disappeared for ever.

One day in the middle of March I saw two long chains of caterpillars, lightly attached to one another by what appeared to be the touch of their antennae, making their way from somewhere to elsewhere across the ground in front of the second garage before the garden. Gray furry tubes with slight touches of deep green on their backs, they crept with the slowness of eternal Nature over the packed earth, one chain occasionally breaking as a link detached its head end to look up and around (at where they were going?), then, apparently satisfied with what it saw, rejoined the chain to continue the gradual traversing of the ground in the direction of the garden, I hoped Finette or one of the cats would not disrupt the journey and promised to check on their progress in a half hour or so. Unfortunately other things intervened and I quite forgot about them until too much time had passed and they had disappeared, safely into the garden I hoped.

In the late spring, Mme Mourre's albino cat Bébé decided that sleeping on our bed at night when the window was open to clear my head of the dust and rubbish of the day was more satisfying than wherever else she spent the night. Occasionally she did not wait until we turned the reading light off but marched over the window sill on to the small desk and gracefully leaped onto the bed to wash herself and curl up for the duration. This usually proved to be rather short because the cat chose a spot where our tossing and turning in sleep forced her to move too often and she finally gave up and left. Nonetheless, the sight of the completely white cat with pink eyes and a crimson collar lying on the bright red bed cover was an interesting contrast in color coordination.

> The albino cat arrived early one night
> Before we'd finished reading.
> Furry white on the red coverlet she
> Washed slowly and thoroughly, then
> Settled down, curled and snug, for the night.
> Soon enough human insomnia

Drove her elsewhere in search of rest
While we paid the price of thought.

Around mid-June Bébé came less and less often at night and we wondered if Mme Mourre had been shutting her up in the evening along with Finette, but we hoped not in the same space.

●

That winter my mornings followed a pattern that rarely changed for the time we lived in the village except for the temperatures and the clothing befitting same. At 7:30 I left the house for a brisk walk through the still darkened village streets and lanes, shoulders hunched against the cold, hands deep in the pockets of the ever-present pea jacket on the way to the *boulangerie* (bakery) and *librairie* (newspaper, magazine and sundry shop) for a baguette and the *Midi Libre*, made worthwhile by the view of the orange lighted sky just above the mountains in the east broken by the mass of Mont Ventoux (we at first thought a blanket of snow capped the mountain, but it turned out to be a startlingly whitish sea of sand and shingle the origin of which remained obscure but related to human degradation of the earth), the streaked orange light heralding the coming of the day and the bowl of café au lait in the kitchen, stove on to warm the room, and the beginning of a new day. On the return walk the young apprentice waiter from the Hostellerie often came toward me, smiled and greeted me with a few stock phrases one uses with someone who does not completely understand one's language. I learned to understand and repeat "*Bonjour. Il fait beau aujourd'hui. La soleil est beau maintenant, n'est-ce pas? Ça va? Ça va, ça va, merci.*" As LM said at the time, "Always bonjour people and smile, even if they don't speak first. It's also a way of forcing them to recognize your existence. And it's the polite thing to do."

Before LM left the university for CELA we entertained our first guests in the Tavel house, or as I should write: they entertained us. In Avignon for a month or so, Pat and her husband Hardy attended the language class where LM met them and Hardy interested himself in various aspects of French culture, mainly associated with food. They lived in the center of town at a hotel called Le Médiéval where a decade later LM and I stayed during the Durrell conference at the Palace of the Popes. Hardy was in the habit of rising at 3:00 o'clock in the morning to visit a nearby bakery to watch how the baker went about his business; he did the same thing in a butcher shop at a more respectable hour, and wished he had a larger kitchen in which to try out a recipe for bouillabaisse he'd found somewhere. We agreed to open our kitchen to his culinary experiment.

One can certainly do better than to refer to Thackeray's not at all satisfactory "The Ballad of Bouillabaisse", the second stanza of which reads as follows:

> This bouillabaisse a noble dish is –
> A sort of soup, or broth, or brew,
> Or hotchpotch of all sorts of fishes

That Greenwich never could outdo.
Green herbs, red peppers, muscles,
    saffern,
Soles, onions, garlic, roach, and dace;
All these you eat at Terré's tavern,
In that one dish of Bouillabaisse.

(The spellings are Thackeray's.) As one British writer on the subject has put it: "The famous bouillabaisse described in Thackeray's ballad is a very Cockney affair and only fit for the ignorant British tourist caught very young on his first trip to Paris."[12] And Mr. Thackeray doesn't tell us much about the nature of what goes into the making of the stew. And "roach"? (A "roach" is a "silver-white European freshwater cyprinid fish with a greenish back." A "dace" is defined as "a small freshwater cyprinid fish." And a cyprinid is "any of a family [Cyprinidae] of soft-finned freshwater fishes including the carps and minnows," all according to *Webster's Seventh New Collegiate Dictionary*.) Furthermore Thackeray is referring to one he ate in Paris. One could, I suppose, find a fine fish stew outside Provence. The great food writer, Waverly Root, insisted in his *The Food of France* that the best he'd ever eaten he'd done at the Restaurant du Midi in New York when it still claimed mostly French sailors, not uptown socialites, as its main clientele. Well, *à chacun son goût*, as it were, or as we used to say in the Bronx that's what makes horse racing.

---

[12] Capt. Leslie Richardson, *Things Seen in Provence* (London, 1928), 132.

Some in Marseille indirectly reinforce that city's claim to being the locale of the first bouillabaisse by telling the story that Venus invented it to serve her husband Vulcan as a soporific to send him off into the arms of Morpheus so she could keep an amorous appointment with Mars. The Marseillaises considered themselves the inheritors of Greek civilization and the ancient Greeks did bring the olive into the region, and olives are a mainstay of the stew in many recipes, so the connection in their minds is not as tenuous as it may seem to others. As Root notes, it is easy to believe that this dish is divine. In any case, ancient Greek food literature often refers to fish soups and it is not out of the question that the Greeks brought some form of seafood stew with them, or concocted it once they'd arrived. We can be sure that the people of Marseille would have invented some form of the stew even without external assistance. All the ingredients were there.

The ingredients for a true bouillabaisse are the subject of controversy in certain circles concerned with the cooking of food. Indeed, the origin of the fish soup or stew is unclear. The following doggerel is one story among many.

> *Pour le vendredi maîgre*
> *Un jour, une certaine abbesse*
> *D'un convent Marseillais*
> *Créa la bouillabaisse.*

(An unrhymed translation: "One day for meatless Friday, a certain abbess in a Marseille convent invented the bouillabaisse".)

The *Larousse gastronomique* defines the stew as "a Provençal dish, made of various kinds of fish cooked in water or white wine, with oil, tomatoes, garlic, saffron, pepper, laurel (bay), and other spices added." This is again of little help if one wants to know how to cook the dish. As Waverly Root claims the best he had eaten in New York, so Joseph Wechsberg stakes a claim for "my best bouillabaisse on the fo'c'sle deck of the *Azay-le-Rideau*, in the middle of the Mediterranean. It was made by my friend Étienne-Marcel, a nonprofessional cook."[13] The amateur cook gave Wechsberg this advice, "Remember just two things about bouillabaisse, *mon petit*. First, never make it for less than a dozen people. Second, never use fish that is merely fresh. Only the *very freshest* is good enough. The secret of bouillabaisse is to blend the different *parfums propres* of all kinds of fish while they still have the wonderful aroma of salt water, algae, and seaweed." All very well and good but not so easy to find "the *very freshest*" if one does not live along the shore of waters filled with a wide variety of fishes. And with the increasing pollution of our shore waters, including the Mediterranean, "fresh" fish is increasingly difficult to guarantee.

Bouillabaisse means "boil down", which indicates the necessity for speed as well as a very high temperature in order to emulsify the oil and water into the desired

---

[13] "The Mysterious Fish Soup" in *Blue Trout & Black Truffles. The Peregrinations of an Epicure* (New York, 1954).

density of broth. Though the different fish must be cooked in order (the denser longer than the flimsier) speed and watchfulness is imperative. The entire cooking process should not consume more than a quarter of an hour once the broth is made.

Len Deighton has a few words of advice for those attempting to make a bouillabaisse: "The cook should remember that if the fish is tasty and the broth thin, the bouillabaisse will be a failure, but if the fish is tasteless and the broth flavorful you will be acclaimed." While a tad exaggerated there is a grain of truth in this.

My own preference is to sauté chopped onion and a finely chopped fennel bulb in a large amount of olive oil, adding chopped garlic after the vegetables have become translucent and cook briefly to release the taste, then add water and white wine and a large bay leaf, bring to a roiling boil, add the fishes, the densest first, followed a few moments later by the most tender and cook briefly, remove from the heat, serve the fishes and broth separately with crusty baguette chunks, to be or not to be placed in the soup bowl, and a spicy *rouille* (*aïoli* colored with paprika and cayenne) which is added to the soup in amounts depending on one's tolerance for its sharpness and pungency. The addition of chopped tomatoes to the onion and garlic sautéing phase is a matter of debate among connoisseurs and one of taste for the rest of us. Sometimes I use them, sometimes not. In his *La Cuisinière Provençal* M. Reboul agrees with me. That is it – *trés simple* and very tasty. There is a fine chapter on the stew in Georgeanne Brennen's *A Pig in Provence* (2007) that includes directions on making a complex broth (called *fond* in Provence) of fish heads, small crabs, small to tiny fishes, leeks, onions, garlic, tomatoes and eel, which turns out to be richer and denser than my own variety.

As time passed and the Côte d'Azur and Marseille became destinations for mass tourism the fish stew served to the tourists moved ever further from the original recipe into a mass produced item made as quickly as possible to serve as many people as possible in the shortest amount of time possible. So in 1980 eleven restaurants mainly in Marseille signed a *Charte de la bouillabaisse* (bouillabaisse charter) that specifies the ingredients and preparation process for an "authentic" bouillabaisse. This is akin to the finger in the dyke syndrome or the attempt by the Académie Française to purify the French language of foreign elements. But it is very French.

O yes, Pat and Hardy and his fish stew. It must be said that he savaged our small kitchen but the dish he made, with perhaps more fennel than I subsequently found appropriate, we thoroughly enjoyed. They left Provence shortly thereafter and we have never heard from them since. I do, however, clearly remember the fennel.

•

We did not expect to freeze in Provence but for many weeks we suffered greatly from the cold in our Tavel perch and used the oven in the kitchen as a heater to warm at least that room where I often worked during the day. The temperature sank low enough for snow and often the mistral blew and roared while the sun shone brightly in a cloudless sky of pale blue and light gray. On occasion it became so cold the kitchen windows fogged over when we turned the oven on. Unless the sun shone strongly the rooms did not really warm up. The dichotomy between the refrigerated rooms and the glaring light outside began to wear me down as I struggled to keep my fingers from becoming stiff by punching the keys on the electric typewriter and consuming small glasses of local *marc*, in addition to the flannel shirt and blue sweat shirt from the Alexandria (Virginia) Torpedo Factory, all of which helped but could not at length withstand the penetrating cold of that winter ("the worst in 20 years," the villagers assured us shaking their heads in wonderment, thinking how fortunate we were to experience this rare phenomenon, an idea needless to say we could not share).

When the unrelenting wind slashed the winter cold through every nook and cranny we wondered why the house had not been constructed in a manner that dealt with this sort of thing. After all, winter is not an unusual event even in the south, but no, the builder had constructed the house for the traditional long summer months. Tile floors may be cool in the scorching Midi summers but do not lend themselves to carrying what little warmth emanates from the radiators.

One day in early December on the spur of the moment I checked the gauge on the heating oil tank in the garage downstairs and discovered we were almost out of fuel. Approximately one thousand liters in one month at a cost of 2,600 francs astounded me and I ran back upstairs and turned the radiators off, despairing that it would be a cold, cold winter, even with occasional mild days and nights. In mid-February the Esso delivery truck pumped 851 liters of oil into the tank and charged us 2,500 francs, confirming that we went through an unusual amount of oil for very little resultant heat. (The invoice I paid at the post office where I purchased a "*mandat*" and mailed it off: Visiting the post office which I did with persistence and often, consumed much time because, not only can one do an incredible amount of various business in French post offices [pay bills, take money out of a savings account, and so on, in addition to actually mailing a letter or a package], but one had to chat with the clerk who knew everyone in town and everyone wanted to hear and impart the latest gossip.)

In fact there appeared to be no consistency in the weather and it remained as mysterious to me that winter as the language, though my ability to function with the latter increased week by week. In mid-December we went through a series of bitter cold sunless days with mild nights, sunny days of bitter cold and the mistral blowing, three days of rain and cold followed by a warm sunny day. One mistral lasts three and a half days, the next less than 24 hours; so much for the local myth that it comes and goes in increments of three. As the days passed we began to look for that hard wind because it blew away the otherwise gray cloud covering which seemed to dominate the winter. There appeared to be some geometric relationship between the sun and the mistral; when the wind blows the sun blesses us, no mistral means overcast sky. The idiosyncratic oddity of a wind storm blowing its worst on a bright sunfilled day continued to impress one whose only knowledge of wind storms included dark, gray usually rainy accompaniment: indeed the mistral remains exotic still.

In his 1837 book on touring (*Mémoires d'un touriste*), Henri Beyle (a.k.a. Stendhal) author of *Le Rouge et le noir* and *La Chartreuse de Parme* writes about "the great drawback to all the pleasures one can find in Provence ... When the mistral rules Provence one does not know where to take refuge; there is in fact fine sunshine, but a cold, insupportable wind penetrates into the most carefully closed room, and aggravates the nerves to a degree which exasperates the very calmest people." (Interestingly enough the word "drawback" is embedded in the French sentence in English.)

Lawrence Durrell has a poem entitled "Mistral" (doesn't everybody?) some of the lines of which are as follows.

> At four the dawn mistral usually
> A sleep-walking giant sways and crackles
> The house, a vessel big with sail.
> One head full of poems, cruiser of light,
> Cracks open the pomegranate to reveal
> The lining of all today's perhaps.
> …
> Where will I next be when the mistral
> Rises in sullen trumpets on the hills of bone?

Even Friedrich Nietzsche has a poem to the mistral that he calls a "dance song" which contains the stanza

Raffen wir von jeder Blume
Eine Blüte uns zum Ruhme
Und zwei Blätter noch zum Kranz!
Tanzen wir gleich Troubadouren
Zwischen Heiligen und Huren,
Zwischen Gott und Welt den Tanz.

Very Nietzschean. It might be translated something like this: "Let's tear from each flower / a blossom for our glory / and two more leaves for the garland! / We dance like the troubadours / between saints and whores / the dance between god and the world."

The great Provençal poet Frédéric Mistral (1830-1914), in his "Pouèmo dou Rose" describes the wind in these words (translated by C. M. Girdlestone),

> ...
> The mistral hurricane
> Is still blowing. The trees, greeting it
> > With groans, bend and shake
> > As if to tear themselves from their
> trunks. The wind
> > Holds back the Rhône, become
> smooth as a mirror.
> Against water and wind the strong
> > teams,
> Nose down, march northward
> With a regular step. Like a mighty
> > bagpipe,

The resounding storm astounds the
    animals
And makes them prick up their ears.
The exasperated waggoners raise their
    hands
To their hats and plush caps,
And, with lips awry, let fly against the
    mistral
A torrent of full-mouthed oaths …
    … And with a clicking
Of whips, they drive on their heavy
    horses.

Even if one doesn't care for the translation (it isn't clear whether it is from Provençal, in which Mistral wrote his poetry, or French, into which Mistral translated most of his work), the power of the poem, driven by the power of the storm, is clear as the Midi sky in autumn.

And in the last decades of the 17th century, the irrepressible Mme de Sévigné wrote to her daughter Mme de Grignan about a recent visit she made to the latter's château on an isolated rocky hillock in Grignan, in the Drome, 44 kilometers north of Orange. The mother thoroughly enjoyed her lengthy visits to her daughter's ménage; she writes with verve about the variety of sumptuous meals eaten there (partridges fed with thyme, marjoram and other herbs, fat and tender quail legs, succulent doves, and so on), the view from the terrace, the grotto where she wrote in peace and quiet, a wonderful life there, except for the mistral, "that bitter, freezing and cutting wind."

Que vous êtes excessifs en Provence! Tout est
extrême, vos chaleurs, vos sereins, vos bises, vos
pluies hors de saison, vos tonnerres en automne; il
n'y a rien de doux, ni de tempéré. Vos rivières sont
débordées, vos champs noyés et abîmés. Votre
Durance a toujours le diable au corps ...

Which might be translated as, "How excessive you
are in Provence! Everything is extreme, your heat, your
serenity, your winds, your rains out of season, your
autumn thunder; there is nothing soft there, nothing
temperate. Your rivers burst their banks, your fields
flooded and full of gorges. Your Durance always has a
devil in the flesh [meaning the river is in a state of
constant turmoil]."

There is a very old proverbial saying in the Midi
which describes the trials and tribulations of the populace
during the *ancien régime*:

> *Parlement, le mistral et la Durance*
> *Sont les trois fléaux de la Provence.*

This can be accurately translated as "taxes, the mistral
and the Durance/are the three scourges of Provence" and
that summed up the vagaries of the state and nature for
those who lived in the region. Without the same rhyme
scheme the sentiments expressed in the saying, I suppose,
could have been applied to anywhere else in France.
With hindsight one might add the Rhône to the list and
make it *quatre fléaux*. The mighty Rhône has turbulently

flooded the region more than once: indeed, the swollen river caused the destruction of 18 of the 22 spans of the Pont St. Benezet (better known as the Pont d'Avignon) in 1670. In 1882, while Henry James wiled away several days in Avignon and environs, the river again flooded, attended by the populace along the upper east bank who enjoyed the spectacle as if in a giant circus tent. It was, he wrote, "beautiful and horrible." One of the townspeople informed James of an earlier flooding in 1856 during which the grand old Hôtel d'Europe, the hostel where he was staying, flooded to within a few inches of the dining room's ceiling "where the long board which had served for so many a table d'hôte floated disreputably, with its legs in the air." When we lived there the Rhône flooded its banks to the point where some roads on the Ile de la Barthelasse became impassable and at least one restaurant, L'Hostellerie du Vieux Moulin, on the west bank in Villeneuve-lès-Avignon, succumbed to such a mass of mud and debris that it remained closed for many years. We waited too long to eat there, and, sadly, still have not done so. It is now called La Guinguette du Vieux Moulin, and who knows? Perhaps one day ...

And those long majestic rows of tall Cyprus trees one sees throughout Provence, though less so in the Gard, were not planted in the 19th century to keep the farmers' fields free from marauding livestock, but to act as windbreaks against the power and fury of the mistral, which is why they are usually bent in one direction, the wind's force has bent them in the same direction for generations and they have become one of the major characters in the landscape of the region. Think of Van Gogh's iconic painting of the stars and Cyprus trees called "The Starry Night."

The erratic weather made it even more impossible to heat the house with any consistency or efficiency. The furnace did not work correctly as we found out later in the autumn of the following year, the knowledge coming too late to be of any use. What turned out to be of great use to us were the flannel sheets and pillow cases our Washington friends, Moira Egan and Jim Vore (more about them in Chapter VIII), sent to help us make it through the winter. We have rarely enjoyed a gift so deeply and long as those warming bed linens. Their remnants rest with other of our goods in the garage of Mme Mourre's house, a rental property now owned by her daughter.

The troublesome weather also influenced one's sanitary habits: more than one bath a week was impossible. The bathroom, separate from the narrow room containing the toilet (a quite civilized way of housing construction unknown in America), held no stand-up shower, but did boast a *Sitzbad* and a hand-held shower hose and nozzle apparatus. One alters one's habits when living in a different culture. Shaving every day was of course out of the question, and one wore the same thick clothing until one's sense of aesthetics or smell became sufficiently offended to force a change. Socks, however, we changed daily and fortunately our deodorants functioned as they should.

When the water in the garden fountain froze tight and we retreated to the kitchen with the oven on full blast, it must be admitted we began to wonder about the myths of warm, voluptuous Provence – did Van Gogh's eyes and those of the other artists who worked in the south fail to see reality? Was the fact that Cézanne only painted bright colorful scenes around his home in Aix-en-Provence late in his life when memory perhaps nudged his brush across the canvas rather than what he saw in the landscape?

The wind scatters everything outside not nailed down, objects fly through the air, odd noises accompany the incessant howling, and walking in the village required a brisk pace as the wind pushed and tugged one down the lanes. The Tom Waits phrase, "colder than a well-digger's ass," comes unbidden but ineluctably to mind. The concept summed up in the phrase "wind-chill factor", I thought, surely originated in this wind-whipped frozen landscape, but the old women of the village continue to saunter through the streets on their daily round wearing only an old sweater over their winter dresses, evidently impervious to or contemptuous of the weather. Thick, heavy stews and soups, glasses of *marc* and hot coffee, brisk march tempo walks around the large terrace surface mark off the hours until it is time to go to bed and allow our bodies' natural heating system to take over under the quilts and open red colored bedroll.

Snow. Somewhere I read that as Vincent climbed down off the train from Paris onto the platform of the Arles railway station he stepped into a snow storm. Ergo, it snows from time to time in Provence. To this we can attest without hesitation and have photographs to prove it. *Alors.*

At mid-month in February the cashier at the Tavel cooperative, having remarked that snow had fallen (or at least skirls of flakes had been reported) in Lirac (three kilometers north of our village) and in Nîmes (some 45 kilometers to the west), told us not to give up hope, no, we would have it by the following day. This, of course, we chalked up to local patriotism and drove off to the Ile de la Barthelasse in the Rhône beneath the crenellations of the Palace of the Popes where our friends Jean and Blair Williams and two of their young boys had ensconced themselves at the Ferme Jamet for part of Blair's six-month sabbatical. We returned to our house very late and not being in any condition to look up into the night sky and murmur something knowledgeable such as "Tonight a cold wind will blow", I took the last of the Excedrins and we went to bed. Ah, the follies of youth, one might think, but I was coming up to my 44th birthday. Ah, the follies of the not very smart might have been a better motto for that night.

Early the next morning, awakening to a sharp pain in the bladder, a dull ache behind the eyes and the penetrating ringing of the telephone, I discovered it was snowing, had snowed for some time, about six inches worth, and the village looked like a kitschy Christmas card. The telephone call was from Mme Mourre asking if one of us could please open the door to Finette's room and let the beast out, a task which I accomplished with a minimum of effort. However, the shoveling of snow meant an expenditure of energy which in my condition I could ill-afford since fighting off a cold and the cold itself was the main focus of existence at that point.

Nonetheless we dug the green gate free and walked into the village to buy the usual baguette and newspaper, achieving success with the former but not the latter: no newspaper deliveries yet. At some point a delivery was made because the son of Mme Mourre's *femme de ménage* brought her a copy which she kindly allowed us to read. The following morning's slippery slush and wet melting snow brought no paper either. Nîmes, where the paper is printed, is a tad more than 30 minutes away on a dry day. Surely the *Midi Libre* folks could have figured out a way to move their product so far on the second day after a snow fall. Like selling ice cube makers to the Eskimos. Then snow began to fall once again and we sat at the table looking out over the cemetery to the hills girdling our valley and watched the small white flakes gently fall, tumbling lazily in the cold air reminding us, should we have needed it, that any talk of spring had been quite premature. Indeed, the snow did not begin to melt for another couple of days because the temperature dropped and the sun refused to appear. We became something we had never in our wildest dreamscape imagined possible: we had become *snowbound* in Provence! Because of the true rarity of the situation few locals knew how to deal with it and the French refused to leave beloved vehicles at home which resulted in many more accidents than usual. How like the Americans.

•

It was frustrating not to be able to work because of the temperature in the house. The ink in the pens coagulated, the typewriter required five minutes just to warm up sufficiently to use. Morning glasses of calvados probably didn't help much, a French myth no doubt, but tasted just fine.

Journal entry for March 8:

Wind almost gone, air chilly, sun bright. Much warmer in Avignon than the village. Beginning to feel the isolation somewhat. It's not a bother when the work is going forward but that isn't the case at the moment. Must work harder.

The chirping of spring birds grows in volume, a pleasing background sound complex (until broken by Finette who has returned to the fold not much wiser for her sojourn in the village). We must begin to think of the garden, layout and content. Tomatoes, zucchini, some herbs, lettuce. Daylight is present until after 6:30. Thoughts of the grill return. At least my cooking goes forward. Little compensation for the lack of increase in the number of MS pages, however.

The sun warms the room in a rectangular block of light formed by the window through which it passes. The door to the terrace stands half open; a soft breeze nudges the faded curtain. Motor sounds from the farm equipment in the lanes below the house commingle with similar sounds from the autoroute three kilometers to the east, somehow soothing to an urban habituated ear. The cock in the courtyard next door crows four times at regular intervals, the sound rising dully above the noise of the trucks. It is 3:30 in the afternoon. Birds in the garden do not sing but chirp their pleasure at the sun and mild gray- blue sky. In the distance Mont Ventoux is hidden behind a haze of dark white. The giant pine trees in the middle distance stand unmoving, their tall green color bleached by the thinning haze. The mimosa in the garden gleams yellow and green as the season's first bees tentatively explore the ground not yet buzzing or entering the house. On the table in the room with the open door lie books and pages of manuscript and letters, one of them explaining that the manuscript is not deemed strong enough to be published at the present time. The sun warms the small of the back dimming the minor shoots of pain; but the brown coffee in the white nude cup continues to cool. A restful pause in a day full of too much convoluted thought and tensed muscles. Knowing the deceptions of this cunning Midi weather, I am not convinced that spring is here.

There is a legend in England to explain its nasty weather: a brewer of beer in the west of England where people traditionally drank high alcohol content cider, incensed at his inability to convince them of the pleasures of his beer, sold his soul to the devil to guarantee cold wet weather during May to ruin the apple blossoms. What excuse, one wondered, did Provence have?

Early April found us gazing out the window to the south over the terrace watching for the spring. While we so occupied ourselves, winter snuck back through the rear gate and bushwacked us so that once again its icy breath numbed the fingers and stopped the breath with shock. The cold, combined with rain, lasted for days at a time. April, it seemed, was truly the cruelest month breeding thoughts of warm, lazy spring weather and then delivering yet another blast of what we hoped was the dying gasp of winter: the mistral forced the cold into the house while the sun shone sovereignly over the hills. I moved from the living room table to the kitchen and the oven in the mornings, then back to the table in the afternoons when the sun warmed the house to a point where I could work for an hour or so there. Sometimes my hands became so chilled I could not close them into a fist, the skin seemed to tighten beyond its normal texture. A vicious joke, I thought, played on innocents such as we, believers in the myth of the southern sun and Provençal summer. Not this April. So we went on day to day telling ourselves that the wind, rain and cold spells were the last of the season. The villagers we talked to fall into the same syndrome, but they have the time and would be there the following year as they'd been there the previous year. We did not have that luxury. But summer hadn't really begun and everything really would have been fine if the bloody furnace had worked as it should. Summer did, however late, finally arrive.

•

The Peugeot unsurprisingly began to require repairs as soon as we arrived in Apt but I cannot remember much about it except that we had it in the garage twice. No doubt my inabilities with the language added to the inability of the mechanic to discover whatever caused the visit to his place of business. We did notice that the vehicle struggled to climb even the smallest incline and required down-shifting to achieve the heights, be they only a meter or two in height, and causing a near riot of blaring horns behind us as frustrated French drivers, not noted for their patience on the road in any case, expressed their intense frustration at what they surely believed to be excessive caution by these bloody foreigners who should have stayed home where they belonged and not clog French roads with their moronic ... and so on and on, and the strain caused the oddest sound from somewhere in the innards of the mechanism. Embarrassing and frustrating for us as well.

At Tavel shortly after Christmas we were fairly sure the problem might be the clutch, and indeed it was about to fall into the street. Fortunately the garage about 100 meters down the street from the house could replace the mechanism, though at what we thought was considerable cost, though the father and son owners repeatedly assured us that they would charge a "*juste prix*". I learned how to say, "The car quacks like a duck" in French to describe the noise it made with maddening regularity, especially when climbing even small hills. The owners of the garage widened their eyes, simultaneously and incredulously replied, "*Comme un canard*!?" clearly thinking I had no idea what I was saying. But I did, though it may have been an unusual formulation of a technical automotive problem, it certainly described one of the symptoms, the other being the lugubrious strain caused by the slightest incline in the road.

Indeed the culprit was the clutch and the visit to the garage to arrange the repairs lasted quite a long time because of the double and triple explanations necessary before I understood what the owners were saying with much gesturing of hands and faces lined with ingrained stains of evidence of having spent many years working with greasy automotive engines and other such parts. They could probably fix the damn thing the following week, but would first have to telephone the Avignon Peugeot dealer to see if the apparently massive clutch part was available. Several days into the New Year the motor car spent two days in the shop (leaving us stranded in the village since the bus service tended to be erratic and curtailed) and emerged with a new mechanism to allow shifting so we would not cause apoplexy in French drivers behind us on inclines.

This was not the end of it, needless to say. At the end of April we paid 260 francs to have the brakes repaired, an unfortunate necessity since tooling down the autoroute at 120 kph without functioning brakes is really rather stupid. Early one morning in July the fan belt broke as LM entered Avignon headed to her 8:00 o'clock French class; she made it back to Tavel at noon and the garage people installed a new one. Then, in August, on the road from Paris to Chartres the car began to drink water at an incredible rate making me think it should be taken to the vet or somewhere. None to be found, but a more immediate problem presented itself: one of the rear tires suddenly sprouted a blister and came close to blowing out. When we picked up Jim and Moira from the airport we briefly wondered about the tires but in the city we never used the car so forgot about it. Fortunately we were able to roll into a roadside filling station where the young fellow said of course he'd change the tire for us but after lunch, come back at two o'clock. So we unloaded the food and equipment from the trunk and plunked ourselves down beside the station and enjoyed a picnic on the grass and it was a gas. And we eventually drove off with the spare tire performing quite adequately. But the inexhaustible thirst?

By mid-September, within six weeks of our extremely reluctant, but inevitable departure, the untrusty blue Peugeot sat once again in the Tavel garage down the street from Mme Mourre's house with water leaking into the cylinder housing, using two liters of water every 50 kilometers. On the road returning from a trip with Andrea to Marseille we panicked when the radiator began leaking and dire thoughts of requiring assistance on the side of the autoroute assailed us. The panic continued until we reached Tavel and turned the motor off. The following morning we drove Andrea to the train station in Avignon and returned to Tavel leaving the machine at the garage to be fixed. The cost of the repairs provoked a feeling of mild nausea and the onslaught of what earlier centuries called a swoon; well, almost. The bill was 1800 francs and included a new radiator; the car was worth no more than 2000 francs total. But in the end that did not matter.

•

We celebrated that Christmas 1982 without the usual festive accoutrements, which we had stored back in Washington. Indeed, we had brought nothing of the sort with us so found ourselves left to our own devices and the necessity to improvise whatever holiday decorations we might wish to set up in the living room of our apartment above what had been the vineyard's storage garage.

The first step would be to find a tree of appropriate size and some mechanism to maintain it in an upright position. So we bundled up and drove our poorly heated battered old blue Peugeot out of the village and down the highway in the direction of the Rhône River and the city. Several kilometers along the way stood a plant and garden store where we found a rather scraggly pine tree approximately a meter high; we took pity on the shy thing (it reminded us of Chester the turkey on the Lum and Abner radio show about Thanksgiving: Lum buys a live turkey to fatten up for the holiday, names it Chester and becomes attached to it so that when the time comes, of course, neither one of them has the heart to kill it), thinking no one else would buy it, so we did. The store also provided a small green plastic stand that served its function just fine.

Pleased with the serendipity of the process thus far we discussed the types of decorations to adorn the tree. Since we lived under the constraints of a rather severely limited budget (savings and no real income to speak of), the purchase of boxes of brightly colored bulbs and similar doodads was out of the question. We were, however, more than up to the challenge: we decided to make our own adornments, an idea that had hitherto never occurred to me, at least. Like the peasants (called farmers in the States) of old who could not afford to dillydally with such expensive frills we would make use of materials we already had at hand and use our imaginations in creating objects that would reflect the spirit of the occasion. No, we did not carve little baby Jesus in a cradle of local plane tree wood nor any of the Santon figures so popular in the Provençal Christmas decorations. We (mainly LM) did, however, wield scissors and colored paper with aplomb, savoir faire and, I must admit, a certain elegance of movement. Both of which items we had already purchased for other purposes.

The tree, now looking less lonely and forlorn sitting in its green plastic stand on a corner table, awaited its adorning with snowflakes of various (some odd) shapes and sizes, bulbs also in various shapes and sizes cut out of red, green, blue and yellow paper and a couple of strings of what may have been popcorn; at least in the two somewhat unfocused self-timer photographs it appears that they are popcorn strings and LM's memory confirms their presence on the tree. This is somewhat surprising since the French are not entirely ignorant of popped corn but they are not exactly enamored of it either, hence it is difficult if not impossible to find the stuff there.

In previous years we had enjoyed decorating trees for the holiday. In fact, the first present I ever bought Lynn-Marie was a Christmas tree at 3 o'clock in the morning in Georgetown shortly after we met, but that is another story. While decorating the trees we naturally played music, particularly an album by the Paul Winter Consort that contained the haunting song called "Icarus," which we nicknamed "The Christmas Tree Song" because we played it several times on our first Christmas together, but also some of the more traditional seasonal songs by Nat Cole (his pronunciation of "O Tannenbaum" in German is endearing), Emmylou Harris, Joan Baez and Perry Como, as well as various jazz musicians who recorded festive holiday songs. And of course we drank champagne and laughed a lot.

In Tavel we had a radio-cassette tape player purchased in Munich on our way south, but this did not play LPs which in any case we'd left in Washington and our minimal tape collection contained Georges Brassens, Willy Nelson, Yves Montand and Jean Ferrat, but no Christmas songs. I think we sang a couple *a cappella*. A bottle of fairly decent, but real champagne would not have been amiss as an accompaniment to the decoration process, and it wasn't. But what about the caviar?

That story is not extensively complicated. On one of the yellowed and spotted pages of a notebook of recipes I collected while there, just below a cutting from the local newspaper, *Midi Libre*, (*Oeufs au curry, macaronie au gratin* and *pêches cuites au sirop* from Tante Marthe, none of which we ever made), I find a recipe for "Mock Caviar Mix or Faux caviar mélange." This series of instructions were written on four different occasions to judge by the handwriting and four different inks. The first of them I wrote in Tavel in the cramped, small handwriting that I used before 1986 when I expanded and opened my scribbles to an enlarged form, much more readable.

> ½ med. minced onion
> 2 ounces lumpfish caviar
> 1-2 finely chopped hardboiled eggs
> Enough homemade mayo to bind other
>   ingredients together. (A light garlic mayo may also
>   be used for as   lightly different taste.)
> Mix above together & refrigerate for 30 minutes
>   before serving with crackers of some sort.
> It may look terrible but il goût bien.

Immediately below the French phrase I added at a later date: "No French would use this term. One learns, after all. *Il est bon* would be more vernacular, not to say accurate."

Some time later still: "More traditionally: do not mix the ingredients, but this method is not so interesting & doesn't provoke comments on the ugliness of the dish prior to eating it."

And as the penultimate gloss, the statement: "It is also difficult to maintain loose ingredients on a traditional cracker without losing one's social balance."

The final addendum consists of one word: "capers," which was LM's suggestion at some point during the last 24 years.

That day, December 24, the sun shone brightly on the frozen landscape, *France Musique* persisted in broadcasting John Cage instead of Mozart or Bach and the *International Herald Tribune* predicted the dollar's continued decline against the franc while the price of cigarettes rose 20 to 40 centimes a packet depending upon the brand. Louis Aragon died at the age of 85 the previous day filling the newspapers with pages of eulogies by prominent politicians and writers in addition to bits of his poetry. The leftwing Socialist *Le Matin* devoted ten pages to the deceased. The French will forgive their intellectuals almost anything if they live long enough. The fact that Aragon was a Stalinist of the first water who sold his soul to the PCF and wrote a lot of tendentious crap appeared to be of no interest to anyone, although one of the editors of the *Midi Libre* mentioned the politics in his piece into which he stuffed the name Brassens as often as possible as if to lend Aragon the prestige of one who did not sell his soul to anyone or thing. Aragon did write some valuable poems and prose, especially in his youthful Surrealist years, and he did perform well in the Résistance during the war, but it was the length of his admittedly interesting and wide-ranging life that brought him such uncritical accolades from the entire political spectrum.

During the final stages of dinner preparation the village lost electric power due to the continued ravages of the current mistral; we continued cooking by candlelight, glad we had a gas stove on which to roast our Christmas Eve chicken pieces (the French eat "*dinde*" [turkey] at Christmas but we had chicken), heat the mashed potatoes, smooth as silk gravy, pungent chestnut dressing (made on top of the stove since we'd no full chicken which to stuff) and young green peas. We finished the well-watered (Mme Mourre had given us a bottle of champagne to which we added our own bottle of Tavel rosé), candle-lit meal with our first *bouche de noël*, which our baker made for us, buttery but not excessively sweet and, after an exchange of presents listening to Georges Brassens, we went for a brief, swift ramble around the terrace in the roaring mistral to render assistance to the digestive process.

The weather and our mood of buzzing happiness decided that we would not attempt to go to the midnight mass in the small stone 10th century Saint-Ferréol chapel in the center of the village. The building rarely opened in any case since a sufficient number of parishioners could not be gathered together each Sunday for services and, as with other village churches in the region, a priest held the mass in a rotation system, one week here, the next there, and so on. Thus we never did see the inside of this edifice at the time, though years later we found the doors ajar and looked in on the spare, cold stone walls and battered wooden benches; an equally ancient and dusty wooden confessional booth stood forlornly against the north side of the chapel.

That Christmas in Tavel was one of the more memorable holidays we have ever created for ourselves.

Several days later we purchased a small inexpensive, black and white television set, justifying the expenditure by noting that a wider exposure to French culture would benefit learning the language. This may have been the case for LM, but in retrospect I doubt it helped me very much. At that point in its development French television lagged about 20 years behind America in technological sophistication: much dead air time, singers all mouthing the lyrics to their records on variety shows, thoroughly silly game shows, the regional news presented in visually boring cardboard sets with off-center timing, no soap operas, and so on.[14] However, commercials did not interrupt the films and television adaptations every seven minutes, but appeared grouped together at certain times between programs. And LM became fascinated with a game show called *Des Chiffres et des Lettres* which required the construction of words and phrases containing, obviously, numbers and letters. The presentation was then so primitive that the judges carried out the calculation of points with pencils and paper during which not a sound was to be heard. Dead air, indeed. Or, as LM put it then, "What kills me is the deadness of this show!" (The program is still running on French TV in a vastly more technically sophisticated and much less interesting presentation.)

One phenomenon on French television we discovered fairly soon after purchasing the apparatus is the concept of the nude human body as something natural and indeed a thing of beauty, a concept that remains as foreign to American popular culture today as it was then. This applies to the non-cable network programs, not the availability of pornographic movies and feature films containing nude scenes with well- and unknown actors. The sight of a nude body, usually female, in advertisements on French TV is not uncommon and no

---

[14] The French finally came up with a wildly popular soap in 2004 when the show *Plus Belle la Vie* (roughly "Life is so Sweet") made its premiere appearance. As of this writing almost a fifth of the French population watches the show at least once a week to follow the complicated plots about several Marseille families.

one seems outraged by it. One of the first situation comedies we watched that winter was the story of a young couple, he a dentist having trouble finding a practice, she in some other professional trade who also could not find work. They found jobs as a butler and maid in a wealthy Parisian family's household. In one scene the couple is preparing for the day, he is dressing and she is ironing a blouse, all quite normal except for the fact that she is naked from the waist up. They carry on a conversation about the possibilities of finding work in their fields, she finishes ironing, dons the blouse, adjusts her lipstick and off to work they go. No muss, no fuss; very French. *Ça va bien.*

The comic aspects of our television watching could not be avoided: outbursts of "What was that word?" or "Did you catch that?" or "Whatidhesay?", with an occasional swift scramble through the French-English dictionary. We also found it amusing that in mid-March the technicians union of the state-owned television stations went out on strike, leaving the stations with a "minimum service" that consisted mainly of test patterns with music or talk, some news and the showing of a telefilm *Come Back, Little Sheba* (*Reviens, petite Sheba*) with Joanne Woodward and Laurence Olivier.

LM at the Nymphenburg Castle in Munich.

LM at the demented Ludwig's castle at Neuschwannstein.

LM at the Hotel Sacher with Sachertorte in Vienna, scene of the Leonard Bernstein incident.

La Petite Mo in Munich.

The Taverne du Septier was located down the alley on the right.

LM on the Apt house terrace.

Keeping the home fires burning in Apt.

LM and Andrea shopping at the weekly Apt market.

At work in Mrs. Potter's tiny but functional kitchen in Apt.

Andrea Anderson at table in Apt; note baguette on the book.

The two Maries being carried out of the Church in their boat.

Mme Mourre's apartment on the left; the gate to the
courtyard in the center.

The main door to our apartment; below are the vineyard
equipment garages.

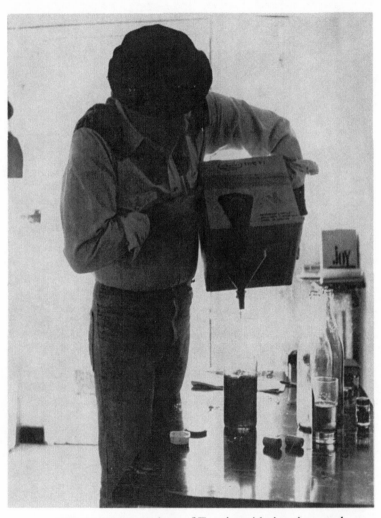

The 11-liter container of Tavel rosé being decanted.

The gardiens await the arrival of the saints.

The Tavel wine cooperative where we spent much time and money.

N° 19   23/10/82

REPAS		
1 langouste 1p 550g	248
1 Timbale	47
1 fromages	40
CAVE	1 estandon blanc	40
1/2 estandon blanc	25
BAR	20
TEL.	
► PRIX NET	420

The infamous lobster invoice.

Chapter III

Paris Interlude: Year's End and Beginning

Paris has come to play a large role in our lives, but it wasn't always so. My first visit to the city took place over a three day period in the summer of 1964 while I lived in Heidelberg. LM was first there in June of 1968 on a college package tour, then again in the mid-1970s for one night on her way elsewhere. Oddly, she has no recollection of the social and political upheaval that took place there in May-June of 1968. (She was also in Prague that summer, but well before the Warsaw Pact troops crushed the Prague Spring of Alexandr Dubček and his hapless colleagues.) Together we stayed in Paris in May 1980 at the start of our trip through France to Spain and at the end of the sojourn. Since then we have been in the city innumerable times and I have written two books on its history and culture. During our time in Tavel we visited the city three times and those visits truly began our love affair with the place.

In November after we'd moved to Tavel we decided to welcome the New Year in the City of Light and made the appropriate plans mindful of our limited financial possibilities. Through Roswitha and Jean-Louis we met an Avignon travel agent who arranged for us an inexpensive package that would include transportation and hotel accommodations, which in this case included taking the train to Paris and a room at the Hôtel Château-Landon on the eponymous street in the 10th arrondissement overlooking the Gare de l'Est rail lines. The hotel reminded us of the Holiday Inn chain, no charm, rabbit warren rooms, but clean and warm.

So much has been written about Paris it is difficult to describe being there with a freshness that might charm the reader and offer a unique vision of what it means to be there. The difficulty does not preclude the attempting to overcome it, thus the paragraphs that follow, not to speak of the two books I've written about the city.

We had planned to visit several museums and bookstores while there, but in the end we were only able to view the collections of the Opera Museum and the Centre Pompidou and two bookstores, as well as the Montmartre cemetery. Of the Opera museum I have very little recollection except for many costumes (scruffy when seen up close) descending from wooden hangers and vitrines of handwritten sheets of music by various composers. It was chilly in the rooms and they smelled of moth balls.

The Pompidou is another matter all together. It impresses with its deliberate eccentricity. In the summer the circus of urban tourist attractions fills the open plaza in front of the building with their trinkets, acrobatic tricks, and outright begging. Even in the cold end of the year weather, a number of magicians, guitar players, tap-dancers and clowns plied their trades with an admirable disregard for the lack of sunshine. Inside, which had the look of being unfinished, a number of exhibitions were open to the public free of charge: the use of the earth in art, the work of four photographers who studied with Man Ray, and a history of French literary prizes. The major exhibitions included selections from the permanent collection of modern art, well worth a visit though we did not have the time or energy to go through it this time, and a massive temporary exhibition entitled "*Éluard et ses amis peintres*" ([Paul] Éluard and his painter friends), which we did spend a lot of time wandering through, and very glad we did.

This was a major production with many pieces not only by his world renowned friends (Max Ernst, Man Ray, Giacometti, Picasso), but also others of somewhat lesser fame (Dora Maar, Roland Penrose) and some I'd never heard of. I noted in my journal, "A series of photographs of Nusch Éluard by Man Ray are especially attractive." What I meant was: in the photographs she is deliciously nude. Many of Éluard's books, manuscripts, letters to and from, his Communist Party membership card, photographs, and Alain Resnais' 13-minute short film *Guernica* with a sound track containing a poem by Éluard, were on display. The curators provided very little explanatory texts; for that information one had to purchase the exhaustive and profusely illustrated catalogue for 90 francs (which we should have done then rather than spending even more than that for drinks in the bar of the ever-elegant if somewhat worn Hôtel Meurice).

Going up the exterior escalator to the top of the building is somewhat akin to rising on the elevator in the Eiffel Tower and equally unpleasant for one who suffers from vertigo. The view, even on a gray overcast afternoon threatened with rain or snow is fine if you have not been surfeited on views of Paris roof tops. Alas, this was the only way we found to quickly reach the uppermost floor of the building where the Éluard show was situated along with an intensely crowded café with absurdly expensive coffee. Éluard wrote a tremendous amount of poetry, all of which, alas, was published in volumes ranging from a seven page three by four inch booklet to coffee table size cooperative volumes with now famous painters. Éluard was similar to the New York poet Frank O'Hara in his continued and reciprocally fructifying relationships with painters of name and talent. On a subsequent trip to Paris we did purchase the exhibition's catalogue.

(The exhibition devoted a good amount of space to the poet and Communist functionary, Louis Aragon, who, as noted in the previous chapter, died the week before we saw the show. In the USA the death of a writer or artist might make page 10 of *The New York Times*; Aragon's death made not only the front page of every newspaper in the country, left-wing or not, including our local *Midi Libre*, but pages and pages of articles, tributes, photographs, TV series, news programs, memorial services, what a circus! No wonder poets and painters like living in France, at least the successful ones. In any case, this added contemporaneity to the aura of the exhibition.)

The mention of the Meurice's bar above reminds me how the temperature's bonechilling tines penetrated even our layered clothing levels, which led from time to time to sitting in bars for a cup of café au lait and a *marc* to warm our insides and thaw our skins. This can be an expensive proposition, especially for those on a limited income. A couple of double scotches in the famous bar at the Hotel Ritz set us back 80 francs, and the bill at the Meurice for two *marcs* and two coffees cost us an astounding 113 francs. A beer at Harry's New York Bar near the Opera was more on our price level, but the infestation of American tourists was hard to put up with so we moved on. Museums were then fairly inexpensive, but those we wanted to visit other than the Pompidou we found closed for the holidays (the Impressionists and Cézanne at the Jeu de Paume and the Orangerie, the Erik Satie exhibition at the Musée de Montmartre).

We did walk by the third edition of the Shakespeare and Company book shop, this one located in an uncertain building on the Left Bank overlooking the Seine and the Nôtre Dame cathedral, but for some reason, perhaps lack of time, we passed on without entering, saving it for the next visit. The American pillar of rectitude and intelligence, Sylvia Beach, owned and operated the first two editions of the book store of that name from 1919 until the German occupation of Paris forced her to close in 1940. George Whitman, the owner of the third edition, appropriated the shop's name, and registered his daughter's name as Sylvia Beach Whitman. The shop is still there in all its shabby glory, filled with books of all sorts scattered throughout the many small rooms on the ground and first floor.

We did enter into both Smith's and Brentano's book shops in the rue de Rivoli across the street from the Jeu de Paume where we purchased several books to see us through the winter including Herbert Lottman's biography of Albert Camus, a lengthy volume for one who died at 47, Francis Crick's biography of George Orwell, *A Tale of Two Cities* (for the life of me I cannot remember why this one), a cheap thriller the title of which I've long since forgotten, and Lawrence Durrell's *Constance or Solitary Practices*, a title that evokes naughty mysterious doings in the Midi (the novel is the third volume of what has become known as *The Avignon Quintet*). The author signed our copy in the chilly spring of 1986 in Pennsylvania, four years before he died.

We have always made it a practice to walk through cemeteries wherever we find them. On this sojourn in the city we toured the Cimetière du Montmartre at the western end of the 18th arrondissement, a few blocks north of the Place de Clichy. We did not tarry there for the temperature may have been fine and comfortable if one were a polar bear, but had dipped too low for the likes of us humanoids. We added the graves of Heinrich Heine and Émile Zola to our collection, then walked swiftly around the quarter to see Le Lapin Agile, once before 1914 host to many of the painters and poets who later became well-known and still, in 1982, open in the evenings as a cabaret of some repute.

Standing in front of what had been the building on the Place Ravignan called Le Bateau Lavoir, some say because it resembled one of the boats along the Seine where women washed clothes, we felt rather disappointed at the reconstruction which did not particularly mirror our image of the place from the photographs we'd seen. On December 1, 1969, at

131

Picasso's urging, André Malraux, then Minister of Culture, declared the building a historic monument. Five months later it mysteriously burned down. And so it was, a historic monument, easily understandable when one considers who lived and worked in the unheated, cold-water studios there before 1914: Fernande Olivier, Max Jacob, Paco Durrio, Juan Gris, Kees van Dongen, André Salmon, Pablo Picasso, Pierre MacOrlan, Joachim Sunyer, Modigliani, Auguste Herbin, Pablo Gargallo, the unfortunate German Wiegels, and the visitors numbered among them Paul Gauguin, Apollinaire, the Stein ménage (the siblings Leo, Michael [with his wife Sarah] and Gertrude [with her wife Alice Toklas]), the dealers Wilhelm Udhe, Kahnweiler, and Berthe Weill, the folk artist Henri Rousseau, the painters Marie Laurencin, Georges Braque, André Derain, and Rudolf Levy.

•

It is a distinct pleasure to eat in an elegant restaurant that provides attentive, professional, well-dressed staff with clean fingernails. We would not often repeat the experience of trusting the gods who oversee public eateries rather than making reservations, especially on nights as celebratory and crowded as New Year's Eve. Fortuna smiled upon us as we wandered through the Beaubourg section of the city, which in the early 1980s was similar to Greenwich Village without the latter quarter's history and tradition of art and bohemianism, which makes the Beaubourg essentially a place for mindless tourists. That judgment excludes the Centre

Pompidou museum and cultural center, which though an architectural horror that assaults the eye and aesthetic sensibility is the only reason for being in that section of the city. Well, perhaps there is one other justification for ending there at dinner time: the restaurants, at least one of them, at least one at the very end of the year 1982.

We had not made dinner reservations for Sylvester's Eve, not very smart to be sure, and contradictory to the advice of several people that without such a thing finding a decent place to eat on that night would be impossible. Nonsense, I thought, no city has as many good restaurants of all types as Paris. So off we went and somehow ended up walking through the Beaubourg section, increasingly frustrated as it became ever clearer that the advice had been well-given if not well-received. Finally, we stumbled upon Monsieur Boeuf, an unpretentious façade but a fabulous interior, subtle, well appointed, but very expensive. This obviously was not the time to be chintzy; a table was free and we took it and settled in with a sigh of relief. The meal could hardly have been better, or more adventurous.

We started with a pastis and, no doubt, a cigarette for in those days we smoked those long, filtered Royale cigarettes with little thought of what we were doing to our lungs (though on some of those "mornings-after" the pain in my head informed me that I should quit the filthy weed, something I did not accomplish until the summer of 1990; LM, being smarter, stopped in 1984). We decided not to eat the animal which gave the restaurant its name. LM ordered what she thought was a cut of veal that looked interesting, and indeed it turned out to be a cut of veal, but from the inside of the animal: For the first time in her life she ate a meal of liver, ate every bit of it and allowed as how she enjoyed it. Woof. I ordered the *rognons de veau* (veal kidneys), not having the opportunity of eating them at home. LM asked to taste a piece, which I found rather suspicious, but gave her a tender morsel which she hesitantly said tasted, well, fine. When I demanded to know why she had always refused to eat kidneys before that, she blanched and muttered something about not realizing I'd ordered innards, a response I also found suspicious. After another tentative taste she admitted that it wasn't bad at all. Another first.

The first course of *foie gras*, creamy and well-herbed, melted on our tongues and the side dishes of mashed potatoes and leeks and creamed cauliflower with onions matched the high level of deliciousness of the main course. A bottle of chilled Sancerre accompanied the meal, which ended with a chocolate mousse in a delicate bluelined porcelain cup, coffee and *eau de vie de poire* (essence of pear high in alcohol content, a tasty digestive). As is traditional and rational in classy French restaurants, the presence of the waiter did not signal a desire to seat other guests at our table after we departed, but rather attentive service, so that, as is traditional and rational, we remained ensconced in the aura of warm well-being for over two hours.

Another tradition in French eateries of all types is the presence of small and smaller dogs at table, a phenomenon not only frowned upon in the USA but banned by the sanitary police. Thus it did not come as a surprise to us when the elderly and elegantly attired couple seated at the table next to ours brought forth from the lady's purse an accessory mutt the size of a large rat and asked for a plate and napkin for the creature. These accoutrements the waiter hastened to supply and madam cut a piece of her own steak into minuscule pieces and fed the thankfully silent pet with her own hand, murmuring incomprehensible sounds of love and devotion. We wondered if she was ever so attentive to her husband, but banished that untoward thought forthwith and smiled without condescension when monsieur gazed at us as if asking for understanding.

The meal cost 531 francs, approximately $76.00 at the then current exchange rate, far above our budget, and worth every centime.

To give some sense of proportion to the matter, the following rainy, cold day before we climbed aboard the train to return home, we ate lunch at a bistro called Le Petit Poulet on the Place de Clichy, an area well-known to Henry Miller and his friends in the 1930s. There, slightly hungover and tired, we tucked into the typical bistro meal of roasted chicken, pommes frites, a baguette and a bottle of Muscadet, the perfect meal for the occasion. Replete, we paid the bill: 80 francs (approximately $12.00). Nothing could have been more satisfactory at that time in that place.

Clearly, the vast difference in price says nothing about the quality of pleasure involved in the two locations. One enjoyed both with the same sensual delight in taste and milieu from the almost stuffy elegance (a bit drafty on the feet) of Monsieur Boeuf where the waiters are attentive to one's every desire to the very laissez-faire atmosphere of the bistro in Montmartre where the waiter saw to one's needs when he could find the time – as a result of this experience we've decided to benignly neglect the restaurants of Paris and concentrate on the bistros and thus save more money for other things. There is a great deal to be said for bistro food if one doesn't expect a Tour d'Argent meal and stays with the traditional bistro cooking. The cost alone, of course, is sufficient to recommend these places.

Paris was cold: temperatures hovered around zero centigrade the entire time we were there and the sun refused to show itself. (So different from the Midi with the mistral blowing once again across a cold bright blue sky in the clear brilliant sunlight.) In Paris one walks despite the weather, at least visitors walk when the subway or bus is not available or goes to an inappropriate location. Thus we walked from Monsieur Boeuf to the section of the city where the people gather in droves to bid a fond or not so fond farewell to the old and welcome the New Year.

The crowd on the Avenue des Champs-Élysées is similar to that in Times Square or Trafalgar Square one supposes (never having been to either location on the night in question): agitated with drink, the cold and excitement, each one reinforcing the giddiness of the others, the masses of them jostled, laughed, kissed, drank and shoved their ways up and down the long avenue.

"*Bonne année! Bonne année!*" and the North Africans ("*les arabes*" to the French) took advantage of the general relaxation to gleefully hug and kiss "white" women up and down the avenue yelling "*bonne année!*", for once in the year at least being able to feel like something other than second class citizens. Indeed, one suspects the leveling nature of the event (or non-event since nothing really happens) and its lack of financial necessity, lies behind the fact that two-thirds of the crowd appeared to be from North Africa. A cheap and amusing way to spend New Year's Eve amidst a friendly crowd, unless one was damaged by the fireworks tossed about with abandon and lack of discretion by sophomoric cretins of various nationalities.

The second time down the Avenue, choked with milling people and those foolish enough to have driven an automobile onto the street (traffic of course barely moved for more than an hour, many simply left their cars in the middle of the street and joined the crowd, some were hauled out of their cars by chanting celebrants to join the circle of revelers in their incoherent but happy song) became boring and the atmosphere with its drunken slobbering mass of moronic humanity, the loud and dangerous fireworks blasting at one's feet began to be annoying. The discovery of the closed métro added to the annoyance. No taxis to be had, of course. The realization that we had to *walk* back to the hotel sent a charge of explosive rage howling through my brain and I almost dropped the mask and screamed out loud right there in the middle of the Champs Élysées.

Quickly suppressing such an untoward notion down to the level of simmering, muttering, sputtering annoyance, with LM's attempting to look on the bright side of the issue ("We'll get to see parts of Paris we'd never have otherwise seen"), we began the trek: down the seething Champs past the Grand and Petit Palais, across the Place de la Concorde through the hundreds of trucks, cars and motorcycles parked on its eastern side before the Jardin des Tuilleries waiting for the starting gun of the Paris-Dakar race, by the shuttered Jeu de Paume, its masterpieces of light and shadow darkened in the cold, the Madeleine church and on around the Place de la Madeleine into the avenue with three names (Madeleine, des Capuchines, des Italiens) with its grand old buildings butting into the night sky, ground floors jammed with brasseries still open and doing a roaring business, until we reached the intersection of the Boulevard Haussmann which just at that point becomes the Boulevard Montmartre and after a few blocks the Boulevard Poissonnère, then the Boulevard de Bonne-Nouvelle, continuing the massive old buildings and brightly lighted brasseries. Checking the street map of the city, LM thought we should turn left soon to walk north toward the Gare de l'Est and the hotel where a warm room and the bottle of Calvados awaited us. So we turned left into the rue d'Hauteville and proceeded up that narrower street empty of people except the sudden intrusion of the arguing couple trying to work out their destinies at two o'clock on the first morning of the New Year. By the time we reached the Place Franz-Liszt and I noticed a sign indicating the Gare du Nord I started to panic, not then realizing that this station lies only a few blocks from the Gare de l'Est. Avoiding a small group of intoxicated bourgeoisie in long dresses and silk scarves we finally crossed the boulevard de Magenta and went up the rue de Valenciennes and down the rue du Faubourg-Saint-

Denis. Two very young and shivering teenagers, a boy and a girl, asked for alms from the doorway of a grocery store as we walked by. Though we did not understand their version of the French language we intuited their meaning and gave them whatever change I had in my pocket. We were now too far north of the train station and had to come back down to circle around the station, closed at this point, to issue ourselves onto the rue du Faubourg Saint Martin, and finally to the hotel. The walk had covered about six kilometers and had taken one and a half hours in the damp cold. The calvados never tasted so good. We set the alarm for an unreasonable hour and slept.

Late on the first day of the year, after the simple but splendid lunch on the Place de Clichy, we took the train to the south, standing the entire trip in the bar car drinking beer, eating ham and cheese sandwiches (on baguettes of course), wishing we could better understand the conversations flowing around us even if they might have been banal, and making lavish plans for a return to the city of light in March or April. After three days sitting under Avignon's ancient ramparts, the car surprised us by starting immediately and we drove home in the winter darkness to unpack the treasures from Paris, drink Calvados against the cold and sleep at home, feeling rather strange that home was Tavel, that we returned to Tavel from a trip to Paris, not back to Washington DC.

Chapter IV

Dealing with the Bureaucracy in a New Language

Bringing an automobile into France from another country may not have been one of the smartest moves we ever made. The process, lengthy, at times frustrating, at times torturous, of registering the machine in a good citizen, formal manner, consumed many months of running about from one bureau to another to obtain a multitude of documents that would, perhaps, finally culminate in the issuance of a license plate number and an official registration sticker. There are interesting lessons to be learned about a different country's rules and regulations, to be sure, but at what cost?

The story begins in Munich in September when we purchased the blue Peugeot from Ute Benz, though she is hardly to blame for any of it. We transferred the registration from Ute to me by bill of sale; since we would not be residing in Germany, we licensed the vehicle with what are called "customs plates", which allow the machine to be driven for a certain length of time in the country of purchase and out of the country to be re-registered in the country of one's residence, in this case France. This appeared to us to be straightforward and simple enough. How off the mark this opinion turned out to be became apparent several weeks after we settled for the month in Apt and the time began to run out on the temporary customs registration.

On October 29, I noted in my journal, "After three days of frustration, anger, despair and hard work the car is provisionally registered and insurance taken care of – for the moment. Anything could go wrong. If there's a possibility of something happening, it will. In any case now the remaining major hurdle is housing. Not having a permanent address makes things difficult with the bureaucracy as we use Le Marquis and hope for the best although we may not be living in the Vaucluse in the end (different license plates)." What this means is, each department's license plate begins with the administrative number of that department, in these cases 84 for the Vaucluse and 30 for the Gard. Thus if one lives in the Gard, one should not have one's automobile registered in the Vaucluse, *n'est-ce pas*?

On a bright sunny morning three days earlier, having dropped LM off at the university, I checked with the Automobile Club de Vaucluse in Avignon regarding the procedure for registering the car since both registration and insurance would expire the following day. Always wait until the last moment is my motto. Insane, of course, but all too frequent. The office manager (*chef du bureau*) spoke German well, which was a stroke of luck. He informed me I would have to pay a custom import duty on the vehicle, despite the fact that it was a French car returning to France! Thus the steps to be followed were: pay custom fee at the appropriate office in the Courtine industrial zone south of Avignon, apply at the prefecture to register the machine, and then buy insurance at the firm the *chef* recommended.

Since the insurance office was located not far from the Automobile Club, I decided to pay a preliminary visit to discuss the matter with what turned out to be a charming lady who said the insurance rate would be *trés cher* (some 8,000 francs), after which the rate would be reduced over the next two years to the normal tariff of 4,000 francs per annum. For a second only, the thought flew through my head that it was we who were insane, but the lady smiled and seemed to assure me that everything would work out just fine, and yes I could return the following day with the custom fee receipt and the registration certificate, whereupon she would issue the necessary insurance documents, after I turned over the cash.

When I met LM after her class we decided two things: lunch would be taken in a café with a glass or two of wine, and since the bank was closed for the long French lunch and since we had not sufficient cash for the customs office and the registration fee, I would handle the matter the following morning whilst she was in class.

Another of those gorgeous late autumn days accompanied my perambulations and I found the custom office without much difficulty at 9:00 o'clock. Thirty minutes later, having filled in numerous forms, spoken in my not only broken, but positively lame French, and having paid 934 francs (30 francs less than the Automobile Club *chef* estimated), I raced to the prefecture (opening hours 9:30 – 11:30, 13:30 – 15:30), stood in line for 30 minutes and observed the face of the young clerk fall to pieces when he saw my pile of scattered papers. After going through the pile he informed me that since I did not possess a paid invoice from the water, gas, electric companies to prove I lived in Apt I would need a *"justification de la résidence"* from the Apt city hall (*Mairie*), and a *carte de séjour* from the *Service d'Étranger. Then* I could register the vehicle. And where might the Service d'Étranger be located?

Waving his arms about, the young man spoke a lengthy sentence which included the words *"à droite."* Fine. After making several directional mistakes, I found the correct office only to be informed that the carte de séjour had to be obtained at the Apt city hall and, by the way, hadn't I read the visa in my passport carefully, where it clearly stated that the said carte de séjour must be applied for within eight days of arrival in France? Eh? A second clerk sitting there smiled and mumbled something about *"les américains"* which probably was derogatory, but I didn't get it, of course. The young clerk repeated the business about the Apt city hall, and a photocopy of the visa for the dossier at the Service d'Étranger (which keeps track of legal foreigners in France). Fine.

I left the prefecture to meet LM for lunch in the park. We decided to return immediately to Apt and the city hall where, in a small, well-lighted office we sat in front of a very young woman who refused to talk baby-French to us but knew exactly what to do: go out to the Prisunic supermarket, sit in a small booth and take four photographs each and photocopy the visas for yet another dossier, a mission we accomplished with a minimum of energy and time. Back in the presence of the all-powerful young woman, we watched her open two dossiers which would apparently also follow us around during our sojourn in France. It was not clear whether this would be the only set of dossiers or if the Service d'Étranger would also create a set of their own. In any case, the dossiers would contain the following information: name, address, date and place of birth, names of parents including mother's maiden name, and so on. Fine.

And profession. This caused a minor tempest in the proverbial teapot. LM mentioned that she was taking a course at the university in Avignon. Ah ha, a student. This LM denied, not wanting to be classified as a student which might prejudice future possibilities. The discussion went on too long and LM finally agreed to be a student and obtain a *"certificat d'inscription"* (certificate of enrollment) from the university for inclusion in her dossier. When I gave my profession as *"écrivain"* (writer) another lengthy discussion ensued between the young miss and an older male colleague at the neighboring desk as to whether or not this was indeed a profession in the French legal system. In France, of all places! Finally she shrugged her young shoulders and wrote it down in the dossier; let Avignon worry about it when she sent the files there to be approved. (Avignon would then return the files to Apt, our putative place of residence. Would they eventually be forwarded to our new residence's *mairie*? What presently unknown troubles would this cause us?)

Now, the young woman said, what about income? "Yeah," interjected her male colleague who had nothing to do with her job, "how do you eat, eh? *Vous savez, manger?*" Here he mimed shoveling food into his mouth, thus carrying baby-talk too far, even for us, but I restrained any retort. After 15 additional minutes of broken conversation about bank accounts, travelers' checks, parents sending money when we needed it, and so on, both officials appeared to be left with the impression we would be living from the largesse of LM's parents (mine having long since disappeared, as the French would say) who would send us cash to live in France. At this point we thought, fine, as long as it works.

After writing all this down, she filled out forms which stated we have requested *cartes de séjour*. Our photographs and her official stamp (or "chop" as the Chinese more onomatopoeically put it) were then affixed; what happened to the three others we never knew. The provisional certificate of residence was filled out for the mayor's signature, which would be executed later that evening to be picked up in the morning. And yes, one can take care of registering the car in another office in the *mairie d'Apt. Alors. Merci bien, au revoir.* Exhausted we drove up the mountain, home to a fire and supper of pasta with a vaguely Provençal sauce we made up for the meal, and sleep. The permanent *cartes de séjour*, which must be issued in Avignon, could take three months: our temporary papers were valid until January next year. On them our address is Apt in the Vaucluse. What would it eventually require to change this when we moved?

145

The following morning the young lady did not seem to recognize us. Odd. But finally she woke up and gave me the certificates (which we should immediately have photocopied, but did not). With some trepidation we trooped upstairs to face the official in charge of motor vehicle registrations: a flighty, heavily made-up young woman apparently in the job until she found a husband whereupon she would quit, having learned the absolute minimum about her work. Extremely anxious to be helpful and speaking English at about the same level as we speak French (which means it would have been easier if she had spoken only her own language), she looked up a number of steps for us to take none of which had been mentioned by the Avignon official the previous day: two different forms from Peugeot headquarters in Paris about the vehicle's specifications, which must be applied for through the local Peugeot dealer, who she obligingly telephoned about the matter; a certificate of inspection for the car, a tax stamp worth 80 francs to be bought only at a *tabac* (tobacco shop), any one will do. Fine. When asked why the Peugeot documents from Paris were necessary when all the information resided in the vehicle's papers which we already had, she replied with the ubiquitous bureaucrat's answer to everything, *"C'est nécessaire, monsieur, alors."* Thirty minutes of this depressing stuff left us drained and we got out of there as soon as politely possible, nodding like puppets, *"Oui, oui, okay, merci ..."* A lump of lead sat solidly in the pit of my stomach.

We discovered very soon that morning that only one *tabac* in Apt sold tax stamps and had no 80 franc stamps available; why one couldn't purchase two 40 franc stamps and be done with it remains a mystery to this day. Defeated again, if only provisionally. LM suggested we go home, eat lunch on the balcony in the sun, then go to Avignon, simply present what documentation we had to the prefecture as requested by the officials there and see what happens. We could also then talk to the motor vehicle insurance lady: perhaps we could arrange insurance before the car was officially registered.

On the way into Avignon, we stopped in L'isle-sur-la-Sorgue where LM found a *tabac* that sold "*timbres fiscales*" in the appropriate amount. Onward, onward. With faint hearts, hollow stomachs and ragged minds we approached the window labeled "*cartes grises*" (apparently meaning vehicle registration papers) in the Avignon prefecture and handed in the paperwork. Astounded and in shock we walked out five minutes later with a temporary registration form and the promise that the permanent form would be sent to us in Apt within four weeks, No vehicle inspection, no documents from Peugeot in Paris, no hassling. *Incroyable, mais vrai.* But, of course, it wasn't.

The insurance lady stunned us even further. Two days earlier in looking through the forms after leaving her office it occurred to me that she meant "*permis de conduire*" (driver's license) not "*permis de séjour*"! With this in mind I jotted a note on the application form stating that I had had a driver's license uninterruptedly since 1956. I couldn't prove this of course, since in the USA a new license or a renewal is required every four years or when one moves to another city or state, but I thought I could explain this to her with LM's help. At the worst, LM could obtain the insurance because her driver's license had two years left before renewal while mine had been issued the previous September because my shoulder bag had been stolen. In short, LM had been documented as driving longer than I, despite the fact that I'd been actually driving at least ten years longer than she. Well.

For whatever reason the nice woman simply accepted my word that I'd possessed a valid license since 1956 and I currently possessed an international driver's license. *Voila*! We applied for and received the minimum insurance at the minimum price (4,000 francs per annum) and a provisional certificate stating that the car was insured. Done in 15 minutes! After a little more conversation about possible health insurance policies, we walked on air out of her office shaking our heads in bafflement, and drove to St. Rémy en Provence to check out house rentals.

Of course the story did not end there; this was but an intermission in the farce that might have been entitled "The Vehicle Registration Labyrinth or How to Grow an Ulcer in a Few Months."

Not all was gloom and doom, of course; that should be kept in mind. Even before we knew we would have the Tavel house we continued to enjoy being in the Midi, as an excerpt from my journal entry for October 29 indicates.

Now 9.30 AM. LM left at 7.30 for her class and some errands in Avignon, the first time alone. She's met some interesting people there whose acquaintances we may pursue. Time for work on [the Berlin novel]. Must find a place to live within a week and all will be well (except for the bureaucratic complications of changing addresses). Chilly here but will wait a bit before starting the fire. The sun is so bright I may be able to work on the terrace. Ah, Provence!

But of course the comedy did continue. Indeed on the tenth of November, a week after we moved to Tavel, we received a form from the Bureau des Mines forwarded from Apt demanding two certificates from the Peugeot main office in Paris. The veritable same stuff the overly-made up young woman in the *Mairie d'Apt* said we'd need three weeks previously, which we thought was no longer required. Why the office of mines concerned itself with motor vehicle matters remains cloaked in impenetrable darkness. It became clear that since we purchased the car in Germany, the French could not accept that it was French until proven otherwise with the specifications included. Only Peugeot headquarters in Paris is capable of providing this documentation. Since November 11 is an important holiday in France, and elsewhere in Europe (at the eleventh hour of the eleventh day of the eleventh month in the year 1918 the belligerents signed the armistice that ended the war that had raged since August 1914), we perforce waited until the 12th to make our way into Avignon and the Automobile Club de Vaucluse. The German-speaking fellow there called an acquaintance at the local Peugeot dealership, the *Directeur de Vente* (sales manager) who said he would take care of the matter. Fine. What he meant was, he would forward the request for the documents with a cover letter to Paris and when he received them he'd mail them to us. This, he assured us, would take 8 – 10 days, or just before our provisional registration would lapse. When the documents arrive we must take the car through an inspection. O yes.

Several days later the insurance lady informed us the car was officially insured, with the wrong address to be sure, but she assured us this would be taken care of. Furthermore there had been a slight reduction in the rate because Tavel causes fewer accidents than Apt (which causes fewer than Avignon). The contradiction of the policy being issued to an address in Apt with a rate applicable to Tavel did not seem to disturb the woman's sense of the rightness of things, so we did not let it disturb ours either.

At the same time the BNP finally opened an account for us after acquiring the necessary note from Mme Mourre attesting to the true fact that we lived where we said we did, plus a copy of an electricity invoice with her name on it attesting to the equally true fact that she actually lived where we said she lived.

In mid-November, the Peugeot dealer, M. Finiels, sent us a letter asking us to come for a consultation. At first we took this to be a simple confirmation of our request to Paris for the documents, but a closer reading with a dictionary changed our minds and we drove out to the industrial park to see him. Paris needed certain papers which we'd given to the Préfecture, for example the original German *carte gris*. M. Finiels called the

Préfecture, which had sent the file to the Interdépartement d'Industrie, which for some reason had requested the Paris documents the week before. He called that office. Yes, they had the file and would make a copy of the contents. We drove to the appropriate office arriving just before the lunch hour and the clerk made copies of the documents for the fee of four French francs, with which we sped back to M. Finiel's office to leave them with his secretary, he having gone to lunch, of course.

A bright spot that week: the *mairie de Tavel* had requested our dossier from the *mairie d'Apt* and received it. A note was made on our temporary *cartes de séjour* that we now resided in Tavel but did not provide the new address. The helpful woman at the *mairie* mentioned that a year or so ago someone in Tavel had purchased an automobile in Belgium which took six months to register in France! And that fellow spoke fluent French. *Bouf*! She agreed that we should complete the process of registration in the Vaucluse and then see about transferring it to the Gard, which she promised to take care of when the time came. Before the 15th of December we had to purchase a tax stamp for the car at a tabac somewhere. The provisional registration would run out on October 28, a few days hence. I thought I could arrange an extension. And somewhat to our surprise I was able to get the Préfecture to make the extension until mid-January, by which time we hoped to have received the documents from Peugeot in Paris.

On December 23, Mme Mourre received a telephone call from someone in Aigues-Mortes asking why we still have German license plates on our car. No explanation given; very mysterious.

On January 5, I noted in the journal, "No word from Peugeot dealer who's allegedly requesting documents necessary to register the car from Paris for the Bureau des Mines." The "allegedly" indicates our faith in the system had declined and we could only shake our metaphoric heads at the fact that it worked at all.

By the middle of the month one of the documents requested from Peugeot in Paris arrived and LM took it to the Mines office in Avignon where the official handling our case, whose hobby was the American Civil War and very obscure aspects of Minnesota history, became upset over the missing document and burst into a paragraph of denunciation of his countrymen's inability to understand French and urged us to write ourselves directly to the Paris Peugeot office, which we did, in English, several days later. Evidently it did not occur to this Civil War buff that the entire procedure was absurd. He did, however, recommend we inform no one we lived in Gard until the process had been completed, echoing the same advice the young woman in Tavel had given us. Amusing that one part of the bureaucracy denigrates the others as narrow-minded and unable to see beyond the directives by which their offices function. Amusing, that is, until one is finally caught in the labyrinth of those same, sometimes contradictory, directives.

Leaving his office with a small smile and a discouraged "*Au revoir*", LM found a success of sorts at the Préfecture when the clerk there extended Petite Mo's German plates for an additional month without a quiver of hesitation. When LM approached the car to make the trip back to Tavel two plainclothes policemen asked to see the vehicle's papers (routine check, *madame, rien plus, s'il vous plait, merci*) which, after a careful reading, they handed back to her and wished her a good day. As luck would have it they did not ask to see her personal papers because she did not have them. I did, back in Tavel, at the mayor's office, where I had taken them with mine to extend our temporary *cartes de séjour* for as long as possible. The pleasant young thing behind the small, neat Swedish style desk informed me that the date for the extension would not be due for another week; could I please come back then because, who knows, maybe, the permanent residence permits might be in by then. If not, she promised to renew the documents on that date. Fine.

In the meantime, the fellow in Tavel who had purchased a car in Belgium more than six months previously continued to drive around with what we hoped were valid Belgian custom plates.

On January 27 we received a letter from one department in the Paris Peugeot main office requesting a copy of the *carte gris* and the receipt for the French import tax, both of which are already in a different department there. What to do? Write a letter explaining the situation? Better to simply send additional copies? But this wouldn't be simple because it meant another visit to the Bureau des Mines and explaining the situation to the Civil War buff. We decided to send the additional copies and hope for the best. By now we'd lost the sense of the entire matter and acted almost by rote in taking the steps that we hoped would end in a clean, clear set of new papers for the motor car, which had begun to require major repairs at the garage down the street.

On the first of February I met the secretary of the *mairie* in the street, small towns having their advantages, who assured me that she was taking care of finding out why we have no permanent *cartes de séjour*. No one seemed to really care about such things, one lived as one could without too much concern about governmental rules and regulations; such things are there to be resisted whenever possible. Nonetheless, on the 7th the residence permits finally nestled firmly in our shoulder bags, valid until September. Sighs of relief and glasses of *marc* to celebrate.

Then, some days later – lo and behold! – the documents from Peugeot in Paris arrived. Progress. What remained, we thought, was the matter of the headlights and the inspection. Headlights? In those days, French law required all automobiles registered in France to have yellow tinted headlights, no doubt because yellow illumination is easier to detect in dense fog and is therefore safer than white light. Fogs in Belgium and the Netherlands are thicker than in much of France but no such ordinance existed there. Nor in Germany, where the fogs in the north can be dense and dangerous. La petite Mo had been sold and resold in Germany, hence had white headlights. Logical, *n'est-ce pas*? So we spent the money and the garage down the street put the yellow headlights in the car.

In order to relieve the tension of this process, I wrote the following doggerel.

With Randolph Scott
on the horizon
how can the stones
lie peacefully
in the grass?

While we entertained our first set of visitors in the New Year for ten days at the end of February and early March, word reached us that the car inspection was scheduled for the first of the month. We drove to a desolate stretch of unfinished highway about 30 minutes east of Avignon where the inspector would test the vehicle for whatever the state thought necessary and total up the good and bad points, thus coming to a mathematical conclusion. Who stood there next to his own vehicle waiting for us but the Civil War buff from the Bureau des Mines! The result of his observances did not inspire confidence that he would put his stamp of approval on the certificate. Indeed, he mumbled something about the fact that any of his colleagues would have failed the car due to various depredations caused by age and use, such a rusted out front end not entirely visible unless one looked underneath the fenders. However, being good of heart, we believed, and probably tired of us and our problems, he passed us with the minimum grade and stamped the document with a sour smile and a vague farewell. The imprimatur of the Préfecture now stood as the last possible obstacle on this devious and twisted course toward the goal of legalizing our mode of transportation. By the middle of the month, as the weather continued its unpredictable erratic course between bone-chilling cold driven by a mistral and sunny, warmish days of spring, six months after we began the process, the Préfecture finally gave us the longed for license plate number, for a fee of 250 francs, and we entered the golden pastel gates of automobile Paradise – for the Vaucluse, that is. Thereafter loomed the question of transferring the paperwork to the Gard, not something we looked forward to with any joy.

Now that we had an official number we had to indicate this in the proper place on the vehicle, there where the license plates are attached, but this meant an expenditure we thought premature if the car would be soon re-registered in the Gard with a totally different number. So we bought some white paint and a small brush and I painted the number on the space provided for the plate itself. There would be no mistaking our car for any other in the country: the paint job appeared to be accomplished by a five-year old let loose on it after a tab of LSD and blindfolded. Other vehicles we'd seen around the region had hand painted numbers where the traditional identification numbers would normally be, so why not us as well? Our friendly garage mechanic/owner cracked up with laughter and wondered aloud how long it would take the Gard authorities to notice the Vaucluse number and insist it be changed. What our friend did not tell us was that those older vehicles in the region with hand-painted numbers rarely if ever left the villages and environs where they lived; they certainly did not travel on the large, high-speed highways. On the other hand, we wondered briefly if the fellow with the Belgian registration had made any progress but we never found out.

The final episode in the long story of registering the car occurred in early May when we drove from Paris where we had picked up at the airport and spent some time with LM's parents from Oklahoma City. We stopped for a brief lunch on the autoroute and had rolled up to the entrance to the highway when the traffic police waved us over to the side of the roadway. "*Les papiers de voiture, s'il vous plait.*" Papers in order, we sighed with that by now known flood of relief. *However*, where is the tax stamp on the windshield? And what's with those painted numbers where the license plates should be? O dear. Well, you see, officer ... Result is the usual lecture about following regulations, applicable for Americans as well as Frenchmen, *vous savez*? Yes, yes, we know, and we promise to have the matters taken care of as soon as we return to our residence, emphasis on the fact that we actually live in this glorious nation of thinkers and poets. Let off with just the warning, we think, we sped down the highway south, well, as fast as the car can go in any case. And we do buy the tax stamp at the *tabac*, and we do have the garage down the street make up a set of plates and attach them to the creaky, aging machine. Everyone including us seems to have forgotten about transferring the registration to the Gard. Why poke around, even with a long stick, in the hornets' nest?

Sometimes the hornets bestir themselves without any outside assistance. In mid-July we received a notice of a 300 franc fine levied against us for not having a tax stamp on the car last May when the gendarme stopped us. *Alors!* We wrote a letter protesting ignorance of the regulation and attesting to the fact that we'd had such a stamp on the windshield since shortly after the meeting with the long arm of the law.

Thus, toward the end of our sojourn in the Midi we finally had the motor car properly registered, taxed, and license-plated, in the Vaucluse to be sure, but *done* at last.

Mme Mourre and LM on the one occasion
we were able to convince her to come up to visit us.

The author as chef de cuisine.

LM and Finette the dog.

The author on his daily rounds.

LM in the unusual snowstorm on our street.

The Christmas tree with hand-made decorations.

Mary in our Tavel living/dining room
(with my water color abstractions on the walls).

LM, Abigail, Kate, Marty and Erin in the Marseille
restaurant waiting for bouillabaisse.

Mary, Erin, Abigail and Kate in the Tavel living/dining room.

LM and Mme Barré at Les Baux.

The painter at work.

An example of the "blown" technique.

One of the totems on packing paper.

An example of the quasi-Cubist portraits.

LM and her parents in the Rodin Museum Garden

The drummer and his guide dog of uncertain parentage
in L'Isle-sur-la-Sorgue.

Blair, Ulrike Joram and the author with Benjamin's back.

The Williams clan at the Ferme Jamet with friends. From left to right: Marsha (Blair's sister), Carma (daughter), Blair, Rick Anderson (daughter Michelle's fiancé), Matthew behind who sits Martine and Etienne Jamet, Michelle, LM and Karin.

Boules at the Lebels: Warren, Blair, Benjamin, Michel
(partly hidden), Matthew, the author and La Petite Mo
with handwritten license plate.

Left to right: Evelyn, Jean, Penny Lipsett (a friend of the
Williams), LM and Freda Williams (Blair's mother) at the
Williams on the Ferme Jamet.

Matthew, LM, Benjamin and the author on the terrace
of the Tavel house.

Benjamin, Karin, the author, Matthew and Jean's arm
in Châteauneuf-du-Pape for lunch.

LM, Evelyn and Warren at the harbor of St.-Jean-Cap-Ferrat;
note the ever-present green Michelin guide in LM's hand.

Evelyn's 65th birthday dinner in Venice.

The over-abundance of zucchini growth inexorably led to
imaginative uses for the expanding vegetable.

The main manse at the Ferme Jamet; the doorway on the far left
leads to three apartments in one of which the Williams lived
during the winter and spring of 1983 and in which LM and I often
stayed over the years.

Chapter V

The New Year: Winter into Spring 1983

The Gypsies do not restrict their travels to the Mediterranean coast, but they no longer traveled in horse-drawn wagons: 20 years before the end of the 20th century they moved about in old Citroëns and Mercedes pulling their wagons and mobile homes. The French call them *"les gens du voyage"*, the traveling people, or travelers. In most of Europe the people themselves prefer the names Roma or Romany (plural) and Rom (singular) and in parts of the continent they are known as Sinti. There has been speculation that the word "gypsy" is derived from "Egyptian", which one supposes is possible, especially when the notion is supported by Webster's 7th edition (my good and constant companion)[15] and the OED (which like a good English product spells it "gipsy"). The fact that most Roma lead sedentary lives, moving restlessly about the landscape no more often than most of us, has not altered the general public opinion of them as migratory tribes of dubious honesty and trustworthiness. There are naturally groups of young and old Roma who prey on tourists and make their living stealing other people's goods, but no more

---

[15] "One of a dark Caucasoid people coming orig. from India to Europe in the 14th or 15th century and living and maintaining a migratory way of life chiefly in Europe and the U.S."

than there are such groups in any given population. This fact does not hinder certain local governmental authorities from various forms of discrimination and harassment aimed specifically at the Romany people. Outside Avignon on a barren strip of dusty ground dotted with stunted brown-green shrubs the city authorities have established a camp site with signs stating the place is for "*les gens du voyage*" and they are not to camp anywhere else within the city limits.

As the autumn turned colder and crisper and edged into winter one saw the younger of the people hunkered down under the ramparts of the walled city, occasionally around a fire, where few tourists venture and where therefore they are not bothered too often by police patrols. The older of them sometimes sold trinkets within the walls where the police shooed them down the street. Only rarely did we see young Romany girls with twisted ankles and sores on their necks holding infants, eyes rheumy, swaddled in filthy clothes, begging in the streets. We thought then the city authorities had over-reacted to what they clearly perceived as a threat to the stability of law and order in the city. Since we never had much contact with the Roma we saw no reason to change our opinion. That bark of laughter from the street corner shrouded in the evening's crepuscule could have been uttered by anyone including one of the bums that gather wherever the winters are mild and tourists plentiful.

There are of course exceptions, such as LM's "Avignon street lady," who LM first saw at the university before she switched to CELA for language instruction. We never learned the woman's name, but her presence

160

on the street was a constant reminder of how fortunate we were and are. Ever dressed in odorous black dragging her suitcase and sack filled with whatever it is the homeless carry with them all day from pillar to post, we never saw her ask for a handout and she looked healthy, if pale and rather dusty, with long dark slightly electrified hair streaked with gray. She had clearly known better days: she possessed a variety of once elegant and expensive shoes, now old and worn with missing ankle straps. We saw her often that year, wandering around the city or sitting on a bench munching on a roll or an apple. LM often saw her studying the course offerings at the university (we heard she sat in on classes from time to time) and in the halls smoking with any student who would offer her a cigarette; she also spent time in the library where she would leave her baggage when elsewhere on the premises.

In later years when we returned to Avignon we would occasionally see her on her rounds, unchanged and unchanging, an integral part of the cityscape we had come to think of as our own. Then, several years ago, we saw her no longer schlepping her goods through the streets and our friends could not enlighten us as to what had happened to her. Did she move on? Did family members take her in and off the streets? Had the social services authorities put her in a residence for indigents? We never knew her name but we have a photograph of her by Julien Charlon in a book entitled *Portraits de Face* (Avignon, 2000) where she appears as "*personage de la ville*" amongst other noteworthy types who inhabited the city's domains in 2000.

Avignon has always attracted the well-off and curious who later became well-known, if not famous, and more often than not they stayed at the Hôtel d'Europe overlooking the Place Crillon. We discovered the hotel and its one-star restaurant early in our sojourn and, while we could not afford the restaurant, we could from time to time in clement weather sit in the courtyard in front of the bar by the entrance and enjoy a *pastis* and a cigarette before seeking a less expensive eatery or driving back to Tavel for supper. I well remember the occasions when we spent an hour or so in the courtyard with an aperitif, especially those late spring or autumn evenings when the temperature dropped to a slight chill and a breeze skirled the leaves from the plane tree across the paving stones and out the gate into the Place Crillon. The mild breeze raised small puffs of dust in the darkening crepuscule as the damp from the river crept into the courtyard.

We did eat there once, but that was many years later when we stayed for a night at the hotel and thoroughly enjoyed ourselves. On another occasion I sat in the courtyard with a small group attending a literary conference sponsored by the International Lawrence Durrell Society, an academic fan club, after a half hour of merriment the management asked us to lower the volume because we might be disturbing the resident guests.

The hotel in one form or another dates back to 1580 and none other than Napoléon stayed there several times, signing in simply as "Bonaparte". Henry James slept there on his little 1882 tour in France and appreciated its comfort, as did James Joyce and his wife Nora for a few days in May 1928. The occasionally effervescent English writer Lawrence Durrell used the hotel as an *espace d'assignation* for nocturnal adventures with young female admirers in the years after his beloved wife Claude's death in January 1967.

•

The French equivalent of public radio, which there, unlike in America, does not pollute the airwaves with commercials, amazed us in its unpredictable eclecticism of musical selections. Indeed, the eclecticism of programming on the French national broadcasting station, *France Musique*, is always amazing to the American ear. The wide variety of types of music often played one after the other jarred one's sensibilities so accustomed to one genre per program. The French station also played far more "modern" works (meaning dissonance dominated or a series of noises, human and manufactured) such as the noisy sounds of Stockhausen and worse, and Middle Eastern quarter tones followed by oriental strings and flutes bending notes in a manner foreign to the European ear, followed by the overture to *The Three-Penny Opera* followed by a lengthy French rock number. French public broadcasting (there were few if any privately-owned stations in the country) took its responsibilities seriously and played music on a cultural level far exceeding that heard in the United States where both private and public stations pander to the lowest common denominator of taste and knowledge.

There were times, of course, when the broadcaster spent 20 minutes at a stretch, alone or with colleagues, in the latter case the conversation took much longer, explicating the music just or about to be heard. On more than one occasion this constituted such a boring disruption that one clicked the off button and listened to the wind and the hysterical hound Finette.

After a while, we no longer expressed surprise at what we considered eccentric and eclectic programming on the station where Keith Jarrett played a long solo piano piece followed by the cerebral sounds of the Modern Jazz Quartet, succeeded by a raucous mélange of noises called "Italian free jazz" and a peppy number by the Swingle Singers. We found listening to a Thelonious Monk tune followed by one of Yves Montand's popular hits and a Tommy Dorsey swing number to be not at all jarring, but we were somewhat taken aback to find that one of Monk's songs is the musical signature of a Marseille radio station.

Excerpt from a letter to Dean dated January 12, 1983:

Radio France Musique has an opera singer doing Love is a Many Splendored Thing. No, really. It's 9 a.m., for christ's sake, I'm sober. This is real! They just did a Haydn piece followed by Lester Young – now this! Arrggghh ...

Excerpt from a journal entry dated February 3, 1983:

Beethoven's 5th before 9 a.m. is a new experience – live Karajan-Berlin Philharmonic performance. Followed by a post-John Cage piece done by un-tuned instruments played by the musically illiterate inmates of the Montfavet asylum for the warped of brain and captive of fantasy – the cock's crowing and Finette's yapping only add texture to the barnyard squeaks and groans on the broadcast.

To which one can only add the encomium I wrote in the journal under the date January 21, 1983: The little radio-cassette player "has seen us through the good and the not so good (haven't had any bad yet) and continues to be a source of consolation with its broadcasts of the crazed eclectic French stations: Brahms followed by Archie Shepp takes some getting used to."

One of the more interesting listening experiences occurred that winter when the station broadcast a series of early morning segments on the history of "*le bebop*", extolling the music of Charlie Parker, Dizzy Gillespie, Monk (though he was not really a "bopper"), Bud Powell and *tout le monde* of the time. As usual on this station, regardless of the subject under discussion, the discussion time drags on and the time for music suffers, but the shows are long so there's room for both. One of the good things about this program is the inclusion of pre-bop (known as swing) and post-bop (known as "hard bop") tunes to give historical context to the music, i.e., where it came from and where did it go.

The high-pitched, speed-speaking commentator continually referred to the musicians as "Charlie", "Dizzy", and so on, as if he knew them well, which we all tend to do, but not on national radio programs. But hearing him announce the next number as "Flat Foot

Floogie with a Floy Floy" in a heavy French accent is a phenomenon one should not miss.

On various occasions the offerings bordered on the unbelievable. At midday in mid-summer we witnessed Screaming Jay Hawkins doing "Put a Spell on You" on the television, rolling his eyes, shouting, hammering away at the piano, rumbling gusts of laughter, surrounded by jungle vegetation into which he loudly mumbled African talk to a shrunken head, in what under other circumstances would have been a pleasant baritone voice. He followed this with a version of "Constipation Blues" accompanied by a white French fellow playing a second piano and interjecting intellectual comments amidst Jay's grunts and groans, verbal gems such as *"Suffite le caca!"* A program about the influence of pop music on fashion followed, a pale shadow of the energy generated by Hawkins, with a Mick Jagger interview in French until his knowledge of the language seriously lagged behind what he wished to communicate and he switched to his own brand of English.

Another example of the variety of musical types heard on the television was the performance one night of a 15-minute piece by five Japanese percussionists flailing away at a considerable number of instruments that required whacking with some implement at regular intervals of very short duration. Dressed in what seemed to be sumo wrestlers' outfits, they banged away, leaping about in a controlled frenzy, yelling what I suppose were samurai phrases, but might have been words to the piece. Quite enjoyable, actually, if loud, for late night entertainment. Had it continued for another minute, that would not have been the case.

There are also musical performances that are less esoteric to one's ear, but nonetheless come unexpectedly in that direction. The French jazz pianist Michel Petrucciani was born in Orange, Provence, on December 28, 1962 with a disease (*osteogenesis imperfecta*) that causes brittle bones and in his case curtailed his growth so he remained during his short life no taller than about three feet. The parts of his body that did not seem to suffer this diminution were his head which contained an amazingly fertile and inventive brain, and his hands which allowed him to play the piano like an orchestra. Since he could walk only with great difficulty, in concerts one of his fellow musicians often carried him in one arm onto the stage and seated him on the high piano stool, his feet resting on special pedal extensions. Over the far too few years he remained active in the business he recorded dozens of albums both as a soloist and in the company of other musicians, including one with his guitarist father and another with Stéphane Grappelli. One of my favorites is an album made on a jazz cruise with Wayne Shorter and Jim Hall on which the interplay of their improvisations is nothing short of stellar. Equally amazing is the combination of his piano and the legendary alto saxophone of Lee Konitz recorded in a documentary on Petrucciani's life shown on French television in the summer of 1983. The fact that we watched the broadcast in Tavel allows me to mention here that wondrous talent and gracious personality that was Michel Petrucciani. He died in New York City on

January 6, 1999 just barely 36 years old, and he is buried in the Père Lachaise cemetery in Paris.[16]

As our collection of tapes expanded, the time we spent listening to the radio diminished, but we've never forgotten the wildly thrown together and astonishing selections of sounds that emanated from that small plastic and metal box on the credenza through the winter days and nights.

We did not lack opportunities to hear live music but often found the price of admission to be beyond our budgetary limits. We made several exceptions for truly exceptional musicians: the pianist Mal Waldron, Mstisław Rostropovich and Stéphane Grappelli.

Waldron is well-known to jazz aficionados such as we, whose tastes in music are varied enough to contain just about every development barring late Coltrane and that egregious stuff called "free jazz" and its derivatives. As in any musical genre, there is room in the house of jazz for dissonance (*cf.* Monk, Mingus and Waldron's own "Nervous" which he played on the historic Sunday evening of December 8, 1957 CBS television broadcast "The Sound of Jazz", an installment on the series "The Seven Lively Arts"), but for my taste dissonance is limited in range and interest. Waldron's piano playing stretches from the eponymous style of the title mentioned above, to the almost painfully melodic and lyrical support he provided for Billie Holliday's heartbreaking ballads.

---

[16] Mike Zwerin, an American jazz musician and writer living in Paris, wrote an obituary that contains the basic biographical facts, printed in The *International Herald Tribune* on January 12, 1999; it can be found as a link to the Wikipedia.com Petrucciani entry.

He played in both styles, lyrical and gritty, on the seminal and vehemently enthusiastic Charles Mingus Jazz Workshop album *Pithecanthropus Erectus* (1956), a group of compositions, partly improvised by the entire ensemble in addition to the individual musicians' solos, that exploded out of the previous limits of the bebop-oriented styles then dominating the field, so radical that the senior class modern dance group at Hempstead High School in the state of New York in the year of Our Grace 1956 refused to choreograph dances to any of them.[17] Woof. Waldron's comping behind the soloists is nothing short of an exercise in extrasensory perception: he intuits the notes they would improvise and he played to their phrases, complementing as well as accompanying their harmonic and melodic inventions.

I've written at this length about Waldron in part because he deserves any and all encomiums and in part to explain the whoop of joy that burst from my throat when I read in the newspaper that he would be performing one night at a small dinner club called L'Alibi in Uzès, some 38 kilometers east of Tavel. It was a dark and rainy night shortly after we returned from Paris when we drove carefully through the back roads (there were no front roads at the time between Uzès and Tavel, a condition that has not changed since then). We found the club, that doesn't exist any longer, with some difficulty. The

---

[17] For an acute appreciation of Mingus and Monk's music, see Brian Priestley, "Thelonious Monk and Charles Mingus" in Bill Kirchner (ed.), *The Oxford Companion to Jazz* (Oxford University Press, 2000), 418ff. Charlie Parker is alleged to have offered this definition of jazz: "It's just music. It's playing clean and looking for the pretty notes." This of course is nonsense. Bird's notes were always engaging and unexpected and terribly moving, but never "pretty."

building probably belonged originally to some 18th century merchant. Fortunately I had the forethought to make reservations for dinner: the room, formerly the merchant's dining room, appropriately enough, could not be described as large for a supper club, possessing no more than a dozen tables, all occupied except ours. At one end of the room stood a baby grand piano guarded by a mass of electronic equipment relating to the volume and dynamics of the music. The crowd ate noisily and anticipation moved about the room with a palpable presence.

Memory fails me with regard to what we ate that night; I do recall that the food did not fall into the memorable category: it was eatable, no more, but the wine tasted fine, and after all no one sat in that room on that evening for the food. As we finished the meal a small, slender black man with a short Van Dyck beard dressed in a suit and tie, the only Negro in the place, walked through the tables to the piano shepherded by the owner of the club who performed the unnecessary introduction, after which Waldron proceeded to regale us with an hour and a half of swinging, at times hard-driving, at times moving lyrical cascades of music whose origins lay in the older blues tradition regardless of the key or tempo of the individual pieces. At the end we were all exhausted.

During the intermission I slipped out to the toilet and almost bumped into the pianist who stood alone just outside the dining-music room smoking a long thin black paper American cigarette. How could I pass up the opportunity? I most assuredly did not. In fact we chatted about this and that (at that point in his life he lived in Munich and we talked about that as well) until the owner of the club ran up to us and said in English, "Mal, Mal, it's time, the others are waiting, please, let's go." The others in this case were several local musicians who wished to play with the great Mal Waldron, a favor which he graciously allowed them. He led them with chord changes and musical nudges to levels they usually did not achieve regardless of the extent of their talents. How long the set lasted we did not learn. We faced the drive back to Tavel in the chilly rain in a not extremely trustworthy motor car, and it was already late for us. We arrived home at 3:00 a.m. The experience remains a solid block of memory in my brain, as you, dear Reader, have perceived. The narrative comes from the depths of my recall mechanism; I find only a brief reference to it in my journal and none in the letters to Dean.

It does remind me of another occasion upon which I met a great musician of the generation immediately preceding Waldron's. Once upon a time, in the mid-1950s, there existed a small mafia-owned jazz club in the old-money, white community of Westbury on Long Island called the Cork 'n' Bib that booked big-name groups to play on weekends and local musicians to fill in during the week. Exactly how this worked is something of a mystery to me because the club's manager, Charley Oil (no doubt someone's needy cousin, so nicknamed because of the amount of goop with which he greased his stringy black hair), obviously knew nothing about the music. One night when he thought the intermission had gone on too long, he stalked up to the clearly sick and dying Lester Young, grabbed him by the arm pulling him out of the chair and growled in a tight voice filled with threat, "Get your ass out there and play, god damn it!" Creatures like that belong on their bellies shinning Prez's shoes with their tongues.

Be that as it may, the club allowed those of us who could not get into Manhattan every weekend to see and hear some of the best performers in the business, from Sarah Vaughan and Billie Holliday (also not long for this world at the time) to Prez and Eddie Costa, George Shearing and John Birks (known as "Dizzy") Gillespie, the point of this story.

It is indeed Dizzy, as everyone called him, whom I met at the Westbury club when he performed there with one of his big bands which included the singer Austin Cromer (of "Over the Rainbow" fame) and the lady trombone player, Melba Liston. During the intermission I wandered to the room in the front of the building containing the bar, several booths and the stairs leading down to the toilets. At the table in one of the booths sat Dizzy taking apart the valves of his trumpet and cutting holes in thin rounds of cork with a pen knife. Not being completely sober and curious as to what he was doing, I walked up to him and said something along the lines of "Hey, man, how are ya, what cha doing, can I help?" Dizzy Gillespie was one of the kindest souls in the business not particularly noted for its kindness to strangers, and I soon wielded the penknife on the wine bottle cork whilst he screwed or unscrewed his horn's valves. As I recall all this activity was in pursuit of replacing a rubber washer in one of the valves that had

172

deteriorated to the point where it no longer accomplished its task of buffering one part of the instrument from another and had begun to affect his playing. I think. In the end, he (I almost wrote "we" but that would be far too presumptuous) repaired the horn and performed the final set to the wildly applauding audience's immense satisfaction.

More than 20 years later at a reception commemorating an anniversary of the creation of the National Endowments for the Humanities and Arts at the Carter White House, LM and I spotted Dizzy standing by himself in a corner of the room, not looking lost by any means, but nonetheless alone, a social situation I thought unworthy of this giant of modern American music. So I walked up to him, introduced myself and shook his hand. He smiled and said in his inimitable high but gravelly voice, "Pleased to meet you, man." I told him the story about the cork and his horn's valves and he laughed. "Oh, yeah, I remember that." He didn't of course, but it was typical of his charm and generosity that he said he did. Soon some others approached and began talking to him and I moved away and back to LM's side as the Marine Band began to play a ballad as its first number of the evening. No one danced, everyone waited for a couple to be the first on the floor. You can guess which couple slid onto the floor with what I hope were graceful movements, us alone dancing in the second story ballroom at the White House in Washington DC in the year of 1979.

I don't know if Dizzy ever played in Avignon, but I like to think he did.

Mstislav Rostropovich, one of the great cellists and humanists of the 20th century, needs no introduction to the readers of this memoir. When we heard he would make a solo appearance at the recently renovated Opéra Théâtre d'Avignon on January 14, LM stopped at the box office and purchased two tickets in the "with restricted visibility" second balcony using her student ID card, the others being too expensive. From our seats, Slava, as he was known in Washington during his years as musical director of the National Symphony Orchestra, appeared smaller than he was in reality. There was nothing small about the music he made: despite a curious lack of fire his intonation was clear as a bell; the volume of his sound, the precision of his technique and the lovely music of Bach's suites for the solo cello could only be described as big. He filled the small faux Renaissance hall with such music that even the stone figures of Corneille and Molière sitting on their tall pediments outside the theater perked up their ears in wonder.

The general impression of the theater itself was one of maroon plush with an occasional cherub on the gold flake trim. The plush was fake, simply a deep maroon paint, not cloth, at least in the second balcony. After the performance we wandered in a daze across the Place de l'Horloge to Pimm's Cup Bar (no joke, so it was named) where we spent more francs for two glasses of Scotch whisky than we did for 11 liters of rosé from the Tavel coop. There's a lesson somewhere here, no doubt, but who's to say where or what it consists of.

The only other occasion on which we attended a performance at the Opéra Théâtre d'Avignon found us in the presence of the giant among violinists, Stéphane Grappelli, who accompanied by his rhythm trio regaled us for two happy hours in early March. Grappelli's career traced an interesting arc from an unknown youth who played improvised street music on a violin he'd studied since the age of 12 in his native Paris, developing his talent and name to become the co-founder with the guitarist Django Reinhardt of the Quintette du Hot Club de France in the 1930s, and finally, after the war his willingness and ability to play jazz, classical, Middle Eastern and Indian music led him to become one of the most well-known, respected and listened to musicians on the planet. His style rarely deviated from the way he played in the Hot Club; that is, a lyrical, swinging music that stated the melody of the song and improvised around it without the noisy excesses many of his much younger colleagues thought they needed to make in order to define their identifies.

Grappelli made countless recordings and concert appearances, but also played in small venues seating as few as 50 people, as he did once in Bethesda, Maryland in the late 1980s when we last saw him. He always ended the concerts and club appearances improvising a piece on the piano in the style of Ravel and Debussy: lyrical slow movements contrasted with equally lyrical faster tempos. Then he thanked the audience and quietly disappeared into the night clutching his violin, one of his musicians assuring that he reached his hotel safely. Stéphane Grappelli died at the age of 89 on December 1, 1997 and is buried in the Père Lachaise cemetery in Paris.

That night in March 1983, in Avignon, the group blew the top off the theater; it was one of the swingingest performances to which I've ever had the pleasure of listening.

Aside from evenings spent in the piano bar on the Place Crillon in Avignon where a very good jazz pianist played several times a week, we only attended one other musical event, the performance by the group Oregon in the ancient Roman arean in Nîmes. It was a beautiful July night, the dark sky filled with bright stars and a clear round moon; a warm breeze gently moved around us as the music spoke directly to us, nudging our emotions to expand as the melodies pursued their fates. Oregon had a sound similar to that of the Paul Winter Consort, they shared songs and occasionally band members. Various guitars, saxophones (especially the soprano, which is not my favorite but in conjunction with the other instruments works fine to my ear), cello, bass, occasionally an electric piano and some marvelous tunes including "Icarus", our Christmas tree song, which the band played as an encore.

Icarus of course had nothing to do with Christmas trees, but as explained in an earlier chapter, it played a role in LM's and my early days when we were "courting". So we happily tapped our feet and didn't mind sitting on the old stone seats for another ten minutes. The South African pianist known as Dollar Brand followed Oregon, but *tempus fugit* and we had to leave for the drive back to Tavel so only heard his first number.

Having mentioned piano playing, a further music-related incident cannot go unmentioned. On Sundays one of the two national networks broadcast a variety show called *"Champs Élysées"*, hosted I think by the energetic and ubiquitous Michel Drucker. Late in our sojourn we watched it one night because the popular singer-actor Johnny Hallyday performed on it; we had not up to that point seen him but I had heard about him since the 1960s. He is known as the French Elvis Presley, a smarter and less drug-addicted Elvis, who some say invented French rock and roll, and is also known as the greatest rock and roll singer completely unknown outside France. However thrilling his act may have been (I can find no opinion on the subject in the sources), the kicker came that night when Michel Piccoli and Marcello Mastroianni sat down at dual pianos to play a Scott Joplin piece, the performance of which convinced us that neither could actually play the instrument, the sounds of which had been recorded earlier. Like movie stars everywhere, they fulfilled their contractual duty and plugged their newest celluloid adventure on national TV, and they seemed to enjoy themselves, as well they should have; we certainly enjoyed their act because it lifted the usually insipid star-advertising appearance to a new and ironic level. (Johnny Hallyday, né Jean-Philippe Smet, by the way, remains as popular as ever, though he is now threatening to retire from touring. What would *Paris Match* be without a regular appearance by the singer, his wives, children and entourages at work and play in California, on Caribbean islands, in St. Tropez or Réunion?)

●

Early April words meander across the page of the journal indicating the condition known to medical science as intoxication and familiar to those who "drinks a bit" (according to the wise Mr. Bojangles) as "transcendent inspiration"; this can be seen from the following excerpt.

Walking through the back road to the postes I was attacked by a bee, small but vicious bee who hit my neck, then as I slapped about fell into my shirt and bit me twice again under the right nipple – the welts lasted four days, waning and waxing in itching intensity until finally the whole mess apparently disappeared into the dusk of vaguely multi-colored rainbows striking down into the next of one's comfort and then gone like the lightning unrecorded upon the sky, brief illumination, oh epiphany! Look we have come through the shit of nighttown's horse parades while the Liliputaners die of unknown diseases. O yes I shot the fire full of wholes when circles have a definite end.
   Stopping the pedestrians on the rue de la République, you see, means no more than too much wine and enthusiasm. Readable or not it is there at the moment of its creation and how many have made their reputations on less? Hein? Panama elicits fragrant songs from novelists of prose with somber rhythms edging into bassa nova and the entire circus of Central American intellectuals who write stuff as coherent and "meaningful" as this stuff done late at night with concrete frog calls, deep, throaty, so laden with sex that

178

the erection finds it impossible to arise. Leck mich deshalb oder deswegen am Arsch. Ca suffit. Los. Vers imagination.

This hardbound book is not going to last the race. Shabby production denies eternity or even the Nobel Prize – it gives out upon a street with no end shadowed by ruins renewed in the solid Stalinist style meant to last as long as a political friendship. Drop ashes from your cigarette on the page and you have the coherence of modern dialogue – a wind blows and the page is blank.

Laughter is the only answer. Henry Miller was right in the end. But this knowledge comes too late, of course.

Well, maybe it does, and maybe it doesn't. That text will not tell you one way or another. And the hardbound notebook may not last the race, but it has endured just fine to this day and it lays open before me on the desk overlooking the tropical lane on which we live now.

●

Journal entry March 16, 1983:

Solitude is far different from loneliness because it is filled with the comfort of work and elation, while the other consists in the dissatisfaction of being alone. Normally, *hélas*, life is more the latter than the former, but this condition allows the sharpness of solitude to be more deeply felt when it is found. One treasures solitude and struggles against loneliness. Neither has anything to do with physical isolation.

Telephone repairman arrived, fixed the phone, puffed a few clouds of Gauloises smoke and left – all within five minutes.

●

Health

Writing as Van Gogh to his brother Theo, only the date and the symptoms are real:

St. Remy, 11.II.1983

Dear Theo – it is so cold the very pages of my MS stick to my fingers and come away with my skin on them. I doubt this will impress the publishers should any of them ever see it. Winter has finally forced its ravages on my body, although I have been careful – really – as you suggested, but my weakened condition has allowed the germs to breach my defenses and my bones ache terribly, my head is stuffed not with colors but phlegm and ugly mucus. Even the sun is conspiring with the cold and does not hang in the sky to warm the landscape. It's too gray for me, but the sisters say I'm doing better now and the physician smiled yesterday and gave me back my pencil. They don't have much blank paper here but they are nice and treat me well. Today I can walk briefly in the garden in a borrowed muffler. If the weather warms perhaps I can go over to Glanum next week when one of the sisters has time (can't go out alone yet). I hear the postman—he must be very cold—perhaps he's brought me a letter from you. I will try and do some work.

Your brother in the "warm" south.

Vinnie

The attempted humor in the missive reflected an obviously unexpected situation with regard to the weather and my general health during that winter.

The problem seemed to be two-fold: pains in the upper torso leading me to believe my heart and/or my lungs had something seriously wrong with them, and blood in my urine together with sharp intermittent pain in the left testicle, leading me to fear a stone had grown and lodged itself in one of my kidneys and was now straining to release itself into the urethra on its way out to a watery freedom. If this were the case, and if a urethral colic occurred, I was, as I knew all too well, in for an agonizing blast of pain unlike any other.

Any number of factors could have contributed to the heart/lungs discomfort that occasionally crossed the border into severe pain: I smoked an ungodly number of cigarettes each day, drank an inordinate amount of wine each day and suffered badly from the unusual cold temperatures freezing the region that winter. From time to time I had stopped smoking for a day or three, then cut down consumption and took long walks in the vineyards to clear the lungs and exercise the muscles. But this, obviously, remained thoroughly inadequate to achieve any noticeable results. And the French did not then make it easy to buy tobacco products: only registered stores, usually sellers of newspapers, magazines, stamps and stationery, can sell them; they are recognizable by the metal red diamond shaped symbol attached to the façade of the store's front. There were no cigarette machines, so ubiquitous in Germany and elsewhere in Europe so as much as the French enjoyed their tobacco habit they were severely limited in access as compared to the USA or West Germany. The French have long since adjusted the scheduling of their lives to accommodate the results of the endless struggle between capitalist greed and age-old traditions.

Another form of exercise was the tennis, which we took up in the early summer: we purchased the requisite equipment and played early in the morning all of three times on the village's public court. Thirty minutes hacking away at the increasingly recalcitrant ball proved conclusively that this was not my game at all. I possessed neither the necessary breath nor the physical agility to achieve any enjoyment at the sport. Though I started out with a modicum of optimism about my future on the court planning to keep at it while expecting little improvement, and in fact enjoying myself until the last minutes when everything fell apart and I knew it was time to quit for the day. After the third attempt I realized it was time to leave the game to those more adept at it. This disturbed me a bit because it left LM without a partner, though she did not exert much effort to find a more suitable replacement for my drag-ass self. And so it came quickly to pass that we quietly retired the equipment, which no doubt lies rotting away in Mme Mourre's ground floor garage to this day. Once we had a television we did watch the French Open (the camera lovingly and slowly moving about the young body of Yannick Noah, the French victor) and the Wimbeldon matches, but our playing days were over.

At one point, after experiencing a feeling of emptiness suddenly filling up with ache or pain, we decided to change our diet to include more health-reinforcing foods, less meat (more fish wasn't really an option because, despite the proximity to the Mediterranean which was increasingly fished out, one never knew how many days the fish at the local markets had been lying in the beds of ice and seaweed and the *hypermarché* fish was inevitably frozen), more vegetables and fruits, the typical swerve of food preparation to which those of our education and social standing turned when the belt had to be let out a notch and one noticed a slight tightening of clothes around the torso. It must be admitted that living in France at that time did not lend itself as readily to dieting as it does today. Grocery stores did not stock low-fat items prominently on their shelves and the notion of denying oneself thick bubbling stews and potatoes was alien to the rural French concept of the good life. Unless one's physician demanded a change in diet because of a life-threatening disorder, the French *mentalité* did not generally consider low fat yogurt, bananas and yeastless flatbread to be anything other than an aberration to be avoided whenever possible. Thus the ambiguity of the situation ensured no real change in my condition based on diet.

The cold became a constant irritation and of course made my health situation even more precarious. The deviousness of the weather in Provence that winter played with our lives like one of the Olympia gods toying with some innocent human to be maneuvered without consideration for his fate. Our heating system could not make much headway, but when we retreated to the kitchen for the oven's warmth the damp heat clogged my breathing tubes and roughened my lungs. The air became thick and sticky and I found it difficult to breathe forcing me back to the clearer but colder living room.

Fortunately, one day in early February I had arranged the purchase of health insurance (shouldn't that be "sickness insurance"?), lying just a little bit about the current state of my health.

As March closed down I made a list of things physically amiss:

Unspecified kidney ailment possibly related to pains in the lower back; shortness of breath, chest pains and nausea all three possibly related to one another; chronic post-nasal drip, inconsistent circulation difficulty in arms and hands; general lethargy (also mental).

Finally, after going through a pain-wracked, sleepless night so disturbing and grave that I made a last will and testament, I consulted a physician in Avignon. I did not do too badly describing my symptoms, having prepared a cheat-sheet before hand with the proper French names. Fortunately the words for many medical phenomena are Latin and thus the same in both languages with differences of pronunciation. Happily, LM was also there to translate. After examining me both verbally and physically, the good doctor allowed that things were "*pas grave*", which I found both a relief and annoying: why did I suffer the pains of hell if nothing major was wrong with me? I had expected at least a diagnosis of a thorough case of terminal emphysema or the necessity for an immediate by-pass surgical procedure[18], but no, he thought it was a spasmodic phenomenon and gave me 125 francs worth of medications to take for the following four weeks and a few tests to be done in a medical building in the center of the city. All the tests came back negative. Hurrah!

On the other hand, not so "hurrah" was the cost of all these tests and consultations: in the end we paid more than 400 francs to determine that as far as they could tell there was nothing wrong with me. (Not at all true, of course, the symptoms remained for the length of the winter weather and in February 1984, in wintry Washington DC, an inadequately trained urologist-surgeon made an eight-inch incision on the left side of my torso, went in and removed a large kidney stone that had attempted to crawl down the urethra and out into the wider world, but become stuck causing a massive amount of pain.)

Of course this wasn't the end of it; as we grow older concern with our health is a ceaseless parade of this pain

---

[18] This traumatic undertaking waited until the end of February 2000, a compulsory, life-saving measure carried out at the Washington Heart Center by an experienced surgeon who had done the procedure over 200 times before he and his team cracked open my chest and fixed my blood-pump.

and that ache, but usually we confront the matter in one of two ways: we ignore the aches and pains and get on with life until a procedure is absolutely required to be able to get on with it, or we consult a medical wallah immediately and enter onto a path of medications leading to dullness of brain and spirit or surgical intervention, after which we get on with life, if we survive the cure.

And the weather plays an ever larger role in one's life. Toward the end of March the erratic climate confused the senses: one day gray and cold followed by several days of such bright sunlight that we needed sunglasses in the living room to work as the sun's rays bounced off the white paper on which I wrote or painted temporarily blinding me. The brightness of the light did not necessarily revise the temperature upwards and we were not quite ready to put the winter clothes away, though some of the signs seemed encouraging: on one of these days LM wore "awful" shorts on the terrace at lunch. I've at this point no idea what these looked like or why they were "awful." Usually LM in *any* shorts is a pleasant sight.

Journal – June 7:

Weather continues to be beautiful … Physically I often feel tired and it is difficult to get up in the morning. Lying down and reading is all I really want to do. This state of affairs is absurd. The physical factor could probably be alleviated by a schedule of exercise and diminished consumption of drink and tobacco (how often have I told myself that!) The mental aspect is something else and probably has to do with my inability to get down to real work on the longer jobs, vol. II and now the Radovic story. Fear of failure? Undoubtedly. The fact that vol. I hasn't sold surely plays a role but what did I expect? Fame and riches overnight? The eccentricity of trying to change careers at 42 on the basis of no previous proof I could even write a decent sentence–and dragged Lynn along on this quest–weighs on my brain.

Perhaps the situation could best be summed up with a sentence from the journal dated September 23: "Not functioning well but cooking good."

As a result of this annoying health condition we became somewhat knowledgeable about the availability of certain medications in France. The United States has ever been a nation of pill-poppers, a situation currently exacerbated by the psychiatry profession which no longer offers analysis therapy to help understand the symptoms and causes of mental disturbances, but now offers a great variety of medications to control the symptoms rather than attempt to remove them. In the USA pills for many illnesses real and imagined were and are available on a mass-produced basis everywhere. Americans freely gobble pills for what they think ails them including masses of inexpensive supermarket vitamins, now called vitamin supplements. One can purchase these pills in huge supermarkets and small corner grocery stores as well as the aptly named drug stores.

In France in the early 1980s one could only obtain such things at a pharmacy at extraordinary high prices,

187

including dental floss. The French did not take pills, and mostly shy away from them today as well, though they have become cheaper and more prevalent than 25 years ago. For a headache then they dissolved an aspirin tablet in a glass of water and drank it, after purchasing the tablet at a pharmacy. Only a physician's order could move a Frenchman to ingest vitamins when some major deficiency existed, and the vitamins more often than not came in the form of dissolvable tablets which complicated the process a bit. Of one-a-day type compounds the pharmacies in Tavel and Avignon had not heard. As the dentist remarked about dental floss, where there's no demand there's no supply. The French advertising industry had not yet caught up on the manipulation front with its American counterpart, which creates the demand in order to sell the supply.

Signs of a change toward a more American way of business did appear from time to time. In early September an article in the *Midi Libre* announced that the supermarket chain Leclerc was planning to attempt the mass sale (at lower prices) of many things then only available in a limited number of outlets at high prices: tobacco, medicaments (non-prescription drugs), and the like. Since tobacco is a state-run business this could have led to government action against the chain, which also threatened to sell cheaper gasoline at night and make cigarettes and medicaments available through the gas stations. In the case of vitamins and medicaments this would have been a positive step, but it did not happen. Tradition and state regulation for tax revenues won over the independent capitalist entrepreneur and, while these days it is easier to obtain certain plant extracts and non-prescription drugs and vitamin C tablets in health-food stores and what the French call *"parapharmacies"* in supermarkets, much as described above remains intact today.

Fortunately ill health rarely invaded LM, but when it did so the effect was doubly intense due to its rarity. Several days of the flu during that winter and an odd stiffening of neck muscles for two days the following summer were her only complaints during our time in Tavel.

●

We took all of our visitors to the gorgeous piece of Roman architecture, the Pont du Gard (bridge of the Gard), astoundingly still incredibly grandiose and massive as in the years after the Roman designers and slaves constructed it. For this miraculous piece of ancient masonry we can thank the talents of the original builders and the French who have meticulously conserved the grandeur of the great arched viaduct and the roadway beneath it, high above the Gardon Valley and its river. When we lived there one could drive one's car across the 18th century bridge built beneath the viaduct, but fortunately this is no longer possible and the foundations no longer groan and crack under the unnecessary weight of human indifference to the wonders of the ancient and modern world.

Tobias Smollett, the 18th century English writer of controversial poems, novels, plays, political essays and histories, saw the Pont du Gard in 1763 and described it as "a piece of architecture so unaffectedly elegant, so simple and majestic, that I will defy the most phlegmatic and stupid spectator to behold it without admiration." One hundred years later Charles Kingsley, the polemical English novelist, noted that his first impression of the beige-yellow blocks of unmortared stone leaping from one side of the valley to the other "was one of simple fear." And this, in the time we lived in Tavel, could be felt by anyone coming upon the great structure for the first time, especially if one walked across the unrailed top from one side to the other and looked down. I suffer from vertigo and could not undertake this part of the excursion, but some of our friends did, and it scared them as well. Many writers have described their responses to this stunning wonder, but I like best Evelyn Underhill's: "The Pont du Gard seems, more than anything else, the completion of a landscape that had been left unfinished by mistake."[19] And we cannot leave Durrell un-cited when on this subject: he speaks of Rousseau as having written the best description of the Pont du Gard and of course gives not a word of it, but he does note that "we must remember that it was dedicated to water, and water was a God ... It took a great deal to shut a man like him up, but the emergence of this mastodon from the featureless garrigues which house the spring that feeds it deprived him of coherent speech so uncanny did it seem."[20]

---

[19] *Shrines and Cities of France and Italy* (Longmans, Green, 1949).
[20] *Caesar's Vast Ghost,* 5.

But all these citations refer to the condition of the structure itself and only hint at the area surrounding it. What once, not very long ago, was a bucolic scene of a flowing river, wild green water grasses and vegetation along the banks populated with tall trees and the sound of moving water, louder in the winter and spring when the river spilled over its shoreline, along which one could rest at a ramshackle hotel and alfresco café for a cool drink or refreshing coffee, is now a landscape infested with the accoutrements that accompany "modernization" and "renovation" and "remolding for the tourist trade."

In 1985 UNESCO added the viaduct to its list of World Heritage Sites, and this is as it should be. Some time later, assisted by financing from UNESCO and the European Union, the French government organized a €33 million "restoration" project to repair great damage to the area (but not the aqueduct) caused by the 1998 flooding and to make the site more "visitor friendly." The restoration's destruction of the natural beauty of the surrounding landscape is not entirely balanced by the banning of motor traffic.

Cut into the side of one of the hills overlooking the valley is a huge, ugly cement and glass mall complete with kitsch souvenir shops and an "up-to-date" and "interactive" museum and, of course, a vast car park to contain the thousands of motor cars and hundreds of buses disgorging their chittering-chattering cargoes to cut another site notch in their tourist belts before rumbling on to the next vast car park and a quick sight of another photograph opportunity. The Romans came to stay and built accordingly, today the diesel fumes of the autobuses corrode the ancient honey colored blocks of stone and the tourists purchase yet another postcard picture before moving on in a daze. One can still, though barely, glimpse the effect of the colossal magnificence of this weather-worn edifice at sunrise or sunset if one stands absolutely still on one of the banks below and focuses one's eyes on the structure, blotting out sound and other sights with a strong measure of will power. We last went there in June 2008 and we shall not return except in our memories.

•

Some ten kilometers southeast of Avignon lies the small town of Châteaurenard which has little to recommend it except the two tall yellow towers, all that remains of the 10th century castle that played an important role in European history. When we visited the grounds on one of our excursions in the region, an old man dressed in clean but well-worn trousers and a faded blue shirt that had seen many washings over the years greeted us with a hesitant nod. Curiously, his carefully cleaned shiny brown shoes could not have been more than a week or so on his feet, a visible contrast to his drab clothing. This agèd fellow, whose name appropriately but surprisingly was Renard, stood guard over the castle remains, or more accurately put, sat guard leaning on his walking stick. He smiled and bid us a good day, which we politely returned, wondering what the visit would cost. No official fee, as it turned out, but at the end of our visit a tip to the storyteller was certainly in order and well-earned. Speaking slowly to ensure we understood his tale, he told us the complicated story of the castle's role in the end of the Avignon Papacy.

It seems that after seven French popes, generally sympathetic to the various French royal houses and their politics, during a period of popes and anti-popes denigrating and excommunicating each other, the Sacred College elected the Spaniard Pedro de Luna as Benedict XIII (Benoît in French), who for some reason lost the support of the mad French King Charles VI. With the support of the majority French cardinals Charles sent troops to lay siege to the Papal city intending to oust the Spaniard, who had his own supporters. Legend has it that, assisted by Robert de Braquemont, a knight in the service of the Duke of Orléans, Benedict slipped out of the palace in the early dawn mist on March 12, 1403, down to the river where a boat propelled by 14 stout oarsmen rowed him quickly down the Rhône to its confluence with the Durance where, muscles straining and sweating profusely in the morning chill, they swerved up the Durance to the closest landing spot to the Châteaurenard. A fellow Spanish cleric, Cardinal de Pampelune (not Rodrigo Pamplemousse and his faithful dog Pommes Frites, as some would have it), awaited him there with a horse and small escort which swiftly moved the exhausted pope safely into the castle. Under the leadership of his nephew, Rodrigo de Luna, his followers in the palace back in Avignon held out for almost a decade, though this did not help Benedict's tenure as Pope. The College of Cardinals elected a new pope in Pisa to whom the French king lent his strong if erratic recognition and the Papacy returned to Rome, ending the Great Schism.

After the story Monsieur Renard seemed tired and older than when he began his narrative; without rising from the stone upon which he rested, he pointed out the door to one of the towers, the Tour du Griffon, and urged us to climb to the top for the *panorama magnifique* of the surrounding countryside where we would observe the town itself, the Montagnette hills, Avignon and Villeneuve-lès-Avignon, the far-off Dentilles of Montmirail, Mont Ventoux and the Alpilles. Perhaps one could see all these landmarks on a very clear day, with excellent eyesight or binoculars. We were able to make out Mont Ventoux and what we thought were the little Alps. The rest remained unseen by the two of us, but we'd had our history lesson for the day and lunch at the small though unromantic workers' café tasted particularly old that day.

●

We visited the city of Nîmes many times with friends, but the first time alone involved a sunny and chilly day at the end of November and an event at the ancient Roman arena known to the non-French as a "bullfight". This term more accurately describes the Spanish *corrida* wherein the goal is to kill the bull with a thrust of the matador's sword after the beast has been sufficiently tortured with pics and banderillas, wounded but still dangerous. In the Provençal version the event is a game that might tire the bull but leave him otherwise undamaged. The young men engaging with the bull are those who run the risk of damage, though this rarely happens.

In this bloodless form of man against beast, called *la Course Camarguaise* or *la Course libre*, a thin wire is tied to the bull's horns and several cockades of various shapes and sizes are strung along the wire. The point of the race, rather than fight, is to run obliquely at the charging bull and grab one the the cockades while twisting away from the animal so as not to be gored or tossed into the air. The cockade grabbers are called *raseteurs* and the best of them are those who tweak off the cockade furthest away from them and emerge undamaged. These events constitute one of the ancient Provençal rituals similar to the ancient Cretan bull games, and they are well attended.

Having seen both the Spanish *corridas* and the Provençal games I must admit that after an hour or so of the latter I become bored: the ugly but exhilarating drama of the *corrida* is lacking; but how often can one watch young men in red sashes and white clothing dash at the animal, twist off the cockade and prance away from the bull, who seems confused by the whole thing but still alive? This is especially true if one has neglected to bring or rent a pillow upon which to sit rather than on the ancient tiered stones that serve as seats. On the other hand, I'll not attend a *corrida* again, but would with a certain amount of reluctance go to a *cours libre* in the Roman arena in Arles or Nîmes. Both forms of the event are performed in those places, the *corrida* less often.

The other great Roman artifact in Nîmes is the best preserved of Roman temples called the Maison Carrée (the square house) set appropriately in a square across the avenue from Norman Foster's modernistic art museum. Somehow the two edifices do not clash. Inspired by the temple to Apollo in Rome, workers constructed the building during the reign of Augustus (late 1st century BCE) with a staircase leading to the portico of 15 steps calculated so that one arrives at the top on the same foot that one begins the climb.

Like all classical temples this one consists of a vestibule lined by a colonnade and a *cella*, the room devoted to a statue of whichever divinity held sway there at any given time. Words describing the structure are very often "purity of line", "harmonious proportions", "elegance of its fluted columns", "Greek-influenced design", and the like. All of these descriptors are accurate and appropriate: it is a beautiful, clean, well-balanced building that pleases the eye and one's sense of aesthetics. It has served a wide variety of purposes after the Romans retreated to Italy: residences for officials and private citizens, stables and a church of the Augustinian order and was sold as public property during the Revolution. Subsequently it became the Gard's *département* archives and from 1823 it housed the city's first museum. Today it contains exhibitions of contemporary art.

There are other ancient and centuries old relics in the city, but, with the exception of the gorgeously terraced Jardins de la Fontaine, we have not visited them.

•

Making Friends

When one moves into a new and different social and cultural environment, especially one where a different language is spoken, making friends, or at least good acquaintances, is an unavoidable and often pleasant necessity. We were very fortunate in this regard: with rare exceptions all of those whom we met and with whom we became friendly in France that year came to us through LM's French language classes, first at the university, then at CELA. The first of these, as noted in an earlier chapter, was a young British-Greek woman who worked in Dubai and had received a sabbatical to study French in Avignon. We called her Mary, but her birth name appeared to be Maria, and we've long since forgotten her family name, which doesn't appear in the journal. We remember her very well, however, because she became our first real long-term social friend and we, especially LM, spent much time with her.

A bubbly, essentially happy person, she had no hesitation in going with us to various events, dinners, saloons and trips around the countryside. Her serious side demanded that she actually study: she and LM would often sit on the terrace in their bikini beach costumes during clement weather and do the exercises to improve their French. LM also helped Mary find a place to live and visited several inappropriate venues such as a form of student dormitory in Villeneuve-lès-Avignon, which was too far away because she had no car, and a tiny room in a sleazy building near our laundromat in the hooker section of town. Finally, Mary found an address on the university bulletin board and LM went with her to see the apartment of a lovely middle-aged widow named Mme Barré in the center of Avignon on the rue des Trois Faucons, where a room was available. A perfect fit; for one thing, Mme Barré spoke little or no English so Mary had to learn sufficient French to communicate with her, a situation similar to ours with Mme Mourre. The match worked and Mary remained there for the rest of her stay in Avignon. We, too, became friendly with Mme Barré and took her on several excursions in the environs. I also recall that she went with a group of us (the Williams, Mary and Karin) to an Indonesian supper at the Loup Garou restaurant near our laundromat, after which she had us to her apartment for coffee but served us scotch as well. A charming and friendly lady, from whom even I learned a few words of French.

Mary came often to our house in Tavel to study with LM and share a meal. If the meal was supper the chances of a lively if not entirely coherent conversation were greater because the imbibing of local wine increased the fluidity of the talk. One evening in early February, LM, Mary and one of the University teachers, Françoise, returned from a hair-raising shopping trip to Nîmes for a late dinner. Hair-raising because Françoise drove her tiny, elderly 2CV with a careless attention to the road and traffic that bordered on the criminal. It was a trip they long remembered with a collective shudder.

Karin Joram, our young German friend, who wanted to study medicine and join the charitable organization called *Médicins Sans Frontières* to work in a third world country, sparkled in her youth and enthusiasm and thus lent the times we shared with her an extra portion of laughter and smiles. The young lady had very little money to spend and we often paid her portion of the bill when we ate out. Those large group outings, often numbering up to nine adults and the two Williams boys, were too much for many restaurants to handle but we always found one, usually with few or no other customers where we ate well and well-watered. On one of these occasions LM and I decided to adopt Karin when well-off American friends came to visit and take us to dinner at gourmet restaurants in Avignon. A sort of share the wealth plan. This worked well since her English outdistanced her French while she and I always had recourse to the German.

She knew an older couple who lived in a small *mas* (a Provençal farm usually with outbuildings) near Roussillon on the floor of the Luberon Valley, the abstract painter Raoul Lebel and his wife Jeanne. They lived simply and frugally, grew most of their own food, drank herbal tea and did not smoke. They lived an interesting life: he apparently sold a sufficient number of his works to bring in a small but regular income, they grew wine grapes which they took to the cooperative in Bonnieux, whence they obtained inexpensive staples and supplemented the supplies with their own chickens, vegetables and goats. They shared the cooking and we talked a lot about various types of grills, one of which for the top of the stove he insisted we take with us and use at home.

His paintings lavished bright colors on large canvases and his brush often sprayed his clothing with the same colors; indeed the colors appeared from time to time on his teeth as well. At 75 his paintings reminded me of the Fauves in his use of color which he applied to the canvas using a system of mathematic formulae related to the Pythagoras system of which I understood nothing at all. He did admire Valéry to the point where he could recite large chunks of his poetry and talk non-stop about his importance to French culture. On our first visit in January, as we ate some of Jeanne's home-made ice cream, he immediately asked if I was anti-Reagan and if I knew Valéry's work. A positive answer to the first brought on a mild tirade against socialism – understandable from a man forced out of his native Romania because he refused to paint socialist realism, a complicated story about which we unfortunately never learned any details. An equally positive but qualified answer to the second led to a discussion of whether or not one can read poetry in translation. This question has occupied considerable time over the years as I've discussed the matter with Dean and others, about which I've never come to a firm and decisive answer, though Dean says it can't be done.

At some point in his life he may have had a gallery/dealer in Paris but when we knew him he sold mainly in the region, though from time to time he showed in galleries in Switzerland and Germany. I quite liked his work but we could not afford such luxuries no matter how good they were. When we left he gave us some literature about his exhibitions, *"expositions"* in French, which led to some interesting twists when he spoke in his idiosyncratic English: "I've exposed myself in many European cities."

Watercolors

I've not exposed myself in Europe or elsewhere except on the walls of our various residences since the time in Tavel. At the very end of our stay in the Apt house I began experimenting with a child's set of water color paints, no doubt under the influence of the artists who preceded me in the Midi, and thinking of writers such as Durrell and Henry Miller who created vast numbers of water colors and oils and doodles with felt tip colored pens. As that winter wore on and I occasionally stumbled over an obstacle in the writing projects, I discovered an additional outlet for the creative urges that swirled around my head: watercolor painting. Not only did this allow the imaginative juices to flow, but it also resulted in subtracting from the effect of the awful wall paper in the living room. (If I print an example of these daublings it is of course purely to show the Reader an example of the wall paper.) The use of water colors and later gouache also allowed me to indulge in fanciful titles for series and individual paintings, such as "Beam Up Tao Captain" combining references to both *Star Trek* and *The Way of Tao*, a title which without an explanation could lead to nothing but confusion, but appealed to me because of the improbable conjuncture of the two.

Since I had no training in any of the plastic arts and could not draw worth a damn, my lack of talent (but not

201

imagination) severely restricted the subject matter of the paintings. My landscapes looked like the work of visually impaired kindergarten pupils and the only portraits I ever made with any success were of a human skull in a tie and shirt and a series of faceted heads described below. This condition left me with no choice but to indulge my fantasies in the abstract, so I became perforce an abstractionist; I'm not sure my work could be called abstract expressionist, but it did express some things in my mind and it certainly was abstract.

I did try to get a landscape or two down on paper and at one point did a view of the village roofs from the living room which I thought had potential and so practiced several versions, none of which got any better than the previous attempts so I stopped. The simpler and more abstract the better became my motto.

On days when I felt especially stymied on writing I could produce ten or 20 paintings, slashing and blowing colors all over the paper and table with the convulsive spasms of the demented and frustrated artist working his way through a tremendous imaginative bind with flailing arms tossing paint about in paroxysm of creative frenzy. Not unlike the behavior of the energy-charged terrier in the courtyard below our apartment. And, it must be admitted, this was *fun*! And no delayed gratification here, the results immediately stared one in the face, so to speak, bad or good.

I thought then that it would be possible that a piece of trashy art might look better well-matted and framed on a wall. It would remain trash, of course, but it would *look* better. I counted on this theory having some visible validity when I framed some of my watercolors. Could I sell some of this stuff, I wondered? Did I know any galleries, and so on? I realized that no to the latter question meant no to the former as well. And I had to accept that there would be no income from that quarter, though my work was as good as some of the junk being foisted on a more than willing public as art. "Need to know the right people. That's the key." It did not occur to me to have a small show in our apartment for friends and their friends and perhaps make some money. (It has occurred to me since living in Key West and knowing several gallery owners, but I've been smart enough not to broach the matter with them.) The fact that during the summer making the water colors raised less of a sweat than typing added to their attraction.

By the middle of October I had progressed to a series of linear geometric forms on slender pieces of brown packing paper that contained the most interesting and ambitious work up to that point. Shortly thereafter I began a series of portraits of imaginary faces in what appeared to be a quasi-cubist style, which I thought much freer in the use of shades of colors, mixing and blending, especially the black and white. Looking at it now (see below) it doesn't seem very Cubist but rather an odd combination of late Cézanne (for whom I certainly will never be any competition) swatches of color, a Cubist flattening effect and Leger outlining. Somewhere in there may be something of my own. The work as a whole may be sloppy and amateurish but it gave pleasure in the doing and occasionally in the seeing: all undigested influences and lack of technical knowledge.   LM suggested I take a course in watercolors when we returned to Washington, perhaps at the Torpedo Factory in Alexandria. In the end I did not do this, though for several months I continued to sporadically push the brush and felt tip pens around pieces of paper. Then other projects and pressures pushed my career as a watercolorist to the side where it has rested, with an occasional and brief burst of energy, ever since. Perhaps this is just as well.

Painting with water colors thus became a substitute for writing then that seemed blocked for whatever reason. If Joyce hadn't been blind would he have painted on occasion? He lacked the visual imagination, at least in terms of physical forms and colors, though his written descriptions of physical phenomena are astounding. At the time I had some hope my pictures would improve in quality; they would at best perhaps make adequate gifts for friends and at worst could decorate our own walls, as they did in Tavel.

At the times when the words did not come, the paint moved across the pages with flowing gestures. I experienced a great feeling of *creating*, swinging the brush around, leaning back to view the work, darting forward to make a dab of color here, a line there – just like in the movies! A real artist at last! The Tao Signals series could have gone on forever in its simplicity but after a while I thought I could see what I wanted from it: without being either minimalist or reductionist (a matter of mind in any case: a Tao painting exists only in the mind of the artist but others can still experience it – the art is not reduced in this manner, rather a way of seeing has been altered), I wanted less to say more. If the less was accurately chosen and carefully arranged it would succeed in saying everything I wanted it to.

•

We knew we had to be prepared for an unknown number of visitors over the course of the year, and we thought it would be wise to ensure that all of them were prepared as well. Toward that end I typed up a list of things they should be aware of. Now, there are a couple of things to be noted about these expressions of mild anxiety and minor trepidation: it is unlikely that we ever sent them, but I had a pleasant time writing them; LM's cousin Greg lived and lives in Spokane not Seattle; and the reference to policy decisions in Paris is as obscure to me now as it is to you The Reader.

Notes for Prospective Visitors
To the
Smith-Chamberlin Hotel in Tavel

For various and sufficient reasons (budgetary considerations, the necessity to accomplish a maximum amount of work in a short period of time, etc.) the following thoughts are offered to those who plan to visit.
    1. Visitors are not charged for room, but are expected to contribute to the maintenance of the usual high culinary standards already established here.

2. Visitors planning to be here for more than two days should not expect either of us to participate in their adventures during the day, as much as we might like to. Consequently, those visitors are expected to provide their own transportation (rental vehicle, moped, bicycle, or other).
3. Visitors staying <u>any</u> length of time should bring their own towels. Everything else of this nature will be provided.
4. Given the number of people who are planning, thinking, threatening to visit it would be helpful to us to know as soon as possible at least the tentative dates of your anticipated presence in Tavel.
5. May is already booked; 26 February to 15 March is booked; the period 23 March to 5 April is tentatively booked. (You see what we mean about scheduling.)
6. The most convenient guests for us are those who plan to spend some time here on their way elsewhere, or on their way back from elsewhere, or both. Those who wish to be here for a longer period should be prepared to do a lot of reading, lying in the sun, or exploring on their own (or all of the above). The situation is somewhat similar to the beach house at Bethany, for those of you who have been lucky enough to experience that, except that here Lynn also works/studies. ("I didn't at Bethany?" LM's addition to the manuscript.)

7. Things to keep in mind:
    a. You are on vacation; we are not.
    b. We expect to be taken out to dinner at least once during each visitor's stay.
    c. There is no reasonable public transportation to and from Tavel. Avignon is 15 kilometers away.
    d. Avignon is easily reached by train from Paris. The fast express (TGV – 4½ hours – no dining car, alas) leaves the Gare de Lyon for Avignon seven times a day. All visitors availing themselves of this possibility will, of course, be picked up at the Avignon RR station.
    e. We cannot plan your trip for you. Please consult a travel agent.
    f. You may be requested to bring some item(s) impossible to find here. Failure to comply with this request will automatically result in Finette being set upon you on your arrival.
    g. We do want to see you, truly, but remember there are a large number of you.
8. A bit of advice: when you think you've packed the least amount of stuff possible, reduce it by 50% (excluding our requests of course) and you'll still have too much to carry.
9. Should you speak and understand the French language, and should we not be at home should you call, and that call should be of some import,

207

the telephone number of our own Mme Mourre
is (66) 50 06 86.
10. Should you show up in Tavel unexpectedly
(NOT recommended), ask anyone in the village
where les Americaines or Mme Mourre live.
Everyone here knows at least <u>of</u> us. The house,
La Rose des Vents, is some 50 meters up the
street next to the Quincaillerie.
11. If any of you can think of anything we omitted
from this list of helpful notions, please let us
know.

Tavel, 15.I.1983

That was not the end of it, of course. As the season
began to bulge with potential visitors, I felt compelled to
write a letter to some of our friends in the States
explaining the situation in some detail.

THE SMITH-CHAMBERLIN HOTEL
Rue du Seigneur
30126 Tavel – France

30.III.1983

Dear Friends,
All of you are planning to make a visit this
summer to our fine hotel located in the heart of
rosé country here in the south of France where the sun
shines all the time and the wine is cheaper than hell.
(How cheap wine is in hell is currently unknown
because recent listings have not been forthcoming from
that region, but it is fairly well-known that things there

are different from elsewhere so there is a reasonable chance that the above sentence reflects the objective reality of the situation.)

We, at the hotel, have come to the conclusion that, in order to avoid disastrous confusion and chaotic eclecticism of visit scheduling, it is necessary for those of you planning a visit to this region of green-brown garrigues, warm breezes (when the well digger's ass cold mistral isn't active) and blazing sunshine to collectively get your acts together.

The reason behind this is the fact that you all know each other, more or less, and the time involved in transmitting schedule information back and forth across the Atlantic at the mercy of the combined ineptitudes of the French and American postal systems. In short, if you coordinated your visits from Washington rather than us trying to do it from here it may be more efficient. The objective truth of this statement should be obvious to all. Alors!

For your reference the following dates have been reserved: 29 April – 29 May, 9-12 July.

Furthermore, we have in hand offers from at least three groups in Germany to visit some time this summer. Since you all have more priority it seems to us, here at the hotel, that early planning on your part would be beneficial, or as they say in certain circles here: de rigueur necessaire. For us, here at the hotel, the only fair basis for making reservations is first come, first served. As much as we, here at the hotel, might prefer to eschew clichés, we must consider our sanity.

As a consequence of the above we, at the hotel, request you all to convene at some time in the near future, if only through the expediency of the telephone, and assure yourselves and us that there will be no conflict in schedules. You may think this early warning is too early. Believe us, here at the reservation desk, it is not.

Also, a cousin of Lynn's from Seattle may visit briefly in June. Dates will be sent to you as soon as known. First come rule still applies. As do the suggestions/recommendations previously distributed to you. Keep in mind that it is cheaper by far for you to call us than the other way around, should such a step be thought necessary.

Remember: we want to see all of you here. In fact, we demand it. But everyone at the same time would present certain problems with sleeping arrangements. (On the other hand, what the hell!)

A bientôt, y'all!

Note that recent policy decisions made in Paris will mean nine million French remaining here in August making hotels, etc. very difficult. Not this one, of course.

In any case, at the end of that chilled February (the coldest in 20 years, the locals constantly assured us) the first visitors of the year from America arrived. As noted in an earlier chapter, the Sullivan contingent consisted of Marty (a long-term chum of LM's from the early days when they were both State Humanities Council directors, she in Minnesota, he in Indiana, whereafter they both worked for NEH in Washington where Moira and Jim also worked), his wife Kate (a former business woman and future librarian and creator of charter schools) and their six-month old daughter Abigail accompanied by Marty's 11-year old niece Erin. We hoped it would be an interesting experience for all of them.

Erin ate her first rabbit dish at the Hostellerie de Tavel which Henri le Kroner recommended to her as a typical dish of the region that he would personally guarantee she would like, or he'd eat it himself! She also sipped a small glass of rosé wine to accompany her rabbit, which Mme le Kroner asked Kate if she might: we all smiled as the young lady tasted her first wine and allowed how it was different alright but not unpleasant. During the dinner Abigail delighted the table with her ever-present smile, then snoozed peacefully in her basket while the rest of us noshed away in the blissful haze that comes with fine food and easy but deep friendship.

Not only was Erin an adventurous eater: one morning she marched off into the village by herself to purchase the breakfast baguettes, impressing not only us but the baker's wife as well.

Indeed the visit contained a number of additional firsts: the first time any of them had been in Europe for one thing; Abigail experienced her first kitchen sink bath in Tavel or anywhere else; they ate their first bouillabaisse in a Marseille old harbor restaurant wherein Kate breast-fed Abigail, an event which caused no reaction at all from the French customers other than the universal traditional *oo la la* at the sight of a cute infant. Abigail was less interested in the windy trip across the bay to the Château d'If of *The Man in the Iron Mask* fame, but the others found it of some interest having at least read or heard of the book and perhaps seen the movie. This is one site LM and I never visited again; I'm not sure why.

The Sullivans were the first old friends we introduced to new friends including Mary and her part time pal, the Italian banker Mateo, with whom we shared the Stéphane Grappelli performance followed by a laughter filled supper at a Vietnamese restaurant. Erin cheerfully stayed home in Tavel to care for Abigail. Since Mateo claimed to have no English and was just learning French, and since none of us had any Italian the conversation that night swerved from the reasonably coherent to the utterly confusing as phrases in all three languages flew around the table like demented bees cruising a large honeypot. At one point Marty grumbled, thinking Mateo was paying too much attention to Kate, who in turn tried a few Spanish phrases on the young banker. However the evening closed with satisfied smiles all around: after all, the music had been fabulous and the food pungent and savory and the wine capacious. We also had meals at our house where we did not have to worry about the drive home.

Despite the cold the Sullivans traveled far and wide with and without our company setting a pattern that we followed with most of our visitors in the eight months that followed: we drove to market towns in the region to give them a taste of country living, to the more traditional sites such as the ancient Roman arenas in Arles and Nîmes, the glorious Roman aqueduct structure at Pont du Gard, the village of Maillane where Mistral spent much of his life and is buried, the high towering mountain top village of Les Baux, abandoned for generations and recently become a mass tourist attraction; and the Fontaine-de-Vaucluse where the source of the river Sorgue has never been explored to its great depth; not even Jacques Cousteau could find the bottom of it.

The first time we climbed the hill at the Fontaine to observe the source of the Sorgue River, Andrea Anderson accompanied us in October 1982; at the foot of the mountain lies the small village called the Fontaine-de-Vaucluse whose small square contains the fountain of its name. The village lies in an "enclosed valley" (*vallis clausa*) that gives the *département* its name surrounded by crags and rough hills through which the Sorgue runs downhill and out of the valley. One climbs from the square up the steep, winding stony path to the huge open pit in the side of the mountain out of which the flashing waters roar and tremble during the winter and spring flood season. In the summer and autumn the river is calm, almost placid as it meanders down the mountain and into the valley and beyond. During the flood season the waters rise to 16 feet above the summer level and race along its watergreen and blackstone bed past the terrace of the Restaurant Philip forcing diners to speak in louder tones than they normally would. It is one of those uplifting culinary epiphanies one can live through, fortunately more than once: fine food and wine sitting out in the spring sunshine with the high sparkling water rushing past. We always order the same things: a small first course of fish and olive mixtures favored by gourmets of the South followed by grilled trout fillets or sole with buttered boiled potatoes and a salad accompanied by a bottle of local dry white or rosé wine. Sitting at the table over the speeding water, large and small shimmering fish swimming against the current, one easily forgets the masses of sweating, cumbersome tourists climbing the path to the great pit.

Indeed it is the "cockneyfication" of the place, as Henry James called it in 1883, that puts one off, especially in the summer when the huge buses disgorge their terrible cargos into the lanes and square of the village before they lumber up the hill past the wooden shelvings piled high with awful kitsch that offend the eye and soul. The sight of overweight middle-aged European women in too tight dresses hobbling about on high-heels up the path is as offensive as the sight of middle-aged overweight American women in tennis shoes and shorts chattering away about how Hazel and Ethel really missed a good site but pictures will be taken. James Pope-Hennessy in his admirable *Aspects of Provence* writes that it was on his "first visit to Avignon that I made the mistake, never since repeated, of going to see the Fountain of Petrarch at Vaucluse ... the beauty of this pre-Raphaelite scene is wrecked by the café chairs along the river banks, the shacks and shanties, the eager touts. All has been commercialized and made vulgar." Yes, yes, one wants to respond, all true, but even so, even so ... Lunch at the Philip is not to be missed and on off-season days the tourists, while always there, are fewer in number and less offensive.

And for those appreciators of love poetry, some of the best of which Francesco Petrarch wrote in his eyrie on the side of the mountain above the river and the

214

village to Laura, his idealized, virtuous beloved whom he first saw in an Avignon church on April 6, 1327. Though she was married, apparently not unhappily, the exiled poet fell passionately and obsessively in love with her. Ten years later, at the age of 33, he retired to the mountainside to escape the corruption and temptations of the Papal city.

Petrarch's sonnets and poems are as popular today as they have ever been, at least among those who read poetry. For personal reasons I like the following verse (in the N. Kilmer translation).

Non alo suo amante più Diana piacque

Diana did not please her lover more
When by some chance quite naked
He saw her standing in cold water,
Than the wild hill girl,
Washing a light cloth in the bright air,
Pleased me.

The sky is burning. I am shaking with cold.

Petrarch died in Italy in 1374, a great humanist and fine poet, if not the most conscientious priest in Europe. Before his disappearance, among many other things, Petrarch climbed to the pinnacle of Mont Ventoux with his brother, a feat he later wrote about as a spiritual experience wherein it came to him that he still loved that which he should not love and he felt shame and sadness about the matter. He is thinking of Laura. There is no doubt that he found the climb to be physically exhausting, the height's thin air making him lightheaded and subject to autobiographical epiphanies. Centuries later, in the autumn of 1865, the English philosopher, journalist, briefly Member of Parliament, social reformer, an early feminist and controversial political polemicist, John Stuart Mill, climbed the mountain but apparently did not experience a spiritual transcendence, though the climb might well have drained him of physical energy. Mill is buried with his wife Harriet Taylor in the Cimetière Saint-Véran on the dusty eastern outskirts of Avignon. How they came to be there is a story worth a brief digression.

In the summer of 1830 the 25-year old intellectual met the vivacious, hungry-minded 23-year old Mrs. John Taylor, mother of two children, at a dinner party in London. To say that they fell head-over-heels in love that evening would not be faithful to the truth, but that they very much interested one another is clear. A few months after the dinner, Mrs. Taylor conceived her third child with her husband. Nonetheless, Mill and Harriet soon became collaborators on writing projects and by the spring of 1832 became so infatuated with each other that Mr. Taylor demanded that they no longer see each other. They dutifully attempted to follow the husband's wishes but by the autumn of that year Mill began dining with Harriet two or three times a week, always in the company of others while Mr. Taylor spent the evening at his club.

During the following 20 years Mill and Harriet lived a life full of frustration, pain, joy and, working together, produced a body a radical reform literature, especially on the condition of women and the institution of marriage. As Mill's biographer, Richard Reeves, writes, "While Wordsworth and William IV were free to squire several illegitimate children across the country, women essentially had only the choice of being a wife, a virgin or a trollop." On July 18, 1849, John Taylor died and, after a suitable period of widowhood, on April 21, 1851, the registrar at Melcombe Regis, Dorset, finally married Harriet Taylor and John Stuart Mill.

In the autumn of 1858 they traveled to the South of France to escape the horrid English winter. At Avignon they stopped for a couple of days at the Hôtel d'Europe where Harriet's coughing increased to the extent she could not move and on November 3 she died of pulmonary congestion. Devastated, a condition from which he never truly recovered, Mill buried her in the Cimetière Saint-Véran and had a memorial made of Carrara marble made for the grave site. It is said, however, that her true memorial is the slim volume called *On Liberty* on which they were working when she died. Shortly thereafter he purchased a small house called Hermitage de Monloisier on three hectares close to the cemetery where he spent about half his time during the last 15 years of his life, cared for by Harriet's daughter Helen. In his posthumously published *Autobiography* he writes, "Her memory is to me a religion, and her approbation the standard by which, summing up as it does all worthiness, I endeavour to regulate my life." He died in the spring of 1873 and is interred with Harriet.

Developers demolished the house in 1961 to make way for the construction of a row of an ugly block of cement flats. But the street than runs along the west side of the cemetery is now called Avenue Stuart Mill, the street sign for which reads, "*John Stuart Mill. Philosophe Economiste et Homme Politique Anglais.*" To the east of the cemetery is the Piscine Stuart Mill in a sports complex. We visited the cemetery on several occasions, first during the Sullivan visit. The guardian (possibly self-appointed) followed us around like a cop tailing a suspect without caring to hide himself and told us in no uncertain terms we could not photograph the grave stone, then stood there watching us hawk-like to ensure we did not commit that felony. Eventually on another visit, in the screw's absence, we did photograph it. The inscription reads,

As earnest for the public good
As she was generous and devoted
To all who surrounded her
Her influence has been felt
In many of the greatest
Improvements of the age
And she will be in those still to come
Were there but a few hearts and intellects
Like hers
The earth would already become
The hoped-for heaven

But to finish the Sullivan visit story: When we put the group on the train to Paris they seemed tired but satisfied that their sojourn in the South of France had been a worthwhile trip. We did later find out that when they arrived in Paris they told the taxi driver to take them to the *Grand Hôtel* instead of the *Grand Hôtel des Étrangers*, which we'd recommended and made reservations for them because it was clean and cheap and we'd stayed there several times. The *Grand Hôtel*, on the other hand, was undoubtedly clean but it could by no stretch of the imagination be called inexpensive. After a conference with the concierge they straightened the matter out and proceeded to the correct hotel where they spent a day or two before flying home.

•

At the end of March we joined Karin, Mary, Mateo and two young men from the CELA faculty, one of whom was Denis Constancias who became a close friend over the years, for a drink and dinner before Karin left with her parents for a holiday in Switzerland by train at 1:25 in the morning. Rain drizzled over the chilly landscape as we crossed half the city to reach the Chien Qui Fume restaurant in the rue de Teinturiers where we enjoyed a simple but varied meal of crudités and a fish-rice dish à la Provence and a solid local red. At some point as the evening wore on Karin discovered she'd left her passport at the Lebels, an hour away by motor car, where she'd been staying for several days. Panic, but to the rescue came the good Sams, only slightly under the influence, who had parked our old Peugeot not all too far away. A mad dash through the dark and rainy night east down RN

100 to the Lebels and an equally mad rush back to Avignon brought us to the train station in time for Karin to hop aboard and find her parents already ensconced in a compartment saving her seat. The following night during dinner at the Williams we all shook our heads at the carelessness with which we had taken the young woman's life in our hands in that condition. Then we laughed and opened another bottle of rosé to accompany the cheese course.

•

As mentioned in an earlier chapter we also met the Williams family through LM's French classes: Jean Williams also studied French at the university and became equally dissatisfied with the haphazard nature of the classes there. She, Mary, Karin and LM decided to switch to CELA, more expensive than the university, but more dependable and consistent with a distinct methodology behind the teaching that appealed to all of them. While the university focused primarily on grammar and writing exercises, François Millet, the founder of CELA, and his staff headed by Denis Constancias, used audio-visual materials and conversation to improve both comprehension and the ability to speak. According to LM, this is the "norm" now in the USA, but it was quite novel (and progressive) in the early 1980s, especially in France. The classrooms were located in the pedestrian zone adjacent to the Place de l'Horloge, which meant readily accessible to cafés where they could take a petite café during breaks in the classes. The fact that Mary and Karin lived in the city, the Williams at the Ferme Jamet on the Ile de la Barthelasse and we even further away in Tavel, hindered gatherings of all of us at our place and the Williams, so they spent most of the time as a group in town, where I and Blair Williams joined them on occasion for dinner and music.

On one unforgettable evening I personally provided the music, however briefly. During the summer between the eighth grade and my freshman year in high school I began taking piano lessons from a woman in our neighborhood who owned a battered upright and smoked unfiltered Old Gold cigarettes one after another, placing them in a small ashtray on the piano when she showed me how to manipulate my fingers and wrists on the keyboard. She smelled of cigarettes and bad teeth, but she did teach me some of the rudiments of playing the instrument. Unfortunately I did not learn very many of these because once I started high school I foolishly determined that I had no time for such unnecessary endeavors and quit going, as any good apprentice juvenile delinquent should do. Naturally, as it turned out I made a mistake of cosmic importance and I have regretted it ever since. So have my friends and strangers in restaurants and saloons where I have played over the years, however briefly each time. The opportunity for me to play the piano arose only once in the year in the Midi: We ate a well-watered dinner one night with Blair and Jean Williams' extended family at the Loup Garou restaurant tucked away on a narrow, obscure street in Avignon. As we finished the meal, and as no other

221

customers appeared, I sat down at the battered wreck of an out-of-tune upright and began to wail away, sounding no doubt like a demented young Brubeck irrationally combined with Liszt at his most thunderous. A hail of small change centimes rained down upon me and the piano, frivolously tossed by our friends to express their pleasure in my wizardry at the keyboard (I hoped) or telling me I had performed at sufficient length and could cease and desist, which of course I did and swallowed another glass of plonk. I no longer perform very often in public, and always briefly, before the management feels it incumbent upon them to toss me out of whatever saloon I am in when the inspiration comes over me. Just as well, I suppose.

LM's French progressed quickly, with the help of Mme Mourre, and by March François, the director of the school asked her to translate some of his publicity materials into English. She also began, if hesitantly, making presentations to the class in French, one of which involved Georges Brassens, self-proclaimed the pornographer of the phonograph and rascal of song, which sounds better in French, which she recited as part of the class presentation.

> *J' suis l' pornographe*
> *Du phonographe*
> *Le polisson*
> *De la chanson.*

Unfortunately I was unable to be there to witness the event. Nor was I able to be there for another of her presentations, this one on the great Spanish cinema director, Luis Buñuel, a man of simple genius, who died during the last week in July. Buñuel had long been one of my favorite men of the cinema, ever since the late 1950s when I saw his powerful film about what we then called "juvenile delinquents" in Mexico City: *Los Olvidados* at the Museum of Modern Art in Manhattan. Consequently I was able to be of some help to her in filling in a few facts about his career and a couple of graphic descriptions of the shocking scenes in his 1928 surrealist short film made with Salvador Dalí, *Un Chien Andalou*, in which a razor blade and an eyeball meet with disastrous results.

I noted in the August 1 journal entry: "Luis Buñuel died last week. They're keeping the news from Dalí. I wish they'd kept it from me."

•

We had a great deal in common with the Williams and shared many references, and perhaps more importantly we got along well with their two young strikingly blonde boys, Matthew and Benjamin. We also shared a taste for the grape and very much liked to cook various kinds of food. Consequently we spent much time at each other's digs and in cafés eating, drinking and laughing. On one occasion at their place on the Ferme Jamet, Benjamin, the youngest son, made several paper airplanes that we all tossed about with reckless abandon making the appropriate airplane zooming sounds. One of the paper fuselages flew out the window up into the ivy that covered the side of the building. I recall resisting the requests to let it be and climbed up on the window sill, stretched far too far out into the ivy and did in fact retrieve the flying paper object without crashing down from the second floor and killing myself. Being a show-off can be a dangerous occupation, the more so when one is allegedly an adult. I like to think that, after climbing down off the window sill, I said to the boys, "Let this be a lesson to you: never climb out a second story window after too much wine." However, I doubt I offered them that eminently wise opinion. They would hardly have believed me in any case.

Another example of our enjoyment of each other's company occurred toward the end of March when we gathered ourselves, a young visiting friend of their older daughters named Danny, Karin and her sister Ulrike and several picnic baskets for a tasting trip to Châteauneuf-du-Pape, 18 kilometers north of Avignon, to celebrate Karin's and my birthdays. We only got to three or four caves because of a long, well-watered lunch under the walls of the castle and a lengthy first game of boules in addition to a local carnival that choked the streets with fun and games. That is to say, we visited the caves and bought some decent, affordable wine, then became so hungry we had no choice but to break off the tasting and lay out the ingredients of a flavor-filled, hugely satisfying *déjeuner sous les murs de la château*. The Williams had conveniently stashed a camping table and stools in the trunk of their car from which we ate the food and drank a fine local red and a bottle of Bernkastler Riesling Ulrike had brought with her from Germany for the birthdays' event.

The fortified castle built by the Popes in the 14th century as a summer vacation spot suffered destruction, as did many such church-related sites and institutions, during the Wars of Religion. Today all that remains is a section of one retaining wall under restoration and the keep which commands a splendid view of the surrounding area including in the distance the Palace of the Popes and Nôtre-Dame des Doms in Avignon and Mont Ventoux. The Popes also planted the first vineyards around the castle and the wine remained a local treat until its reputation for excellence began to spread in the mid-18th century. An influx of phyloxera in 1880 ravaged the vines after which the owners replanted and gradually rebuilt the wine's renown. In 1923 the winegrower's association issued a set of strict rules governing all aspects of the cultivation of the vines and vinification in the area: vineyard management, harvest dates, grape selection, decreeing the 13 acceptable wine types and vintage labeling. This set of rules resulted in the improvement of purity and quality of the wines which are now known world-wide as some of the best red wines available anywhere. I can personally attest to the fact that the growers have not yet achieved an equal level of success with their whites.

This was the first occasion, but by no means the last, that we used our own boules purchased earlier that month from one of those huge stores out at the mall (which the French call *les grandes surfaces*) on the road to Marseille. Once or twice we even brought the balls with us when we revisited the Midi in later years, until they became too heavy for the airlines which began charging extra for their transportation. As long as the Williams remained at the Ferme Jamet we played the game in the courtyard there.

After the boules we decided to visit a couple of additional caves to taste and possibly purchase some bottles to take home. So we drove the two cars back into the town and parked them on the main square; this was not the smartest move we made that day. For one thing, the caves were all closed due to the carnival parade loping slowly through the streets; secondly the parade and its observers locked the cars where they stood and we could not move them until the parade had gone by: many floats, performances by children and adults, including a troupe of *commedia dell'arte* characters in full colorful costumes. This fête entertained everybody but we thought it went on rather too long. Finally, we extricated the cars and drove slowly south, taking care not to exceed the speed limit or make any unduly sharp and undignified moves on the road that might attract the attention of the officials associated with law enforcement and traffic control. Safely on the Ile de la Barthelasse at the Ferme Jamet we could not bear the thought of closure on such a fine, sunny late afternoon, so we stayed for supper at the Williams', ate an enormous amount of food and drank all their wine. A fine ending to a fine day with good friends in the South of France. Nothing could have been better – until the next fête.

We often ate out with the Williams in groups of anywhere from just the six of us (four Williams and the two of us) to 12 or 14 depending upon the number of visitors visiting and who else from CELA happened to be there (Mary, Karin, et alia). It is hardly a matter of boasting to write that on occasion waiters and cooks cringed in fearful astonishment when we marched into their place of business. We could be somewhat raucous but on the whole we behaved ourselves. Henri and Nadine le Kroner at the Hostellerie de Tavel did not join the cringing crowd, but did place us conveniently in a small private room whenever the group exceeded the core six of us. I still remember Blair's veal tongue that seemed to melt on our tongues drenched in a saucy dressing of reduced white wine and the meat's juices. The roasted guinea hen on a bed of salad leaves, drizzled with a savory vinaigrette, remains a revelation of the cook's art. When Monsieur le Kroner stopped by to ask if we had eaten a satisfactory meal we out did each other praising his talents in a mixture of rushed and garbled French and English. He smiled modestly and allowed that our praise had lifted his spirits to hitherto unachieved heights that night and he graciously thanked us for our continued support and custom. The bill that evening did not include the round of marc that finished the meal. There are advantages to being known as a "regular" in certain restaurants and saloons.

On a cold, damp Monday, the 25th of April, in the year of Our Grace 1983, I wrote two sentences in the journal which perfectly captures the nature of our friendship with the Williams. "Dropped in to see the Williams Saturday and stayed for five hours. Too much Corsican wine."

Toward the end of July LM met Heidi, a young German brushing up her already fluent French at CELA, who came to dinner several times with her companion Guy, a dentist; the two of them planned to move to the French island of Réunion in the middle of the Indian Ocean, where he would open a practice and she would raise the children they planned to have. And they did so in September after a final meal at our house with Roswitha and an American girl Sandra, barely out of her teens, who was visiting her cousin married to a French auto mechanic and trying to find a space to open a gymnastic studio, which as far as we know she never did. For several years thereafter we exchanged Christmas cards with Heidi and Guy; he operated a successful practice and she indeed raised their two children, of whom somewhere we have photographs.

•

As noted earlier, we also quite regularly shook with the cold that winter. There were, however, climate surprises that tended to confuse our senses.

Journal, Tuesday, January 18:

Either something is wrong and I don't know it yet or something awful is going to happen: the world (or at least my world) can't continue to be so beautiful! Another absolutely gorgeous day in Provence– temperature is up, sun shines like summer, sky is blue and clear. On a shopping walk into the village I saw smiles on everyone's faces and a willingness to chat even with me; the fish vendor is back at the market and gave me a long story about obtaining oysters in winter of which I understood about 1%; the alimentation lady mentioned the weather – a first for us! Even Finette didn't attempt to escape when I opened the gates. Made an appointment for LM at the coiffeur this afternoon. On the back of the Pepito biscuits box: "Biscuits half enrobed in chocolate."

The matter of the coiffeur I no doubt mentioned because for me to conduct such business in French was a step forward and had to be duly noted. A certain amount of naïveté followed me like my own pale shadow for the first several months of our time in Tavel, but at least I realized that this mild interruption was an anomaly.

In early May we thought spring had finally arrived in Provence, and about time, too. The bakery lady noted it had been the worst spring in ten years. Of course, after all, we were there. If the November hurricane had been the worst storm in 30 years, why not the worst spring in ten? During the third week in May the cold and rain savaged the land once again for two days, but two days after that LM sunbathed on the terrace. Unpredictable, irrepressible and often frustrating weather, but on the whole we did not mind given where we lived!

By the end of the first June week we had traversed the space between winter and mid-summer with no real spring to speak of and began using the wooden shutters to block the sun.

Chapter VI

Paris and Italy Interlude: May

By letter and telephone we arranged for LM's parents, Warren and Evelyn, to come for a visit in May via London to Paris where we would pick them up, assuming La petite Mo would still be running with a modicum of efficiency. The plan was to visit some of the sites in the city, then make our way south stopping at a castle or two, rest in Tavel for several days then drive into northern Italy to visit Venice and one of Evelyn's relatives in a town not far from the canal city of the doges. LM and I arrived in Paris four days before her parents to visit some of the places they would find boring and a couple we had met in Washington just before we left, Dean and Jean-Jacques Ferrier, who lived in the St. Cloud suburb to the northwest of the city.

We drove north, stopping for a picnic lunch at a roadside rest stop (we had become sufficiently French to insist on lunch no matter the locale, something like the English and their tea). After lunch we stopped at Fontainbleau, a mini-Versailles worth a visit and less frequented by busloads of tourists than its big brother on the western side of the city, because we'd not seen it before, then made the mistake of taking N7 into the center of Paris. A mistake because the road passes through horrible suburbs filled with spastic French drivers eager to get home for the weekend. Entering the city through the Port d'Italie, LM driving in the middle of the rush hour, we moved directly to the Grand Hôtel des Étrangers on the triangle corner of rue Racine, the boulevard St.-Michel and the rue de l'École de Médecine. The hotel was a recommendation of friends where the rooms were small, comfortable, relatively cheap and susceptible to street noise, of which there was plenty given the neighborhood: the Sorbonne and the Quartier Latin. We had recommended the place to the Sullivans the previous February. (The hotel is now an expensive renovated palace with small rooms, no doubt comfortable and still susceptible to street noise.) This hotel remains in our minds, among other things, for the sign on the bathroom door that read *"En dehors des petites dejeuners il est interdit de manger dans les chambres,"* which someone translated into English as "Except the breakfast interdiction to eat in the room."

The days that followed belong in another book about Paris and, in any case, even a week later they blended vaguely together into a blur of too many places seen too quickly. A brief excursion into the first two days of our stay will give the Reader an idea about how the rest of the sojourn went. What one does after checking in to a hotel is to have a drink and think about the next meal. Since it was supper time when we arrived, the minute tines of hunger had already begun their tap dance along the rim of my stomach. We chose to walk down the Boul' Mich' and cross the Seine on the Pont de la Tournelle to L'île Saint-Louis where we plunged into the narrow streets of the island which somehow all lead to

231

the rue Saint-Louis-en-l'île along which most of the island's restaurants and hotels stand. Rain threatened and, although by this time hunger gnawed at our innards, we chose the restaurant carefully with regard to the cost. Given the location and reputation of the island (all tourists with any pretensions to being readers of literature want to eat there), we discovered a small family owned and run eatery painted white and blue with a Mediterranean waiter and a reluctant chef with an amazingly inexpensive *prix fixe* menu: 37 francs for two courses and dessert; wine and coffee extra. While it is true that Le Minestrel (for such was the name of the beanery) was not necessarily a place to linger over one's coffee because of the noise level in such a small space, it could be recommended for its good simple food, price and location. Do not look for this restaurant in your red Michelin, it is not there.

After dinner we strolled around the island and crossed to L'île de la Cité over the Pont St. Louis, but did not look in to Notre Dame, there would be time enough for that with the Smiths. We crossed the Pont au Double to the Left Bank but the darkness precluded seeing the statue of Charlemagne (or did we simply miss it, thinking of other things?). Passing the Square René-Viviani we could not see the oldest tree in Paris so turned left into the rue Saint-Julien-le-Pauvre from which we entered the tiny park through the typical French low irongate that keeps stray dogs out of the park. (You find them in most parks in the city, but they do not serve their function very well because French people have an odd relationship with dogs that I cannot remember experiencing elsewhere and so they open the park gates for each and every stray mongrel around.) Satisfied that the tree still maintained its position vis-à-vis the iron and wood crutches holding it up we began to move toward the hotel by edging into the Algerian section by way of rue Saint-Séverin.

You won't find a section of Paris called the Algerian on any map that I've ever seen. The maze of twisting streets and small squares lined with restaurants representing the kitchens of all the Mediterranean lands, especially couscous-based cuisine, is usually referred to on the maps as le quartier Saint-Séverin. A small number of us, however, took to calling this labyrinth of gorgeous smells and darkskinned waiters "The Algerian Quarter" after the dominant style of cooking there. It is not only the exotic quality of the section that recommends it to us but also the fact that we have never eaten badly, and once very well indeed, or expensively there. Now it is true that one must watch one's purse or it will be snatched (some nimble-fingered thief lifted LM's wallet out of her shoulder bag the following night there) and the crowds can be molasses-like in their closely pressed flowing and ebbing, but none of this matters when one eats and drinks there. Unless one has all one's dough in the burgled wallet; then, of course, there could be a problem. Fortunately LM had only 100 francs, credit cards and a driver's license in hers, so the trip did not fall apart in ruins. Back at the hotel we canceled the credit cards and sipped a final glass of our own calvados and slept well, if annoyed.

The following day overflowed with walking great distances and dodging both the rain and the acidic reek of teargas, or its French equivalent called "irritation gas" – and it does do that. The government proposed to reform the university system by passing a complex new law named after the Minister of Education, Savary, that, in effect and among other things, would give the government control over the choice of study fields which would allow it to begin to fill projected holes in the economic life of the nation: in 15 years we'll need 30% more chemists in industry, so we will put a limit on all other fields of study and anyone who wants to go to university above those limits will study chemistry. Very logical, very French, and the state owned all the universities. So naturally students and would-be students flooded into the streets led by the medicine faculty (just down the street from our hotel) in a demo the extent of which had not been seen since 1968. Not that it equaled '68 in massiveness or intensity, but the protesters disrupted the city well enough.

Escaping the gas by ducking into the métro station at the Place St.-Michel, we began the day by riding to the Opéra Quarter which put us in striking distance of a number of places we wanted to visit. A brief stop at Smith's Bookstore reinforced the opinion that only the well-to-do could afford to buy new books in France, particularly if they were imported. This opinion has of necessity been extended to include all first world countries. Indeed, on this occasion I purchased only a copy of Theodora FitzGibbon's memoirs of the 1938-1946 period in Paris and London called *With Love* (silly title), mainly for the gossip about the Left Bank would-be artists, Dylan and Caitlin and that crowd during the war in London, but discovered that she writes very well about living in the war and the life in bomb-racked England.

Smith's is on the rue de Rivoli just about across the street from the Musée Jeu de Paume (the former royal handball court) and once again we made our way through the maddening pack of tourists and French school groups with no real interest in the paintings past the glorious Cézannes and Renoirs and Degas and Monets and Van Goghs and ... glorious all of them! The Manets had disappeared into a major retrospective of his work hanging at the Grand Palais which we saw the following day. In those days I never tired of walking through the halls of the Jeu de Paume, revisiting with pleasure and edification those magnificent Impressionist and Post-impressionist works that so moved me with each viewing.

Of course, one can no longer do this: in 1986 the French government in its infinite wisdom caused the old Gare d'Orsay on the other side of the river to be renovated into a giant cavernous space into which they poured everything from the comfortable space of the Jeu de Paume. Further back in time, prior to moving the collection to the Jeu de Paume, curators maintained it in the Musée du Luxembourg at the north end of the Luxembourg Garden, where Hemingway famously often visited the Cézannes for inspiration. Since the egregious move to the Musée d'Orsay, the Jeu de Paume has become the venue for installations posing as art and other forms of post-modernist excesses that grate upon one's nerve endings like sandpaper rubbed on the tongue.

235

One of the positive aspects of the Musée d'Orsay is the restaurant, which isn't cheap but the food is fine and the view out the windows is not lackluster, if also not extremely inspiring. You may have trouble entering the building: it has become the Mecca of every tour group, family and individuals who want to be able to say when they return to their friends at home, "Well, of course we went to the Louvre, the Orsay Museum ..., you can believe it, Ethel, it was beeyouteefal." The lines of people awaiting entrance can be depressing and send one away to some other less touristed temple of art and culture.

Lunch that day consisted of cheese, a baguette, sausage and a bottle of Vittel mineral water on a bench in the Tuilleries, and the sun finally decided to bless us with its light and warmth. Interesting, if eccentric, folk wandered about the grounds or slept on the benches. The Tuileries lack one thing: grass, the very thing that makes the Luxembourg Garden so attractive not to say comparatively bucolic. And so it went, museums, walks, a pleasant hour in the house and garden of the Hôtel Biron (the Rodin Museum), a post-impressionist show at the Palais de Tokyo, and so on.

We also saw a fascinating but sad memorial retrospective exhibition of Yves Klein's work. A decade earlier Klein splashed the nude bodies of young female models with a bright Greek blue paint and pressed and rolled them on large pieces of white canvas, the original body painting. Scenes of this activity appeared in the sensationalist movie, *Mondo Cane* (1963) and shortly after the film's opening Klein killed himself. He was a serious artist, there is no doubt about this, but everyone laughed and considered his work as no different from the other weird freakish oddities in the movie. He was literally ahead of his time – and the blue canvases were the best part of the show.

Somehow we found time to see *Sophie's Choice* in English with French subtitles which confirmed the rightness of the choice of Streep for the Oscar award. And the time to drink a glass of scotch and listen to Lester Young records with our friends, the Ferriers, in St. Cloud.

After we picked up Evelyn and Warren at the airport we conducted them on short tours of places we thought would be of interest to them: a boat ride on the Seine, an inspection of Napoléon's tomb at Les Invalides, a walk around the Eiffel Tower (which Evelyn and I refused to ascend), a métro trip to Montmartre to see the great Sacre Coeur basilica overlooking the city from one of its three hills and the Place du Tertre flooded with colorful kitschy paintings so tourist-friendly and easy to digest, and a walk through the Luxembourg Garden at the western edge of which, where it exits into the rue de Fleurus, stands a statue of the poet Paul Verlaine, which is as it should be, but ten meters or so away from it is an odd, almost cubist bust by the sculptor Jean-Antoine Injalbert of the poet Gabriel Vicaire (1848-1900) about whom one knew nothing at the time.[21] We walked down the Rue de Fleurus to number 27 where a plaque on the wall informs

---

[21] There is no entry for him in *The New Oxford Companion to Literature in French* (1995), but the French Wikipedia has a brief entry for this successful in his day poet and friend of Verlaine.

the viewer that the American writer Gertrude Stein lived there with her brother Leo and her companion Alice B. Toklas from 1903 to 1938. Over the years this has become a pilgrimage site for many as interested in the Gertrude-Alice relationship as in Gertrude's writings.

As I have written elsewhere,[22] one of the most impressive memories of the Smiths' first and last visit to Paris remains this one: We had walked around the Sacre Coeur basilica and began walking slowly down the steep steps of the rue Foyatier admiring the stamina of the older men and women who lived on the streets off the steps who climbed up and down every day. On the way down, Warren, limping from arthritis, former gas station owner from St. Paul, Minnesota, half-lamed but not defeated by the savage winters there, stopped to talk about the stairs to an elderly citizen of the neighborhood. Warren was nearly 70 at the time. I wish I could have heard that conversation. I know he asked the old woman how she survived the steps every day and what did she call her dog? LM, her mother and I dawdled too far away to hear the talk. Warren spoke no French and the old woman had no English. They understood each other perfectly.

On the way south we stopped at Versailles, several castles in the Loire Valley, the grand Ste.-Madeleine basilica at Vézelay where we stayed overnight–and the motor car behaved.

•

---

[22] *Paris Now and Then*, 293-294.

While we rested in Tavel before driving into Italy, we took the Smiths around the region to some of the by now usual haunts, not too many because we did not wish to tire them out. Within easy reach lay one of our favorite spots in the Midi: the canal-divided and encircled town of L'Isle-sur-la-Sorgue at the foot of the Plateau de Vaucluse, once known as a bustling small industry village with ten massive waterwheels driving its tanning, paper, dying, weaving and grain and oil mills; eight of the mills still exist though they have lost their original functions. Today visitors come for its popular Sunday markets, the morning for food and ingredients for all sorts of meals, the midday for second-hand anything and everything from 19th century books to huge armoires for the closet-less houses the Europeans used to build. Almost every Sunday would find us roaming the narrow streets and lanes, along the canals, stopping to buy a bit of this and a bit of that for the evening meal in this dusty town of about 15,000, 23 kilometers east of Avignon along the National Road 100. We also never failed to stop at the lovely restored 18th century French classical building and garden called the Hôtel Donadéï de Campredon (Centre Xavier Battini, also known from time to time as the Musée René Char) which is now a museum with grand ambitions: Matisse, Miro, Otto Dix, Raoul Dufy, Henri Manguin have been given exhibitions there. The first one we saw consisted of materials relating to Char including several letters written to him by Albert Camus in the ubiquitous French blue ink; you think somewhat differently about some writers after you've seen their handwritten letters and manuscripts: I found Camus more *sympathique* after that experience. Later, I did not have the same response to Sartre after an exhibition at the new Bibliothèque Nationale Mitterand in Paris.

The market is centered in the streets around the Nôtre-Dame-des-Anges church constructed in 1222 and rebuilt in the 17th century set in the middle of the old town (as in all too many of these picturesque old villages suburban sprawl has infected the outskirts of the original settlement with its cheaply-built, faux-Provençal residences and air-polluting motor vehicles). The guidebooks point out the rows of plane trees lining the avenues in the suburban areas and the branches of the Sorgue River that justify their use of the word "charming." One might consider the site charming, but not on market day when thousands mill about the narrow lanes looking for a deal and exclaiming over the wares the farmers and other vendors have laid out on trestle tables. On market day the influx of locals and tourists elbowing their ways through the crowds, especially in the summer, deny the concept of charming. In fact, in the summer weeks it is all but impossible to get into the Café de Paris with its large jazz concert posters for a coffee or a *pastis*. You would never know by its current appearance that the village suffered a long history of pillage and plunder by various religious and political factions since the 14th century, the latest attack taking place in the summer of 1944 when the Allies bombed it for some inexplicable reason since it contained no military targets.

One finite aspect of market day that could still have been termed charming, even in the summer, consisted of an older gentleman in a kepi, unlit pipe in the corner of his mouth, a small snare drum slung from his shoulder on which he played mild march rhythms accompanied by melodies played on an ancient cassette tape player hung from his neck as he made his way through the crowd led by a small dog of indeterminate species dressed in a red and yellow plastic coat that matched the color of the drum's drapery. Warren and Evelyn had never seen such a sight and thoroughly enjoyed walking along behind man and dog as they made their rounds of the town.

We spent the morning there with the Williams then drove as a group to the Lebels' farm near Roussillon where Karin was staying while the artist and his wife spent ten days in Bad Homburg for the *vernissage* of his opening at a gallery there. We picnicked on the open terrace and introduced Warren to the local sport of *boules* (*pétanque*), which we played with the local handyman, Michel.

Finishing the game without keeping score but with much laughter and wine, we sat and talked for a spell before taking the group to Tavel and our house for scrambled eggs and more wine. After the Williams left and the Smiths went to bed I watched a chunk of the 1949 Hollywood version of Dostoyevsky's *The Gambler* with Gregory Peck and Ava Gardner, in a dazed fog it must be admitted. This Sunday was not untypical of Sundays as long as the Williams remained at the Ferme Jamet, whether we had visitors or not.

241

One of the advantages of living long enough in a place is the ability to take visitors to see friends one has made over the previous months. Our friendship with the Williams served this pleasant function for us. In fact, we liked them so much that our visitors could not help but like them as well. They were (are) of course eminently likeable people. So we took our friends to see our friends and the Smiths were no exception. The several meals we ate in the Williams' apartment are memorable for their warmth and *joie de vive*, and the food of course.

We decided to skip Rome on the Italian trip, which turned out to be a smart decision. So in the second week of May, trusting La Petite Mo would remain healthy and functional, we drove off early in the morning south to Saint-Paul de Vence to visit the Fondation Maeght, one of the most charming modern art museums tucked away in the hills above Nice in the same town as the legendary Colombe d'Or restaurant with its equally legendary terrace where we did not dine that day but did many times in the future. The problem the Maeght shares with other similar institutions is that of fame and fulsome mention in the tourist guide books. The Maeght's grounds, buildings and collection are impressive and worth several visits, especially if one can avoid days when it is stuffed with loud tour groups shuffling along at great speed with noisy, inane comments as they stream by some of the iconic works of modern art. When we left Saint-Paul we continued south then west along the coast to Monaco to visit the Palace and Casino of great fame. Typical of the Smith-Chamberlin luck: the running of the Grand Prix had closed everything in that small principality so we moved on to Saint-Jean-Cap-Ferrat, where we searched unsuccessfully for Willy Maugham's villa, enjoyed a seafood meal and slept in clean, neat if tiny rooms with toilets and baths.

The following morning we moved into Italy at the Menton-Ventimiglia crossing having discovered that Ascension Day had closed the Cocteau museum in Menton, another bit of typical Smith-Chamberlin luck. We drove slowly through Albisola, a town on the Italian Riviera where LM had spent two weeks with her friend Christine Watkins visiting the latter's sister and her family 12 years earlier; this time LM did not recognize any of it so we drove on to Viareggio, a resort town with nothing to recommend it. The beach sand resembled a welcome mat that hadn't been cleaned in years. The next day found us in Pisa for two hours viewing the religious works and the tower which has something oddly appealing about it deriving from its actual leaning; a minor mystery. I thought the sculpture in the baptistery actually modern in its execution and expression of that transcendent state of suffering in ecstasy.

Florence, Firenze, the fabled city of the Medici, Dante and the Carabiniere Marshal Guarnaccia. So much great art, so much blood-soaked history, and a lesson in why one should not travel in tourist cities in high season without having made hotel reservations beforehand. Upon entering the city we quickly decided we should have taken the train: horrible traffic snarls coexisted with terrifying mass motor vehicles racing from one stoppage to another with blaring horns and obscene gestures made with a non-violent vehemence only the Italians can achieve. An hour of panic, anger and frustration resulted until we finally found a suite of rooms at the Continental Hotel at the foot of the Ponte Vecchio, which we arranged at the hotel reservation counter in the railway station. The area around that large ugly building presented a situation found in big western cities where everything is geared to the automobile rather than people, a typically Fascist accommodation to modernity, a vision of hell in modern dress. Dante would have been both horrified and amused. We were just horrified – at least until we got the car legally parked and rested in the suite.

Venturing into the old town horror shook us again, but this time a more familiar horror: tourists have taken over everything. This is hardly new, but after having been away from such places for a time (Avignon had not yet that year suffered its annual summer fate) it came as a shock to be pummeled by the herds of culture vultures and blank-eyed tour groups being led around to touch briefly on each shrine before hustling off to a lunch about which they will complain until dinner gives them another subject to whine about. The first of our two nights there LM and I escaped to Harry's Bar for a drink. (Yes, there was one in Florence, too.) Escape is the wrong word of course: we moved from one chaos to another. Even if someone paid the (high) price of my dinner I would refuse to eat in that traffic jam of disgruntled waiters, loud Americans and their Italian counterparts (all being very "in" being in Harry's) and disoriented elderly tourists clearly out of their element but able to afford the tariff. The only pond of tranquility in the place was the small area in which the bartender, Leo the Lion, stood working swiftly and efficiently with an eerie calmness one had to admire.

We visited all the usual shrines to Renaissance art accompanied by thousands of others and left the city without regret.

Having telephoned Venice beforehand (LM did a truly magnificent job of arranging rooms and maintaining a degree of stability in a situation fraught with possibilities for anger and frustration), we motored there directly and with surprisingly few contretemps. We parked the car in a huge garage at the edge of the mainland and took a vaporetto (water taxi) to Saint Mark's Square in the area of which we settled into the Astoria Hotel, rather primitive without a shower curtain and overpriced after the Continental but sufficient to our needs. From the window in our room we could stretch across the alley to the house on the other side, from which the next morning at 8:30 snapped the surprising but welcome sound of Bird's "Scrapple for the Apple", an unlikely music for Venice that did not disturb the atmosphere. It reminded me that John Lewis had written the score to the 1957 Roger Vadim film *Sait-on jamais* (known in the USA as *No Sun in Venice*) and the Modern Jazz Quartet had played it on the soundtrack. The film had a small release in America but did fairly well in Europe and is no longer available for obscure reasons. Although we know the music well, we've never seen the film. *Dommage.*

One of the two nights we spent in this museum-city we celebrated Evelyn's 65th birthday at a restaurant with tables on one of the larger canals, an event we all enjoyed.

We toured the usual sites but what most appealed to LM's parents was the absence of automobiles and they felt more self-assured in Venice than elsewhere, going off by themselves and enjoying the music on the big square eating elaborate ice-cream concoctions at vastly inflated prices. LM and I went through the former residence of Peggy Guggenheim, now the Guggenheim Museum on the Grand Canal with the Morandi horse and rider on the terrace where the gondolas brought the guests she invited to evening soirées. Each year when the bishop glides down the canal in the procession to bless the city's waterways an employee surreptitiously removes the rider's prominent erection and replaces it after the procession of boats has disappeared down the canal. Peggy Guggenheim's life would hardly be believable if it appeared as fiction. She lived in the right places at the right times with an intelligent taste in art and the family funds to indulge it. Her unfinished *palazzo* ("villa" is a more appropriate word but the Italians inflate everything) of white stone and the large garden is a perfect setting for the art she collected and must have been a wonderful place in which to live, small and beautiful as opposed to big and ornate as the other buildings on the Grand Canal.

Unfortunately the place was jammed. "O Hazel-Mae, look at that! Isn't it gorgeous!" Loudly, harshly, referring to the trashy-cute paintings by Peggy's daughter. When they got to the Braque and Pollocks they shook their heads, muttered, "Yuk!" and hurried on to something

246

more befitting to be drooled over. The city has always drawn tourists and has always been crowded, of course. Goethe approved of this because it afforded him anonymity. For those of us who remain anonymous wherever we are it is simply annoying. The gondola tour was a rip-off, if such modern jargon can be used about this architectural marvel, but the Smiths enjoyed it and that was more important than thieving Venetians.

On the morning we left Venice proper we drove north to a small town, the name of which escapes me, to visit a distant relative of Evelyn's named America; the family had been enamored of the USA, indeed many if not most of them migrated across the Atlantic to make their fortunes and establish families. Evelyn surprised herself and us by dredging up a fair amount of Italian from wherever in her brain it had been stored for 50 years, which helped a great deal because America and her husband spoke no English. We had a drink with them and toured their store of linens and gold jewelry, of which Evelyn purchased a table cloth; our purses could not bear the tariff for the jewelry.

That afternoon we sped across northern Italy on the *autostrada*, moving fast toward the border at Ventimiglia and Menton. Before we got there we descended once again on Albisola, discovering this time that this indeed was the town where LM had spent two weeks 12 years earlier, but like the entire coastline "villas" and high-rise buildings infested the shore and the town itself, and the beach had eroded by half. The photographs of LM, Christine and Italian boys on the beach clearly show a large expanse of sand, and large amounts of youthful flesh.

We decided to stay the night and checked into a new "modern" hotel with papier-mâché walls and damp sheets. The dinner in the hotel dining room is best left undescribed, though we all survived it. The meal did bring to the table differences in European (French and Italian at least) and American eating habits, similar to those the Smiths had run into while in France. Warren did not drink alcohol so either ordered a soda or a cup of coffee as close to the American variety as possible. Waiters looked somewhat askance when he did this before the meal, but looked horrified when he asked for more coffee *with* the meal. In Italy, pasta is a first course followed by meat or fish, a veg and a salad. When Warren ordered a second plate of the same pasta as his second course, the waiter gave up trying to understand American eating habits and silently brought the pasta, mentally shaking his head in disbelief. Warren enjoyed himself with gusto; the rest of us tried rather successfully to hide our discontent with the meal. At least the wine was palatable.

Both LM and I slept poorly that night, blaming the mediocre food and the damp sheets, but the Smiths seemed unfazed by the accommodations, though they did bring up with some consistency the odd if not bizarre customs of the French and the Italians and their inability to speak coherent English, complaints that many non-Europeans voice whilst visiting the continent.

In any case, the next morning we got on the road early and drove into the absurdity of Monaco traffic so they could see the Palace (only from the outside because it was closed to the public until July) and Grace's tombstone in the small cathedral visited by thousands who read the boulevard press and live plain, insipid lives working and watching *Dallas*, the American bourgeoisie's substitute for royalty at the time; the Europeans who dragged themselves through the cathedral noticing only the tomb, not the magnificent decorations of the building itself, have real royalty but watch *Dallas* anyway. We did enjoy a brief lunch at an outdoor café located in a less heavily trafficked part of the town, and drove off to see a bit of Cannes. This plan turned out to be unrealizable due to the masses of motorized vehicles clogging the roads and polluting the air with burping clouds of diesel fumes and detritus.

Ergo, we turned north and made our way as swiftly as possible back to Tavel where LM stood on the terrace and announced, "It's good to be back in France," a sentiment with which I completely concurred, especially after Mme Mourre informed us that whilst we motored around the Mediterranean shore and through northern Italy it had rained every day in Tavel. The day after we returned from the trip, Nature gave us perfection: the sun blazed in a cloudless sky blessing us with great warmth and a steady breeze ensured that we could not complain about the temperature. Two days later we drove the Smiths to the Marseille airport, whence they flew to London and on to St. Paul, exhausted but satisfied with their first European experience. LM and I went back to work, glad we could have offered them the trip but also glad to be alone again.

(Years later we did get them to Rome where they found the outdoor cafés to be a blessing, since Warren's partially frozen knees did not allow extensive strolling about without regular pauses for coffee or ice cream. That trip involved driving from Rome through Switzerland and France and flying from Paris to London, where we thought they would feel comfortable in an English-speaking country. They said they missed Rome: London had no outdoor cafés thickly scattered about the city and this circumstance forced them into a McDonald's for coffee, which they now admitted the Italians made much better.)

Chapter VII

The Summer of 1983

Naturally we cultivated a small garden below the terrace at the back of the property, after a brief discussion with Mme Mourre, whose response to our question was simplicity itself: "Well, of course, you will tend the garden, that is why it is there."

So we began, that is to say LM took charge and did most of the work, though I assisted in the heavy duties of preparing the ground by weeding and turning over the earth with a spade and pitchfork. By the end of the first April week my hands had become worn and aching and covered with small blisters from a mere two hours of spading and weeding which made our space ready for the seeds and plants that would constitute our contribution to economic eating and protest against processed foods. After we turned over the rest of the plot LM planted lettuce and tomatoes. Because I was at the time at an impasse in the second volume of the Berlin novel, it felt good to sweat at some honest and productive manual labor, the first sweat of the year is often memorable, as it should be. Even the aching paws evoked a certain amount of gratifying satisfaction, an almost metaphysical uplift of the spirit: at least I was doing something constructive with my time. Nonetheless after we'd spaded and weeded half the space I counted six blisters on my previously un-manual-laboring hands and I wondered if I would be able to stand straight the following day. Some of us go to extremes: from doing nothing to doing too much. Silly, true, but my hands still felt like asparagus stalks – tubers with lumps getting in the way of functioning.

It was not untypical of our sojourn in the Midi that after weeding and spading the first half of the garden I allowed myself two glasses of the local rosé which, given my generally weakened condition from the winter's tribulations, caused me to slip the tight moorings of my mind and drift away from the wharf of practical reality into the foggy bay of nebula we all construct at moments of exhilaration, fueled by alcohol or not. Nonetheless, I created a tasty supper of curried veal chops braised in vegetable bouillon, fresh green peas and a mixed salad accompanied by a local white wine.

Furthermore we had to deal with the Finette threat. The cats seemed indifferent to our gardening efforts, but the dog was something else again. Micheline solved part of the dilemma by building a provisory fence around the entire garden to keep the beast out of her portion as well as ours, to which we added a bamboo gate. Of course, we wondered, "Why not get rid of Finette?" But that would have been seriously asking too much of Mme Mourre and our lips remained sealed in that regard.

As noted previously, the villagers informed us that the spring of 1983 was the worst they'd seen in ten years. This did not cause us to dance in the back lanes of the village but somehow it did follow logically from the worst winter in at least the same span of time. The sun continued to bless the landscape when the rains let up, but the mistral ensured that the temperatures leaped about the thermometer with something approaching abandon, that is to say without any reference to the tradition of mild springs evolving into warm and sunny summers. The swerve from flannel sheets and sweat shirts under the quilt and sleeping bag to the glories of nude sleeping with only a light coverlet can be disconcerting if not deranging of the senses.

In early April we could report the cherry tree blossomed with full blooms, the tulips raised their bright red centers to the sky, other flowers spread yellow color throughout the Mme Mourre's part of the garden, and the bush climbing up the garage wall held one lone pale red rose. We planted 15 heads of lettuce, seeds of lettuce, green peppers, tomatoes, string beans, zucchini, and four basil plants. Then we said a brief prayer to the gods of gardens requesting that the rains not wash away the seeds before they had taken root.

Despite the undependable weather, by mid-May the zucchini (*courgettes*) at least remained a stalwart of the garden, growing rapidly and proliferating like mushrooms after a rain. The lettuce and tomatoes crept along their petty paces and soon blossomed as the figs in Mme Mourre's part of the garden began to burst out of their winter garments and bloom into their luscious, nutty selves, mature and ripe, ready to drop. But the green peppers refused to march to the same drummer as the other vegetables. Had we not fertilized sufficiently? Had a series of voracious insects attacked the young and vulnerable seedlings? We never discovered the answer.

After a few hours of working in the garden my bones and muscles ached and moaned, rebelling against the

253

unusual uses to which they'd been put, but the garden looked fine and almost immediately gave us fine leaves of lettuce, and that somehow made it worth the effort. It is said that Provence is not a single real geographical location, but rather a series of geographical locales drifting through time, ever-changing. Some say Provence is a state of mind. After several hours of working in a Provençal garden it seemed to me that the place existed, solid, earthbound, in the present, and it gave back what you gave to it. There is nothing romantic about aching muscles after weeding and spading in the stony ground of the Midi, but there is a great wave of satisfaction, many of them in fact, at seeing your garden grow.

By mid-June the garden had become a constant joy and an occasional frustration. Lettuce, radishes, basil and the ubiquitous zucchinis overwhelmed us with their abundance and we looked forward to a July with the produce of 20 tomato plants and innumerable green string beans (*haricots vertes*). We began to give bunches of zucchini to our friends, occasionally when asked with advice on what to do with them. The huge amount of them forced me to come up with a variety of stuffings, often using whatever I found in the *frigo* at the time.

With Mme Mourre's help we rounded up a sufficient number of stakes to re-do the tomato plants which the wind and an unknown type and number of night animals had conspired to almost flatten. Mme Mourre assured us that at some point we would have "*beaucoup de tomates*" – and we did. The string beans never did fulfill their early promise of abundance but we ended up having to toss lettuce because we could not eat it fast enough and for some reason did not give it away to our landlady or friends. Hard rain caused the usual problems with washed away seeds and bent stalks requiring re-plantings and re-staking, all of which we (mostly LM) accomplished with enthusiasm that the ups and downs of the weather did not diminish through the summer. The weather plays a greater role in one's life when one lives close to the natural world: matter over mind.

One day in early August just after the sun had risen to brighten the warm summer earth but before the village came alive with the mundane gestures of daily life, LM slipped down the stairs and into the garden in nothing but a light robe. Amidst the tomatoes and zucchinis she took off the robe and began hoeing the rows of vegetables slowly up and down the lines of round ripe red tomatoes and the deep green thick tubes of zucchinis, back and forth, back and forth, until the sun began to gently pinch her skin and the morning sounds of the village waking nudged her back into the robe. It is unfortunate I continued to sleep whilst she weeded the garden in the nude; had I been up and about I would have grabbed the camera and clicked away madly imagining a poster-size image of the event on the bedroom wall. At breakfast she told me about her mini-adventure with a satisfied cat-with-the-canary smile and said, "You can get so much done in the early morning, in the summer time." With this sentiment I could not but agree, but to this day I wish I'd been up, camera in hand.

By mid-July, in the intense sunlight and heat, the string bean plants had turned brown without giving forth any beans, despite constant watering. The tomatoes remained small and green but continued to grow and soon turned the appropriate color. The zucchini plants seemed exhausted after so bountifully producing, but new blossoms indicated another round of the tubes in the near future and by the end of the month they appeared in all their size and number. Radishes grew to plentitude, bursting deep red through the surface of the earth into the light of day.

Journal, September 2:

Lynn making zucchini bread for dessert and breakfast and anytime until it's gone. Tied up more tomatoes last night and watered the garden just before it rained again. Many tomatoes are cracked and have to be tossed. Erratic water and sun no doubt the cause. Snails seem to have eaten all the lettuce seeds. Radishes growing rapidly. Courgettes unstoppable.

Mme Mourre gave us a bunch of figs the size of baseballs that Micheline picked from the fig tree in the garden. Juicy and sweet. Mme Mourre laughed out loud when LM told her I ate a fig with a spoon. The following morning I ate another by hand: even sweeter!

Tavel Morning
Baking bread smells friendly
When the heat cracks walnuts softly
Muted by the iron oven door.
Café-au-lait snuggles strong and hearty
In wide-mouthed breakfast bowls

Steaming in the rain-washed air.
We smile silently without knowing why.
Summer's hinges begin to creak
As autumn pushes against the season's door.

23 August 1983

Interlude: The Glories of *Aïoli*

> Well I'll tell ya, Mr. Jones, if you don't
> know what it is, you'd surely best learn
> because it's gonna be the salvation of us
> all.
>
> - Eden the Perfect Bartender
> at The Edge Bar, Cutchaguog
> NY, 1952, speaking of garlic

One doesn't deliberately set out to argue with a world-renowned expert in her own field of expertise, but in writing about garlic one cannot avoid Elizabeth David's hardened stricture about the evils of the garlic press, about which she allowed no compromise. In a book review entitled "Garlic Presses Are Utterly Useless," Mrs. David writes, "I regard garlic presses as both ridiculous and pathetic, their effect being precisely the reverse of what people who buy them believe will be the case. Squeezing the juice out of garlic doesn't reduce its potency, it concentrates it and intensifies its smell."[23] It is difficult to conceive of something simultaneously both ridiculous and pathetic and there is a bit of twisted logic

---

[23] *Tatler* (February 1986); reprinted in *Is There a Nutmeg in the House* (New York, 2001), 52.

here: no one in their right mind would ever have considered that pressing garlic would *reduce* the potency of the spice; the whole point of using the object of her derision is to *concentrate* and *intensify* the taste. Mrs. David serves up a red herring and magically turns it into a rollmops. Clearly this won't do.

In addition to mincing garlic with a large kitchen or chef's knife and pounding it in a mortar with a pestle, Mrs. D. suggests processing it by smashing it with the side of the same knife. The novelist Len Deighton, in his idiosyncratic but highly readable, *The ABC of French Food*, calls the press a garlic "crusher" and recommends its use, thus placing himself in my camp, warning his readers, "don't imitate those foolish TV cooks who crush garlic by thumping it with the side of the knife." Why not? Because the bits and pieces and the juice resulting from the thumping "will stay in your clothes and turn rancid, producing a smell almost impossible to remove."[24] Well, one could wear a chef's apron, *n'est-ce pas*? In actual fact, I use the knife's side to thump the garlic clove to loosen the skin so it is easily peeled off. All cooks know what a frustrating and time consuming process it is to peel the clove by other methods. So much for thumping and pounding.

I, in any case, regularly make use of an old metal press that has been in the family for 25 or 30 years, not always, to be sure, but regularly when not chopping the cloves into tiny pieces with my trusty Solingen chef's knife. To expend the time and effort to crush and mash

---

[24] (New York, 1989), 4-5.

peeled garlic cloves in a mortar with a pestle is for me wasteful of both, in short supply anyway. The sharply luscious taste of the spice is as pure coming out of the press as it is had it been mulched in the mortar; I have done this many times to prove my point: never fails. (What fails from time to time is of course the quality of the garlic bulb: the stuff one buys in the supermarket is bland and innocuous compared to the real thing.) Furthermore, the press gives you the very essence of garlic because it filters out the stringy skin whilst exuding the fruit of the clove.

O la la la la la
How I loves me garlic O
Pressed through the little sievy-o
A blasting taste of paradise
And that aint ring-a-leerio!
O la la la la la.

And I also admit, in the interests of full disclosure, whatever that really means, that a meal without garlic is to me the equivalent of an egg without salt or a man without a mustache. I've been known to mix minced garlic in a strong tea (but not in coffee). Some of us are rather intense about the spice.

But what about *aïoli*, the ostensible and true subject of this noodling?

A simple recipe for *aïoli* reads in its entirety: "The garlic, say 2 large cloves for four people, is pounded in a mortar, 2 yolks of eggs stirred in, then the oil added drop by drop at first, and faster as the *aïoli* gets thick."[25] Note the elegance of the brevity, but also the assumption that lies behind the advice: that the reader already knows how much oil to use and that it is olive oil, not some other variety.

An even simpler statement by our ubiquitous author lies in another of her books, to wit: "Start by pounding 2 or 3 cloves of garlic, then put in the yolks of eggs, seasonings, and add olive oil drop by drop, proceeding exactly as for mayonnaise. Add lemon juice instead of vinegar."[26] At least we are told that the oil comes from olives, but how much, what seasonings and how many egg yolks? If we look a few pages back we find the recipe for mayonnaise, which includes a little tarragon vinegar and a squeeze of lemon; perhaps these are seasonings. One is also instructed to "stir steadily but not like a maniac." A sense of humor is important in writing cookery books, but adding breadcrumbs to an aioli is surely beyond the pale, so to speak. To be fair, elsewhere Mrs. D. notes that along with the garlic, egg yolks, and a bit of salt, one should use a third of a pint of olive oil, so the amount is specified at least in one place in her oeuvre.[27] And one should also note that a more detailed description of the place of the sauce in Provençal culture and a recipe appear in Mrs. D's classic *French Provincial Cooking.*[28]

---

[25] Elizabeth David, *French Country Cooking* (London, 1951/1966), 67.
[26] E. David, *Mediterranean Food* (London, 1950/1965), 188.
[27] E. David, *Summer Cooking* (London, 1955/1965), 78.
[28] (London, 1960/1965), 302-303.

But the simplest recipe of all, indeed what the author calls "dead simple," is found in Mort Rosenblum's fine book, *Olives. The Life and Lore of a Noble Fruit*, to wit: "For each four or five people, take two cloves of garlic, one egg yolk, a little salt, and a half liter of oil. Then beat it all together until your wrist throbs with pain."[29] A sense of humor, yes, but only *two* cloves? His garlic must be far more pungent than any I can find in the Florida Keys.

To thoroughly transgress the word according to Mrs. David, the great James A. Beard tells readers they can use a blender to make *aïoli*. *Um Gottes willen*! "It will emerge as a dense, mayonnaise-like mass, highly fragrant and flavored with garlic, a change from anything you have ever tasted."[30] Amen. Indeed, one's first taste of a dollop of *aïoli*, regardless of its carrier, is an extraordinary two-fold experience: first the rather mild but clear flavor of the garlic when it first enters the mouth, followed by the explosive crack of the full blast in the throat as the peristaltic swallowing wave sends the fiery rocket into the deepest wells of taste and emotion – one's eyes bulge, one gasps for breath, and, inevitably, one quickly reaches for the next mouthful that will send the senses spiraling up through the multi-colored stratosphere of the mind's limitless open space. Why bother with LSD or other artificial stimulants when one has *aïoli* at hand?

---

[29] (New York, 1996), 173.
[30] James Beard, *Beard on Food* (New York, 1974), 286-287. This is also the source of the information about the Spanish form of aïoli.

As one might expect, the Rombauers have a brief workman-like standard recipe with the curious addition of "one slice dry French bread without crust, soaked in milk and wrung out." This is curious not only because of its presence in the recipe (somewhere Mrs. D. also mentions breadcrumbs!), but because of its near physical impossibility of implementation.[31]

One should also note that the Rombauers' advice on making mayonnaise is applicable to *aïoli* as well. "Don't try to make mayonnaise if a thunderstorm threatens or is in progress, as it simply will not bind." While I've never actually attempted this, I implicitly believe it because, after all, it is printed in *The Joy of Cooking*, an all-American classic.[32]

During the year we lived in Tavel we had ample time and occasion to taste a large variety of *aïolis* and so learn the qualities that make it such a success on the tongue. The one infallible test for a good *aïoli* is this: does it bite the back of your tongue? Mrs. David used the phrase "tingles in your throat as you swallow it,"[33] but "bite" expresses the notion quite well. Indeed, one might say that *aïoli* is so ubiquitous in Provence it has taken on an added meaning: when one sees a sign announcing a weekly "*grand aïoli*" organized by the village mayor or a local association one realizes that the word describes the entire meal as such. This is also referred to as an "*aïoli garni*." (The *grand aïoli* is often associated with *la*

[31] Irma S. Rombauer & Marion Rombauer Becker, *The Joy of Cooking* (Indianapolis/New York, 1975 edition), 365.
[32] Ibid., 363.
[33] *French Provincial Cooking*, 303.

grande randonnée, or weekly hike through the countryside by senior citizen groups that ends with the grand meal. Many things are grand in the Midi.) *Aïoli* is often referred to as *beurre de Provence*, for good reason.

Almost anything you like can go into the *grand aïoli*, but there are a number of standard ingredients that one eats with the sauce: poached fish, salt cod, hard-cooked eggs, snails cooked in water flavored with fennel, various cooked vegetables (boiled potatoes carrots, onions, green beans, artichokes, zucchini, fresh peas, etc., all served cold); possibly tongue, boiled beef, and so forth. In certain areas of Spain, *ailloli* includes chunks of garlic or baked potatoes mixed into the sauce for a denser consistency, but this is frowned upon in Provence. Bread crumbs are added by some recipe writers, but I find them an unnecessary hindrance and eschew them. Once I made sautéed slices of a Provençal sausage and absentmindedly left them in the cast iron skillet too long so that they turned out much crisper than anticipated. A hefty dab of *aïoli* on each one saved the meal. If you are a fan of what the Americans call baloney, try thick slices of *mortadella* with fresh baguette pieces and *aïoli*.

One of my favorite writers, on any subject but particularly and sensuously on food and drink, the American national treasure (as Auden called her), MFK Fisher, notes that a *grand aïoli* can be "a devastating festival" the interruption of which for a "quick salubrious toss-down of local *marc*" to offset the density of the sauce is often necessary. She also reasonably notes that, since the tendency to overindulgence concentrates on the sauce rather than the various accompaniments, "if one is psychosomatically ill-adjusted to a plain robust meal, accompanied firmly by the flavor of garlic, the whole thing should be tucked into a gastronomical Siberia." She also rather restrictedly says this is a winter dish, "always served at noon in French families," to which one can only respond by adding "in *some* French families," since I've been served a *grand aïoli* in the late afternoon and in the evening.[34]

I must admit that occasionally when time was short I've made use of non-fat ready-made mayonnaise as a base for the *aïoli* – non-fat doesn't taste as good as the regular kind (and certainly no where near the kind one makes oneself), but not wanting to go through a second quadruple by-pass procedure I maintain a fairly rigorous low-fat diet. Regardless of my condition, this usage is considered cheating and, in fact, a trespass against the traditional commandment that governs such culinary matters.

It should be added before we end that almost all the sources consulted for this brief essay agree that if the sauce curdles or separates during its creation, mix an egg yolk in some olive oil and slowly add the curdled mixture into it stirring all the while, preferably with a wire whisk.

And what better place to find things traditional than an actual Provençal cookery book, namely J.-B. Reboul's *La Cuisinière Provençal*, wherein we find the following recipe for *aïoli*: Use two peeled garlic cloves for each person, crush them in a mortar reducing them to a paste with a pestle, add a pinch of salt an egg yolk and begin to

---

[34] *With Bold Knife and Fork* (New York, 1969), 152.

pour the oil very slowly stirring the mixture with the pestle without pause. When you reach three or four tablespoons of oil, add some lemon juice and a tablespoon of warm water, then continue adding the oil until it is all in the sauce. Should you find the sauce too thick, add another bit of warm water. An *aïoli* for seven or eight people will absorb circa a half a liter of oil. Thus speaks the master. Variations are possible, but this is the basic text.[35]

As with a *salade niçoise* or a bouillabaisse there are many variations on the theme of an *aïoli garni*. My own, found in a notebook written whilst we lived in Tavel, makes some of its own variations. The notebook entry reads as follows:

This traditional Provençal meal is normally cold, but I have taken certain liberties with it to indulge my taste for boiled potatoes and fried eggs. Essentially it is a meal of raw vegetables and sausages. Add or subtract these as you wish. My version includes raw carrots, black olives, celery sticks, sliced green pepper and thinly sliced *saucisson d'Arles* or *rosette* (a hard salami-like sausage). The major ingredient is the garlic mayonnaise into which the various items are dipped. The amount of garlic is a matter of taste but the more the better according to traditionalists here.

For about one cup of the sauce: 5 large cloves of garlic, 2 egg yolks, ½ pint of good olive oil (note: American taste usually prefers a lighter oil than is available in Provence [1982, things have changed since].

---

[35] 23rd edition (Marseille, n.d.), 83.

Crush the peeled garlic cloves to a pulp, add yolks and a pinch of salt. Mix well with a wooden spoon, then *slowly* begin to add the oil, drop by drop at the start, faster when half the oil is used. The *aïoli* should be almost solid. Add a ½ teaspoon of lemon juice at the end of the mixing.

With the above serve small boiled potatoes and eggs fried in butter and shallots sprinkled with ground paprika. Do not turn the eggs whilst cooking: spoon some of the hot cooking butter over them or cover the pan. Add to the eggs small thin slices of hard sausage which have been previously fried to a crisp. Serve with a dry white wine or a Tavel rosé and a baguette. For those who find the *aïoli* sauce difficult to digest a small glass of marc midway through the meal (as well as after it) is recommended.

Finally, one should note that *aïoli* is often confused with its sibling, *rouille* (literally meaning "rust"). This is a garlic sauce served with fish stews (bouillabaisse) in the south, especially in the restaurants of the Old Port in Marseille. In her book, *Julia's Kitchen Wisdom*, Mrs. Child offers the following recipe for *rouille*. Purée 6 to 8 garlic cloves with ¼ teaspoon of salt; pound in 18 (not 17 or 19!) large fresh chopped basil leaves, then ¾ cup of lightly pressed down fresh bread crumbs and 3 tablespoons soup base or milk. When the paste is smooth add 3 egg yolks pounded, then in a blender beat in ⅓ cup diced canned red pimentos and by slow dribbling ¾ cup to one cup fruity olive oil. Season with salt, pepper and

Tabasco.[36] The addition of bread crumbs and soup base or milk is unusual for this sauce, as is the Tabasco, but who is to question an icon such as Mrs. Child? One can, however, note an inconsistency here, minor to be sure, but nonetheless clear.

In her posthumously published memoir she reports on the widely divergent advice given to her in the 1950s when she and her husband Paul lived in Marseille relating to the composition of a "true" bouillabaisse. The French, she notes, have only one truly negative characteristic: they arrogantly and loudly proclaim what they know to be the final and only truth about anything at all, in this case the use of tomatoes in a bouillabaisse: *jamais!* *"Nous, nous de la vrai Méditerranée, nous ne mettons jamais les tomates dans la bouillabaisse – nous jamais!"* One can see the fishwife shaking her finger, the dogmatism of her statement reflected in the absolute conviction of rightness in her rigid facial expression. *JAMAIS!* Mrs. Child went to the bible of Provençal cooking, Reboul's *La Cuisinière Provençal*, and, lo, he puts tomatoes in his bouillabaisse. *Voila!*[37] On the other hand, Reboul makes no mention at all of bread crumbs, Tabasco or milk in his recipe for *rouille*, limiting himself

---

[36] (New York, 2000), 8.

[37] With Alex Prud'homme, *My Life in France* (New York, 2006), 174. Mrs. Child died in 2004, which means now three great women of the food-centered life are gone: Child (b. 1912), MFK Fisher (1908-1992) and Elizabeth David (1913-1992). For biographical details see Artemis Cooper, *Writing at the Kitchen Table. The Authorized Biography of Elizabeth David* (New York, 2000) and Joan Reardon, *Poet of the Appetites. The Lives and Loves of MFK Fisher* (New York, 2004).

to the barebones version which includes garlic, Spanish pimento, a nut of bread dough, olive oil and a small amount of fish broth. I suppose the bread dough could be replaced with bread crumbs, but I doubt it would have the same consistency.[38]

Writing about *rouille* Deighton in an aside notes that when they go out to eat (presumably in the university restaurants called *Resto-U* or in places with cheap meals that cater to students and other lower income folk like poets and anarchists) poor French students order fish soup in the knowledge that they will also be able to satisfy their immense hunger with the stack of sliced baguette and large bowl of *rouille* served with the soup. Then he adds the plaintive statement, "Writers do the same thing."[39]

Clearly, *aïoli* does not accompany a meal, it stands on an equal footing with all the other elements on the table. *Aïoli* is one of the glories of Provençal cooking, a regional cuisine that boasts many such glories such as a particularly flavorful *soupe de poisson* (also served with a large dab of *rouille*), the famous bouillabaisse, *bourride*, *soupe au pistou*, the infamous *haricots verts de Nice*, the incredibly tasty *rougets grillés* at the Colombe d'Or's terrace in Saint-Paul de Vence, various kinds of garlic sausages, *tapenades*, and the list could go on and on; after all, Reboul's book is 468 pages in length. *Aïoli*, however, would be my choice if I had to choose just one Provençal ingredient to eat the rest of my life. For one thing, it goes with so many dishes and garlic is good for

---

[38] Reboul, 82.
[39] Deighton, 180.

sentient human beings' health and quality of life. What more can one ask?

●

When September finally snuck up on us the flora in the garden began to decline in volume and quality of produce. The tomatoes grew small and often cracked for some secret reason known only to Mother Nature. Micheline thought the tomato plants would survive with sufficient watering and they did straggle on for a while, as did the zucchini tubes inspiring various forms of ratatouille and other uses.

Not too much time passed in Tavel before we introduced to France a dish we'd learned to make whilst still in Washington. Because we first sampled this odd mixture in the dining room of a Korean friend, Dai-Sil Kim-Gibson, we called it Seoulburger. One marinates burger patties in a sauce containing soy, chopped spring onions, a bay leaf and a mystery spicy sauce known only to Korean chefs. Then one grills the burgers until charred on the outside and pink in the middle, places them in buns with a slice of Bermuda onion and eats them slowly accompanied by a strong, tough red wine or a glass of German or Austrian beer. We do have the recipe for this but Dai-Sil wrote it out in Korean characters, sly fox that she is, so for us it remains a mystery.

Since we did not at first have any of the mystery sauce handy, we improvised to achieve the same level of spicy heat. Success in this endeavor can only be termed erratic, the biggest problem being a too heavy hand with the soy which is liquid salt and must be used with the utmost care not to overdo. We added what we could find in the local stores to approximate the taste we'd learned to previously know and enjoy: purée de piment, cayenne pepper, and the like. We tried these experiments out on ourselves before we offered the results to guests, who, it must be admitted, generally looked upon the dish with some suspicion until they bit into one; thereafter they either rejected another meal of the same or loved it. With regard to the latter, their enjoyment increased when Dai-Sil and her husband Don mailed us a CARE packet containing the real thing. This was not an inexpensive matter: they spent $16 on postage and we spent 19 francs on import duty fees. Whatever was in that mystery mixture it definitely added to the quality and taste of the burgers.

Our friends Jean and Blair Williams did not particularly care for the burgers but their young sons could consume two thick examples with noisy appreciation whenever we made them. In fact, with some sadness we made Seoulburgers on the grill on the Ferme Jamet as a farewell dinner for the Williams in early June. The sabbatical over it was time for them to leave the Midi, fly off to Montreal and the summer semester at the university for Blair and the flower store for Jean; the boys had to make up the schooling Canadian education officials believed they had missed during their six months in France, despite the fact that they attended school on the Ile de la Barthelasse and learned school kid French with ease and fluency.

We came to know the Barthelasse fairly well because we stayed at the Ferme Jamet for weeks at a time over a period of many years after we left Tavel. Originally all farmland, after the war the farmers began selling bits and pieces of their properties to developers who added restaurants, camping facilities and small housing tracts. But when we first knew it, the old almost pre-industrial agricultural milieu still maintained its grip on the island; the dusty roads mostly unpaved, long stretches of which had no streetlights to guide the unwary, great swaths of farmland still dominated the landscape except where the camping cropped up. Etienne Jamet, the son and grandson of the original farmers, had recently sold off much of his land to another farmer and was about to sell his vineyards as well, to devote his and his wife, Martine's, time to operating the rentals of the five cottages and apartments in the main buildings.

During the summer of 1983, on the Ile de la Barthelasse in a pizzeria called La Capriciosa owned and operated by a 45ish semi-dwarf named François who claimed to be a Sicilian, we tasted the best pizza ever, bar none, anywhere, any time. Both of us had grown up with pizza of all sorts; if my memory does not fail me I first ate pizza in the 7th grade; it must have been in early June just before school ended for the summer, and there must have been a fête of some kind at the school because I associate the pizza with the sight of a girl named Carol walking down the street after school that day in shorts, the ring indentation made by the garters that had ealier that day held up her stockings visible on her thighs. All

271

memories of one's first pizza should be so pleasant and innocently mysterious.

What made François' pizza the best, or perhaps it should be "so different"? All the traditional elements went into "La Reine", our favorite among the choices: extremely thin crust, tomato sauce with chunks of peeled tomato, Emmenthal cheese (not the tasteless mozzarella usually found in most pizzas), a generous pouring of spiced olive oil, an equally generous pinch of *herbes de provence*, black olives (preferably those from Kalamata), a small tossing of ham, chopped garlic, mushrooms, minced onion and fresh parsley, and a wood fire of olive tree branches in the special oven next to which the pizza sits until done. The small amount of each ingredient is important and must be strictly adhered to if the desired results are to be achieved. With this we ate one green salad and a few pieces of baguette, and drank a bottle of local red or rosé. This constituted our supper and evoked a mild reaction of consternation from François: in France and Italy pizza is normally eaten as a first course and salad is served toward the end of the meal. Eventually the chef came to accept our, to him, odd eating habits.

He also claimed to be related to Frank Sinatra. In a mixture of French and broken English he explained that since they both had Italian mothers from Sicily they must have been related. Whether or not Sinatra's mother came from Sicily or Hoboken is unknown to me but it made no difference whatsoever to François, as of course it shouldn't have. This was his story and he was sticking to it! One night early that summer we drove in a thrashing mistral to the pizzeria, just outside of which the wind buffeted a huge plane tree to the extent that it took on the appearance of an enormous mute monster trembling and shaking in a wild rage about to engorge the entire building. François ignored the dramatic antics of the tree and continued to play his usual role of host, comedian and cook in several languages, all of them garbled. ("I born in America! Frank Sinatra my cousin! You like music? I turn it up!") One additional charming aspect of the place turned out to be the sign at the entrance way reading "*Attention! Chien méchant!*" under which a small black dachshund peacefully rested on the tiles. The dog, whose name we eventually learned was, rather inappropriately, "Sauvage", slowly lifted himself to his feet to sniff at our feet each time we entered the yard, then, satisfied that he didn't need to be mean to us, lay down and closed his eyes.

La Capriciosa unfortunately lost François sometime following 1989 after which it became a Tex-Mex joint, an "Italian" restaurant, a leather and chain sex bar and a "club privé"; the last time we looked the building was shuttered and forlorn, another bit of "our" Provence gone with the winds of greed and indifference to tradition and local culture. In our own kitchens ever since LM has made a La Capriciosa pizza, about which I have written elsewhere,[40] not a perfectly exact replica, but close enough to be classified as the second best pizza in the world, bar none, anywhere.

---

[40] For a different take on the story, see my essay "Gunsmoke and Provençal Pizza Sundays (A Cowboy Culinary, Euro-American Adventure" in *Mediterranean Sketches. Fictions, Memories and Metafictions* (Port Jefferson NY: Vineyard Press, 2005), 71ff.

On the occasion of one of our dinners with the Williams we met a 70-year old Frenchman, René Thibauld, and his younger American wife Eve, who lived in one of the apartments at the Ferme Jamet and were about to depart for Washington where they believed they could find more lucrative employment as translators than they could in Paris or Avignon. René entertained us with stories about Paris in the 1930s and his immigration to the USA after the Germans occupied that city. A charming fellow with definite opinions on anything and everything, he also believed himself to be an expert on the subject of cheeses, a trait common in Frenchmen of a certain age and social standing. At the end of May they had us to lunch and, among other things, served a large wedge of Camembert with chunks of fresh baguette. He'd ordered the cheese by stating the exact time he would present it to his guests. The cheese monger had insisted on knowing the hour it would be eaten so he could provide a piece that would be sufficiently ripe to consume at that hour and no other. René professed himself to be satisfied with the choice. *"Un frommage formidable!"* I thought it tasted just fine, but hardly *"formidable."* The French are somewhat eccentric about their cheeses.[41] Charles de Gaulle once noted in almost despair that it was impossible to rule a nation that boasted 375 types of cheeses, each claiming to be, if not

---

[41] After we returned to Washington we had dinner once or twice with René and Eve at their apartment on Capitol Hill in a "transitional" neighborhood. Their employment situation had not worked out as they expected and they were in the process of searching for cheaper quarters. As is often the case, the acquaintanceship never developed into a friendship and we lost track of them soon thereafter.

better than, at least quite, quite different from any other, stated in a manner that left no doubt the word "different" really did mean "better."

But, then, the French consider cooking to be one of the fine arts and the respect for chefs is commensurate with the respect for food itself. Somewhere I have written that good food, meticulously prepared can be found just as easily in a family owned small roadside establishment with a gas pump by the front door as in the eateries the Michelin inspectors award their much sought after stars. The talents and gifts of a chef are regarded as not qualitatively different from those of a poet or painter. This is the land of great debates among a group of plumbers at lunch as to the composition of *herbes de Provence*, about exactly and in what amounts the various herbs should go into the mix. Everyone considers himself or herself an expert on some aspect of cooking and the selection of ingredients to flavor a given dish. They might argue about the relative merits of this or that football club, or who in the village is the greater boules player, but they also will argue with some heat that this way and not that way is the correct and only way to roast a chicken; and one should exercise caution before entering into an intense discussion of which olive oil is best for sautéing foul, fish, vegetables and meats.

And so we gradually took upon ourselves certain characteristics of our neighbors and friends: we, too, began to experiment with various methods and procedures of preparing and cooking our food. We were fortunate that a farmer's market was held every day in one or another of the villages and towns in the region, and on Sundays the sprawling market that wound its way through the streets under the plane trees and along the waterwheel dotted swiftly flowing canals of L'Isle-sur-la-Sorgue, the birthplace of the poet René Char.

For several months after we moved from Apt to Tavel I kept a running list of dinners we made. Later on, after LM began attending mid-afternoon language classes at CELA, I would post a handwritten menu of the evening's meal on the front door to our apartment so she would know what she would be eating, and I hoped be pleasurably surprised. This usually worked quite well.

Several dishes appear more than once on the list including a number called *"Veau au Marquis"* named after Mrs. Potter's house in Apt where I first made it, according to the recipe book on October 4, 1982. Some have found the recipe itself amusing so here it is, as I wrote it down then.

Escalope du veau for two

4 bashed veal escalopes
4-5 sliced shallots
1 clove sliced garlic
1 chopped green onion
a pinch of thyme, sage & tarragon
olive oil
freshly ground pepper
1 cup chicken bouillion
light cream
flour or egg yolks
fresh mushrooms

fresh lemon juice
dry vin blanc

Alors! Prepare veal with a mallet by hitting it several times. Sautée shallots, onion and garlic in olive oil (preferably extra virgin bought at the Apt market). Push aside; add more oil and brown veal on both sides. Add bouillon, wine, herbs and cover. (Note: you probably do not need a full cup of bouillon and in any case boil the liquid down a bit before the next step.) Cook over medium to low heat until the veal is done. Time depends upon the thickness of the meat. Remove meat from pan along with enough liquid to dissolve 2 heaping tablespoons of flour. Add cream to pan with flour mixture depending upon desired thickness of the sauce. At this time add mushrooms sliced thick. Turn on a Monk tape and cook until you like the thickness of the sauce, adjusting seasoning to taste, and adding a healthy squeeze of half a lemon. Return meat to pan and let simmer for another moment or two. (NB: be careful you don't cook meat too long. Remember you can always cook more but not less, eh?)

Serve with a limited quantity of mashed potatoes and a fresh green salad. Accompany with dry white wine or Tavel rosé and pieces of a fresh baguette to mop any left over sauce. (You may want to try substituting Madeira for white wine in the cooking process.)

Another meal that appears several times is *"Côte du porc èchalotes au sauce crème à la Rose des Vents."* In addition to the pork chops and the shallots, the note tells me that green onions and sliced apples went into the pan and that corn cooked in white wine accompanied the meat dish. It has been many years since we've cooked such a thing since we do not regularly eat meat any longer, but apples and pork do complement each other. We also ate a considerable amount of lamb in various forms, especially in *daubes* (stews), that winter. Omelets with a variety of ingredients figured often in the evenings, as did chicken, but little fish (probably because we could never tell how long the seafood had been journeying around the region from market to market and the fish available in the *hypermarchés* was invariably frozen, a condition that has changed since then).

There is no way around the ubiquitous chicken in its manifold forms and sizes. One night we made a roasted chicken using whatever we had in the kitchen at the time. We stuffed the two-pound roaster with chopped zucchini, a chopped lemon and a handful of dried tarragon, following which we oiled the skin with olive oil and placed it in a baking tin with a quarter inch mixture of white wine and water. We cooked it in the oven (never did know at what exact temperature but assume it was about the equivalent of 350 degrees Fahrenheit) for an hour and a bit, basting every 15 minutes or so and halfway through the process scattering more tarragon on the bird. Once we removed it from the oven, LM made a sauce using the remaining liquid, some flour, hot milk and a squeeze of lemon to maintain the lemony flavor. Serve with mashed potatoes and a veg, if you don't want to eat the stuffing which I found too tart for my taste buds. A dry, white Bordeaux goes very nicely with the meal. And a baguette, of course.

But as Henri le Kroner of the Hostellerie de Tavel once told us, "For all the allure of French cooking when read with sympathy in a book or a recipe, it is nothing to the ultimate tantalizing of the tongue when one actually *eats* the food." And he knew whereof he spoke.

●

The Light in Provence

Not only the light that is luminous in the Midi, but the colors its brilliant gossamer sheen brings strikingly to the eye. In Provence color is light and light is color. Each is more intense than elsewhere. But there are differences as well: in the Vaucluse everything is tinged with a lush green that comes from the luxurious vegetation in the valleys and hillsides; in the Gard (technically not part of Provence but the eastern border of Languedoc, though traditionally the Pont du Gard, Uzès and Nîmes are considered in Provence) the garrigues are rougher, strewn with aromatic bristling herb bushes and trees of pale colors in a gravelly desert-like ground which influences the beige-yellow aura to the light there.

Journal entry, 15 July:

The heat and light indicate that we are truly in the south, and it's summer time, too.

I think the sunlight here is not the same texture of brightness as Van Gogh and Cézanne or even Renoir, Matisse and Picasso experienced. From the mid-1950s the thick yellow light has become thinner as a result of industry and tourism which means motor cars and diesel powered trucks. The noxious gases released over the last 30 years have dissolved the heavy substance of yellow that contrasted so clearly with the green-brown vegetation and blue sky. Now everything is bleached out, everything fades into everything with no clear lines of demarcation. The sky is gray-blue, the flora colors are faded and graying, the sunlight itself is diluted and thin. It is still beautiful, but one convinces oneself that one has been born out of joint with time, that it is too late. It was much better then. This thought is a constant companion, unfortunately, and it detracts rather from the enjoyment of the present. Degraded coin cannot equal pure gold, but one doesn't have to add nostalgia to reinforce the degradation.

24 July:

Finally made the drive to Mont Ventoux today. Picnic on the eastern flank, then through the long winding Gorges de la Nesque. What we thought was snow atop the mountain is gravel. Entire top is man-made landscape of large rocked gravel, radar and electronic equipment, a restaurant, etc. All rather ugly but temperature very cool despite the sun. The view usually saves it but in the summer there is no view in

Provence. Pollution has so severely damaged the atmosphere that we have not seen Mont Ventoux from here since last spring. A permanent blue-gray haze hovers about the hills and the distant skyline. The quality of light has changed because of man and his inventions. Ironic that those machines we've created to make our lives easier are endangering life at worst and at best shortening life – to say nothing about degrading the quality of life.

30 July:

Driving on the *autoroute* on the way to Aix looking at the hills covered in a dusty haze reinforced my theory about a radical change in the light of Provence. Where can one find pure light today? Certainly not here.

Finally, in early August we could clearly see Mont Ventoux off in the distance grandly jutting skyward commanding the Rhône Valley to the west, the Vaucluse plateau to the south and the small Baronnies range to the north, the most visibly distinct natural phenomenon of the region. "Vent" is wind in French and the summit of this mountain is sometimes caressed, sometimes battered by the wind, the latter especially during a mistral. This probably causes the temperature at the top to be an average of 20° Fahrenheit (11° Celsius) colder than at the bottom, which is 6,263 feet (1909 meters) from the summit. Petrarch may have walked up there but we drove our elderly Peugeot up there where little vegetation grows. On a windy day, a picnic is a difficult meal to enjoy – but we did.

One is not sure if the connection can be scientifically proven beyond a shadow of a doubt, but one strongly suspects that the dust-rain that fell on the region several times during our sojourn there is somehow related to the deterioration of the natural light for which Provence was once famous. At some point during the spring we first experienced this uncomfortable form of precipitation: after the brief rain ceased when the drops dried they left a circle of sandy dust on every surface including the rose bushes and windows that had been clear and clean prior to the rain. With cosmic concerns about such matters as acid rain slithering around science circles one wondered what that "dust rain" might portend. Some days a yellowish light accompanied the rain fall, a morbid phenomenon. How could the usually clean air be full of dust activated by falling rain? We never discovered the answer, but we knew, we absolutely knew that the answer boded no good for the planet.

There is, of course, the necessity for artificially created light in the life of modern man, and we manufacture it in the form of electricity. This works well to allow post-crepuscule activities, but curtails those things when the power in the village cuts out for whatever reason, and we rarely discover the reason. When we do discover the cause we are sometimes embarrassed because we neglected to act in a reasonable manner to correct it. Toward the end of August our power went down, but we didn't think too much about it because it happened with some frequency and eventually returned to allow the use of electronic equipment. Gas powered our stove so we could cook to the light of candles or kerosene lamps. On this occasion one of us happened to mention the loss of power to Mme Mourre upon whose face appeared a look of skepticism if not downright astonishment. *She* had power, why didn't we? Had we entered the garage where the fuse box existed and pressed the green button? *Non? Alors,* try it, she recommended with a sly fox smile hovering about her face but not actually emerging. *Voila!* Electricity returns, and we could have had it the previous night had we considered the most obvious first step in rectifying the situation. These days, living on an island where the power disappears with some frequency, the first thing we do is check the fuse box and the neighbors. Whether or not Goethe actually said, *"Licht, mehr Licht!"* with his dying breath, it is a true fact, as Penrod told Sam, that we require light to live a civilized life of depth and pleasure.

Light became even more important after I began experimenting with water colors. The sun in the Midi rarely failed to inspire warmth and observation: it forced one to look, if not to see. But the views of Provence diminish in the distance in the summer: pollution of various sorts has not only reduced distances but altered the quality of the light. Cézanne would not recognize it today, despite the increasing use of nuclear energy generated in stations along the rushing Rhône.

Indeed the evanescent quality of the light, while still visible from time to time, can best be imagined if not seen in the works of the painters whom that brightness captivated before 1939: Cézanne, Van Gogh, Gauguin,

Matisse, Dufy, Braque and the other Fauves, Picasso, and many others not so well known in the popular mind. The art critic Karen Wilkin has written that Van Gogh's "superheated palette ... is often discussed in relation to the blazing, color-intensifying sunlight of the South of France" and his "desire to encapsulate the ravishing, constantly changing Provençal light" and one cannot disagree with her.[42] Indeed, today it is his work that glows with luminous light, not today's reality of the scenes he painted then.

In the summer of 1888, Van Gogh wrote to the painter Émile Bernard, "Oh! that beautiful mid-summer sun here. It beats down on one's head, and I haven't the slightest doubt that it makes one crazy. But as I was so to begin with, I only enjoy it." But the dark of night also fascinated him and he painted night scenes with the same passion and intensity as the sunblasted flowers and fields. "It often seems to me that the night is much more alive and richly colored than the day ... The problem of painting night scenes and effects on the spot and actually by night interests me enormously." Thus did he write to his brother Theo in 1888. His enormously iconic *The Starry Night* he painted in his room at the Saint Rémy asylum and considered it a failure of abstraction. Do we know better? In 1885 he wrote to Theo, "One of the most beautiful things by the painters of this century has been the painting of DARKNESS that is still COLOR."

For anyone who wishes to understand the Midi beneath and beyond the shallow tourist-guide

---

[42] "Van Gogh at MOMA" in *The New Criterion*, November 2008.

comprehension, a close reading of Van Gogh's letters from the south to his brother and Bernard is mandatory. One reason for his acute perceptions of the region and its multitudinous colors and shades is the fact that he was a northerner and came to the Midi with a northern mentality and habit of seeing. This is one of the reasons his work is so different from that of Cézanne, for example: the latter was born and bred in Provence and did not have to think about it. The Dutchman did not have that advantage and thought about it a great deal.[43]

Less than 20 years later, the light of Provence struck Braque's eyes and invaded his painting. About his early experience in the South he wrote, "It's there that I felt all the elation, all the joy, welling up inside me. Just imagine, I left the drab, gloomy Paris studios where you were still working in bitumen. There, by contrast, what a revelation, what a blossoming!"[44] He appreciated the variety of brilliance ranging from soft pale to sharp-edged brightness. Nonetheless, Braque remained a man of the north, for whom the southern sun retained an element of mystery and suspicion, as his post-Cubist paintings attest; Picasso, despite the years in Paris, remained a man of the Mediterranean with the sunburst violence and traditional social attitudes that often ran counter to the vehement experimentalism in his art.

---

[43] For a detailed explication of this point, see Douglas Lord's introduction to his edition and translation of Van Gogh's *Letters to Emil Bernard* (Crescent Press, 1938) and Pope-Hennessy's *Aspects of Provence*, 48-49.
[44] Alex Danchev, *Georges Braque: A Life* (New York: Arcade Publishing, 2005), 41.

•

Apropos of something now unknown, I entered the following quasi-haiku in the journal on August 4:

> Westerners in Japan
> The herring swallowing
> The swooping seagull.

•

Romans in Provence

For three centuries (ca. 51 BCE – ca. 410 CE) the Romans ruled the Midi and their ghosts inhabit the landscape to this day. Indeed, Durrell had good reason for titling his idiosyncratic final book *Caesar's Vast Ghost: Aspects of Provence* (1990), though he does quote part of Van Gogh's September 1888 letter to his brother Theo on another spirit of place influence on the region.

> There is still a great deal of Greece all through the Tartarin and Daumier part of this queer country, where the good folk have the accent you know; there is a Venus of Arles just as there is a Venus of Lesbos, and one still feels the youth of it in spite of all. I haven't the slightest doubt that some day you too will know the Midi.

But it is the Romans that interest us at the moment, because we took practically all the visitors who flooded in upon us beginning in February to the relics of Roman rule in the area. There are several Roman settlements in Provence still containing monuments to their creators' architectural and artistic genius including the arenas in Arles and Nîmes (in which also sits the exquisite Maison Carrée). On the outskirts of St. Rémy de Provence across the road from the former monastery of Saint-Paul-de-Mausole where Van Gogh committed himself for a year in May 1889 when it housed an asylum for the mentally deranged, sit the triumphal arch Julius Caesar had built to celebrate the conquest of Marseille, the 60-foot high pyramidal monument (miscalled a "mausoleum") with its two enigmatic figures in togas, and the great archeological dig at Glanum which contains the only Grecian houses known in France. And of course there is the great architectural miracle of the Pont du Gard that dominates the valley it spans. All of these sites are best visited in the late autumn, winter and early spring to avoid the busloads of tourists. To expatiate on each of these would break the integument of this chapter and many of them are described more fully elsewhere in this memoir. However I cannot escape the compulsion to offer a statement by James Pope-Hennessy regarding one of these sites.

I may add that the Plateau des Antiques and the ruins of Glanum Livii are among several places in Provence that I should not recommend imaginative persons to visit alone by the light of the moon.[45]

---

[45] *Aspects of Provence*, 44.

Another of those places, I would add, is the Val d'Enfer at the foot of Les Baux which I find rather scarifying even in the daylight.

The Roman presence in Provence is inevitable and ubiquitous; it is also the subject of many volumes lengthy and short, illustrated and not, into which the Reader is urged to delve if additional information is desired. Pope-Hennessy's *Aspects of Provence* (1952) and Durrell's *Caesar's Vast Ghost* (1990) are still in print and well worth reading.

•

One aspect of French provincial life appeared to us to be particularly obnoxious, in part because of its ecological significance, in part because of its gross ugliness, and in part because it was, and is, completely unnecessary. In *Tristes Tropiques*, Claude Lévi-Strauss writes, "The first thing we see as we travel around the world is our own filth, thrown into the face of mankind ... [Travel books] create the illusion of something which no longer exists, but still should exist." As we drove around Provence examining Caesar's vast ghost we found countless saddening examples of this phenomenon.

The landscape of the South of France has been permanently altered by the invention of the plastic bag, which may not be a perfect receptacle for garbage because it tears easily but which is almost indestructible once it has itself become a piece of garbage clinging obstinately in wind-driven tatters to the flora of even the most remote valleys and gorges.

Another point about garbage: everyone here is aware that the mistral blows long and hard during the winter; yet the public garbage dumps were unprotected and open to the wind. While paper products will eventually be destroyed by nature's activities (wind, rain and the like), the newer, non-biodegradable products of man's incessantly creative sense of destruction remain to ruin the beauties of the natural work still left to us under the relentless march of industrial and post-industrial "progress". Garbage has become the singularly ugly exemplar by which the late 20th century has come to identify itself. We have gone so far as to mark our technological development in outer space with the same sign: we have left our debris on the moon and in space. Indestructible garbage, the refuse of our civilization is what we have come to give as the hallmark of our maturity. The blue plastic bags that littered the garrigues and hills of the Midi stood and still stand as examples of the indifferent stupidity of too many humans who blithely toss their garbage out of their speeding motorcars into the innocent landscape in which they live.

While this ugly phenomenon is not limited to the South of France by any means (take a drive through your own countryside), it may be instructive to recall what Prosper Mérimée wrote in his book *Notes d'un voyage dans le Midi de la France* (1835): "So far as civilization goes, this is a sad country and instead of a Constitution what these people badly need is a tyrant who would make roads for them, and force them to keep themselves clean and to live better." *Plus ça change, plus c'est la même chose?* Perhaps not quite, but the point remains the same.

•

By the end of June, after an unusual winter and spring, we knew summer had finally arrived. Not only did we receive a steady flow of visitors, but the sounds of the region altered not so subtly: in addition to the usual year-round farmyard and countryside, which seemed so much louder even with the windows closed, we now heard the grind of small airplanes from the field near Pujaut several kilometers to the east and the rhythmic swack-swack of folded newspapers smacking furniture and windows and, with accuracy, flies. Flies presented a constant problem during the summer months as they swarmed through the open doors and windows, annoying not only with their presence but also the jagged buzzing as they flitted about one's head. I am not at all clear as to why we did not purchase bead curtains seen everywhere around the Mediterranean basin in the summer to keep flies and other flying insects out of houses and stores. We tried solid anti-fly material from the local hardware store, but that had no effect on the recalcitrant buggers. Finally we purchased several plastic fly-swatters at the Sunday market in L'Isle-sur-la-Sorgue. I thought in passing that anyone who could construct the perfectly balanced fly-swatter, adjustable to the hand and strength of any individual could certainly make some money. And anyone who could sell mesh screens for the windows could make a fortune but it would be, or would have been, a hard sell in a land where such things are not well-known and viewed with suspicion as an unnecessary American invention unneeded in France. Ridiculous, of course. Without screens we found it almost impossible to read at night: the lamps attracted flying insects like maple syrup attracts ants or feral cats attract fleas.

That summer the presence of various types of insects disturbed our sleep as well as they wormed their way into the bed and under the light sheet. Fortunately LM did not suffer as much from this nightly invasion. The bites appeared to be mosquito-inflicted but we saw no such insect. The use of vinegar liberally applied stopped the itching temporarily, but added to the disruptions of sleep. We also wondered if fleas from the various animals which wandered around the courtyard and the house might be biting us but the bites themselves did not look like those made by fleas. We took the thin, shabby old rug out onto the terrace and whomped it for 15 minutes anyway. We also had to be careful walking barefoot in the house: not only did the constant wind blow dust through the rooms after a lengthy dry spell of several months, but walking on dead flies that stick to one's feet is a nasty business. By mid-October, with two weeks left before our departure, the flies disappeared and I no longer sat at the table working surrounded by the corpses of the swatted insects.

●

Visitors

Visitors to Tavel from elsewhere in the world were both inevitable and on the whole welcome, even when they arrived within a day of the departure of the previous group. No matter how independently they conducted themselves, their presence interrupted our writing and language class schedules. They also reinforced an unfortunate tendency I suffer from: the inability to imbibe reasonable amounts of wine during dinner and the conversation that bubbles on before, during and after the meal, or, much more rarely, the bubbles bouncing along preclude the meal. This behavior I summed up in brief journal entry: "Too much wine and no dinner Friday cancelled Saturday."

Once again in the guise of Van Gogh in the asylum St.-Paul-de-Mausole at St. Rémy writing to his brother Theo in Paris I wrote to mine in York Harbor, Maine.

My dear Theo,
They've taken away my colors once again. I don't blame the sisters – they are just doing what the medicos tell them, but it is a hard row to hoe nonetheless. The problem, as you well know, is that without the colors I can do nothing that makes living further on this earth worthwhile and so I think of ending this vale of calvados before I become certifiably committable. (Not that this stage has not already been reached – but I hope I've covered it well enough to have hidden it so that no one other than you and I know it.) The very parentheses speak for my sanity. The sisters still do occasionally allow me pen and paper

and I spend the time and the paper writing to you even if you find it difficult to read or understand – the sisters do allow me *some* rosé occasionally and visitors occasionally bring me something to drink other than the usual pabulum which tends to dilute my spelling and thoughts in any case. Visitors are somewhat responsible for this missive being written so baldly having returned from the Côte d'Azur one day earlier than I thought, thus throwing off my usual schedule and upsetting the sisters (the physicians – what a silly name for those who cannot even heal themselves) cannot understand the wild enthusiasm of my sneezes in any case and I hear them coming down the stone hallway to take away my last pen – I have sneezed 12 times and will close the door.

In early June my old friend Karlheinz Schwaner stayed with us for a whirlwind visit. I had not seen him for several years, but we maintained a lively correspondence in German and English and he had called us in Tavel several times. At the age of 72 he had not changed a bit from the time I first met him in 1963 while living in Heidelberg: opinionated, supercharged with enthusiasm for life and things that provoked his imagination, and obsessed with the same themes: censorship, sexuality and the freedom of the individual vis-à-vis the state, to which he has added anti-communism and the ingratitude of children. Talking to him brought back the old days in Heidelberg and Frankfurt – nothing exempt from constant analysis, no subject passed on without first taking it apart and refitting the pieces.[46] Language meant a great deal to him (his apartment groaned under the weight of dictionaries and etymologies and this hadn't changed a bit. He was also the perfect guest: stays a short period of time, is exciting intellectually and brings gifts of a functional character: food and wine.

He drove an old red Volvo convertible sports car with a careless, if not reckless, disregard of speed limits: on the *routes nationales* he chugged along at speeds that frustrated the French accustomed to zipping along as if chased by a mistral; in the villages and towns he drove at speeds that made me close my eyes and pray for salvation, talking at top speed; at least he had given up cigarette smoking (on the subject of which he chastised both of us, the converted being holier than the Pope). The trip to Nîmes might be described as heartrending if one means by that the pumping muscle stopped several times that day. We ate a fine lunch at a café on the main street and later that evening he sharpened our long carving knife admonishing me not to use it again to cut up chicken bones, the proximate cause of the pitted edge of the implement, advice I have followed ever since.

On the other hand, he could not get over the resemblance between LM and his living companion, Renate, whom I had met briefly in the early 1970s, and we heard the refrain many times during his brief visit: "You look so much like my Renate. *Unglaublich!*"

---

[46] For a description of our meeting in Heidelberg, see my *Paris Now and Then. Memoirs, Opinions, and a Companion to the City of Light for the Literate Traveler* (Vineyard Press, 2004), 36-37.

The night before he arrived we had supper with the entire Williams ménage: Blair and Jean and the two boys, Blair's farmer parents from the Canadian west, Blair's sister Marcia and her friend Penny, Blair and Jean's older daughters Michele (20) and Carma (19), and Michele's friend Rick, whom she married a year or so later and moved to Bethesda outside Washington where we saw them during a visit by Blair and Jean. The evening was notable for two reasons: the size of our group, which generally discombobulates waiters, and the episode of the beer mugs.

This social faux pas occurred when we all met at the Place des Corps Saints (which I translate as the Holy Bodies Square, the name of which is of interest if only because this is one of the parts of the city frequented by hookers and their clients) and ate a well-watered meal full of laughter and witty remarks. After we paid the bill, each contributing our fair share, and as we milled around the tables preparing to leave, two waiters presented themselves and demanded the liter-sized glass beer mugs be returned to the table from wherever Blair's sister and a daughter had placed them in their handbags, accidentally it goes without saying. Once the participants clarified the matter, we went on our way, sated, happy, buzzing and innocent.

The evening before Karlheinz left for Nice and an eventual return to Frankfurt-Neu Isenberg, we drove out to the Ferme Jamet to say hello to the Williams entourage and introduce them to our friend. The flow of events that night was typical of the Williams' warm openness and immediate friendliness: since we had conveniently arrived at 7:00 they insisted we stay for pasta, salad and wine, which we gladly did, though we had not truly intended to impose upon them. The meal went splendidly.

A week later, on the 9th of June we again assembled at the Ferme Jamet for a last game of boules and a final meal with Jean, Blair, Matthew and Benjamin. Since they had put everything away and cleaned the apartment, LM and I cooked Seoulburgers, which Jean had for some reason not yet tasted, on the grill in the outdoor kitchen. We tried to carefully limit the wine consumption because they would leave very early the following morning. That day, for the first time since we'd been there, we stumbled out of bed at 5:30 in the morning to drive over to the Ile de la Barthelasse to take them to the Avignon railway station. We had no idea when we might see them again. They had been a constant in our world for six months and their absence would leave a hole in our lives there. We got along so well so quickly: the fact that we all enjoyed the product of the grape and the sun added to the immediate sympathy. And we played our first game of boules with them. We smiled as the train began to move away, but we were unsuccessful in repressing our tears.

•

Shortly after they arrived in January, Blair had placed a notice at his sons' elementary school on the Ild de la Barthelasse advertising for a private French tutor. One of their classmates, a young girl named Anaïs, informed her mother, Sylvie Devaux-Sigayret, and the latter became Blair's tutor. She and Anaïs lived on a converted barge tied up along the Ile de la Barthelasse shore across the river from the Palace of the Popes. Sylvie had previously lived on such a boat in Paris, a part of her life that prepared her for the ups and downs of waters and the occasional damage storms and winds could cause to such residences. Before the Williams left for Canada, Blair introduced Sylvie to LM who took her on as a tutor, driving to the barge several times a week for conversation and iced tea. We became friends with Sylvie and Anaïs and had them to dinner several times before we had to leave. LM's French improved still further and by autumn the combined teachings of Mme Mourre, Denis Constancias and Sylvie resulted in an ability to conduct a fluid conversation that helped us greatly in the following years as we spent more time in France. Somehow Sylvie also purchased our small black and white telly and the blue Peugeot, in spite of the fact that we told her the full story of its repair history. And she never once complained about its ability to function in an appropriately motor car manner. The next time we saw her and Anaïs a couple of years later, they had moved into an apartment in an old section of Avignon and no longer owned La Petite Mo. Indeed, they welcomed us warmly and fed us well. That was the first of many meals we shared over the years. The last we heard, Anaïs had become a physician and Sylvie was living in Perpignan on the French border with Spain, but that was several years ago.

Throughout the summer the visitors came and went, many briefly on their way elsewhere, stopping off to say hello, eat a meal or two, drink some of the local wine and see some of the sites: my old friend from graduate school in the mid-1960s, Tom Quigley and his wife Wendy, came from Frankfurt (Tom taught for the University of Maryland's European Division for many years, as I had in the early 1970s, and we talked at length about the possibility of my again teaching for that institution when our money ran out in the autumn); Marsha and Eberhard von Dürckheim came on separate occasions but both with their two children from Bonn on their way to Corsica; Brigitte Gruss and her three children from Kassel whom I had not seen for almost a decade; Heiner Adamsen (a former OMGEESE member who became a good friend) and a lady friend from Bochum; and Mike and Ilse Fichter and their daughter Sarah from Berlin. Mike is another former OMGOOSE who has remained a close and valued friend ever since we first met in 1975. Sarah lived with us in Washington on and off for several years while she attended Brown University. She and her husband, Navin Vember, were married here in Key West in December 2007.

In September of the previous year we had begun our sojourn by staying at Wolfgang and Ute Benz's house in Munich for a month. They and their two children, Benjamin and Angelika, came for several days that summer, a visit notable for several things including a conversation that lasted until 3:00 o'clock in the morning the subjects of which no one could remember the following day, a trip to the bamboo forest and pottery

298

studios in Anduze and the witnessing of the regional wine masters' parade down Tavel's main street as part of their annual meeting, marching into town from the cooperative and back in bright colorful costumes (as if all the older European universities sent delegates in their unique gaudy gowns and hats), 50 strong, accompanied by a team of Aïda trumpeters trumpeting the procession with appropriate blaring and honking.

As much as we liked having these and other friends visit, we felt relieved to some extent when they left and we could return to our "normal" schedule of work and pleasure in living there.

●

The Avignon theater festival is an annual circus-like four-week event stretching from July into August. In 1947 the art critic and collector Christian Zervos and the poet René Char organized an art exhibition of modern painting in the Palais des Papes and invited Jean Vilar to stage his production of T. S. Eliot's *Murder in the Cathedral*, a hit in Paris at the time, in the grand courtyard of the palace to be performed during the run of the exhibition. Vilar thought the courtyard too vast and shapeless for that play but suggested the creation of three new productions instead: Shakespeare's *Richard II*, not at all well-known in France at the time, Paul Claudel's *Tobie et Sara*, and Maurice Clavel's second play, *La Terrasse de Midi*. They accepted Vilar's offer and for the next 17 years the summer theater festival fulfilled his vision of offering productions of work and styles not seen in Paris in order to capture a young, fresh audience, to "renew theater and collective forms of art by providing a more open space ... to give a breath of fresh air to an art form that is stifling in waiting rooms, in cellars, in salons; to reconcile architecture with dramatic poetry," as he wrote at the time.

Vilar organized a group of actors who performed in the great courtyard in unusually staged plays that attracted a growing audience and renown. Gérard Philip, Charles Denner, Jeanne Moreau, Alain Cuny, Maria Casarès, Georges Wilson and many others lighted the summer stage with brilliant acting under Vilar's direction. In 1963 he began to expand the festival to include new venues and he brought in other directors and expanded the types of disciplines to include musical performances, ballet, and the cinema to fill the extended schedule now set for several weeks rather than the original one. The generational and other conflicts that tore the nation apart in the spring and summer of 1968 did not bypass the festival; Vilar found himself in the center of a storm created by young directors, writers and actors who knew less what they wanted than what they did not want at all. The festival's founder, who had always considered himself to be open to new, different ideas and concepts, suffered from the relentless attacks of the younger enrages, and never truly recovered, dying in 1971 of a heart attack. He is buried in the large hill-side cemetery in the coastal port of Sête close to the grave of the great poet Paul Valéry.

On the last day of July 1983 we sat in the overflow audience in the great courtyard to experience a flawed dance performance by the Tanztheater Wupperthal in an "avant-garde" piece entitled *"Tanzabend: Nelken,"* choreographed by the often controversial Pina Bausch. The group performed the work on a raised stage filled with plastic *Nelken* (carnations) from Bangkok. I described it at the time in these words: "A loose, sprawling piece with little dancing, each scene drawn out way beyond its limits – a series of children's nightmares full of shouting, violence, bureaucratic repression, authoritarian sadism and lots of jumping around. One and a half hours should have been cut out of it and the remaining, compressed, ideas would have worked better." I do remember even now all the jumping and running around the stage, but I have no recollection at all of what sounds, music or otherwise, accompanied the physical exertions.[47]

Many years later, in the late 1990s we attended the only other performance we've seen in the great courtyard: Euripides' *Medea* in French with the lovely Isabel Huppert in the title role. Two problems marred the experience for us, especially me: the unspeakable, uninterrupted length of the damn thing, and the location of our seats. The fact that a chilly mistral blew down the Rhône Valley, apparently did not bother those in the audience with seats close to the stage level, but those of us perched way up in the last row of the towering, and slightly swaying, structure that served as the cheap seats, experienced the situation quite differently. Some of us up there closer to heaven spent more time and energy

---

[47] Pina Bausch died of cancer at the age of 68 in Wupperthal on June 30, 2009.

fighting vertigo and holding onto the wooden benches for dear life than attending to the theatrics far below. The fact that I could only understand every 20th word in the script did not contribute to my enjoyment of the play either. An unusual experience, no doubt, but not an entirely pleasant one. Fortunately we had read the play in English the day before so we were not completely lost in that regard.

Over the last two decades the Festival d'Avignon has consisted of two parts, the "In" (the official state supported events) and the "Off" (the "fringe" events scattered all around the town in all kinds of venues inside the ramparts). There are now more of the latter than the former and some of them have been quite charming and less expensive. I well recall during one of our almost annual visits to Avignon and environs sitting in a narrow space in a building on the rue de Teinturiers listening to a singer imitating Serge Reggiani singing all his hit songs so well that if one closed one's eyes one could readily imagine the real Regianni actually standing there. A dazzling performance, but of course I cannot remember the fellow's name. Alas.

●

While that summer brought with it the elegant joys of warmth and sunshine, it also became a time of some long-lasting sadness at the inevitable departure of many of the friends we'd made since winter. At the end of June I noted in the journal, "We're just a way station here." Good title for a C & W song!" The sabbaticals ended

Blair's father Ken, LM and Karlheinz at the Ferme Jamet.

Sylvie and LM aboard Sylvie's barge on the river.

Ute, Angelika, Benjamin, LM and Wolfgang at the Bambouserie in Anduze.

LM, Jim and Moira in front of the hotel.

At the St.-Paul-de-Mausole asylum outside St.-Rémy-de-Provence;
thieves stole the bust a decade ago.

At the by-now terribly familiar Pont du Gard.

Karin, Mary, author, and Denis at one of the many meals at this table.

The "Algerian" and LM in conversation.

The author at the Fondation Maeght in Saint-Paul de Vence.

LM and Christine in St. Tropez.

The entrance to Douglas Cooper's villa, le Château de Castille, a fabled residence in the history of 20th century art.

Claudia and Stan on the Uzès wall at lunch.

Baudelaire and Shy Cat on the terrace.

The author at Daudet's windmill.

LM and Brewster at the old Avignon railroad station seeing
the Williams off; another farewell in a season of farewells.
(Photograph by Jean Williams)

and our friends returned to their non-French lives; not all of our friends of course since some of them lived in the area, but those to whom we had become close: the Williams, Mary, Karin ... they all slipped away one after another. Visits by friends from abroad partially filled the gaps they left in our life, but living there could not be the same without them. At the end of June we put Mary on the train for Paris and Karin on another train for Germany. We had already put Jean, Blair, Matt and Ben on the train north where they would spend several days barging up and down several rivers before flying back to Montreal. These departures increased our sense of melancholy at the thought of our own eventual departure, which we knew would be in November at some point because our funds would be expended by then, unless we could find other sources of income. In June, we half believed we would be able to do this.

Chapter VIII

Paris Interlude: August

We had long planned to drive to Paris in early August to meet our friends Moira Egan and Jim Vore whom LM had known from her NEH days. From there we would drive leisurely through the Loire Valley eating well and visiting castles as we made our way south to Tavel. LM and I arrived in the City of Light after an uneventful trip pleasantly interrupted by a picnic lunch in a small, rustic rest area on the highway, and made our way from the Port d'Orléans to the Grand Hôtel des Étrangers, which had become our regular Paris residence due to its location and affordable prices. After two days of wandering around the squares and streets, visiting museums and bookstores and generally having a quiet good time, we drove to de Gaulle airport early the following day to gather up our friends.

On the way to the airport we noticed something wrong with the car, as if we drove over a series of bumps in the road, and thought it might be the right *front* tire which needed air. The plane was not unexpectedly late and the temporary loss of Jim's luggage caused an additional 40 minutes of waiting before we left for the hotel. On the road back into the city we filled the tire, which did not appreciably alter the situation, and decided not to think about it until we left for the south. After checking them into the hotel we walked to the nearby corner of the boulevard Saint-Michel and the boulevard Saint-Germain where we sat on the terrace of the Café de Cluny for a long, relaxed breakfast/lunch of eggs, *pommes frites* and cool beer. Jim's taste in vodka mixed with grapefruit remains in the mind if for no other reason than the look on the waiter's face when he ordered this barbarous concoction: astonishment coupled with interest bordering on curiosity combined with a vague thought that he ought to have felt a form of contempt for this American aberration, but didn't. After a brief pause, during which he ostentatiously looked at his watch, he served Jim his distinctly un-French libation.

Several events stand out in the memory of this visit: an extensive "Bonjour, Monsieur Manet" exhibition at the egregious Centre Pompidou, an exhibit of Dalí prints and lithographs in his former suite at the Hôtel Meurice on the rue de Rivoli, a failed attempt to gain access to the bar at the Hôtel Ritz, a literary walk following more or less the walk described in Hemingway's *The Sun Also Rises*, several meals of varying quality, another river trip on a boat without a WC (fortunately the trip was short) and the theft of my wallet from my shoulder bag on the métro after dinner on our final night in the city.

When we left the Meurice we decided to have a drink at the Ritz bar where LM and I had imbibed some expensive scotch the first day of the New Year. Dressed in our summer duds we approached the place Vendôme entrance intending to walk through the corridor to the saloon on the rue Cambon side of the building. As we neared the few steps leading into the palatial edifice a

305

young hotel flunky, smartly dressed in the hotel uniform, strode quickly toward us and asked if we had rooms there. Well, either the men had rooms there, or they wore ties, neither of which conditions met our pocket books or sartorial accoutrements. So we did not have a drink at the Ritz bar.[48]

The literary walk began at the Panthéon and wound its way down the rue du Cardinal Lemoine past the place de la Contrescarpe (where the police picked up a clochard suffering from what appeared to be a massive case of the DTs), through the Jardin du Luxembourg, down the rue de Fleurus and the rue Nôtre-Dame-des-Champs to the Closerie des Lilas at which in the 1920s a not-quite-poverty-stricken writer could afford a glass or two of beer whilst scratching away in a blue French school kid's notebook drafts of some of the great short stories in the English language. No longer, alas, but we sat under the protective statue of Marshal Ney and his drawn sword facing an abominable construction of glass and metal housing an insurance company across the square. Poor Ney; he has seen so much from his stone pedestal. The beer was (and is) very expensive but the toilets are very good indeed. Down the boulevard du Montparnasse past the boulevard Raspail we found the Le Select, a café known as one of the places where expatriate writers and artists, and the inevitable tourists, gathered. An English-language Parisian magazine, the no longer extant *Passion*, named the croque-monsieur sandwich at the Select the best in Paris; after we'd

---

[48] For a more detailed, and one hopes amusing, narrative of this event, see *Paris Now and Then*, 34-35.

consumed four of them we could not quarrel with that judgment.

Anywhere one spends time eating out has good and not so good and downright bad eateries and we've had our share of all of them. On this trip we experienced the first two categories. At the brasserie called Le Nouveau Siècle, the service was terrible, Moira's food was a disaster and Jim's only fractionally less so after he sent the blue steak back to the kitchen to be cooked. LM and I ate well that evening, though I cannot recall what and the sources give no hint. In the neighborhood of the Hôtel Georges V, where six Rolls Royces belonging to uncounted oil-Arabs in flowing robes and headpieces rolling out barrels of cash parked helter-skelter in the street, we found a comfortable restaurant with excellent food and horrid music turned up too loud. The management claimed it could not turn the crappy sounds down or off, which these days would cause us to get up and leave, but then we put up with it. Why even elegant and expensive eateries think disruptive music must accompany the meal is a question with only two answers: one, managements believe people have nothing to say to each other so must have white noise to distract them from their discomforts and discontents, which is of course sheer stupidity, and two, managements are airheads with nothing to say to their own dinner partners and thus welcome the distraction.

On the métro back to the hotel a racially integrated trio of thieves removed my wallet from my shoulder bag whilst we laughed with gusto at Jim's Polish joke. Warsaw's retribution, perhaps. The operation is rather

307

simple in execution if the thieves have made the appropriate choice of a victim: a happy individual in a small group laughing after a well-watered meal paying close attention to his or her friends and standing close to the doors. Then you wait until the train is slowing down for the stop jostling the passengers, reach through the false bottom of the large bag on your shoulder, quickly unzip the victim's shoulder bag and swiftly with practiced fingers extract what feels like a wallet. The train has stopped and the doors slide open; LM looks over my shoulder and says, "What's going on there?" The wallet-holding thief slips quickly out the door amidst the unsuspecting, milling about passengers whilst his two colleagues block the exit for the few seconds before the doors slide shut and they are away with the loot.

The "take" in this case was probably of little use to the thugs: the wallet contained no money except for a lucky five mark German coin, but they did make off with my *carte de séjour* and Washington DC driver's license, which would extend the bureaucratic hassle in Tavel when I tried to replace the former document. Now that I think about it, perhaps they could have sold the documents to a forger for a certain amount of cash; the forger would have doctored the papers to fit an order made by a professional assassin who needed cover identification pieces for his next assignment. We sat in a café across the Boul' Mich' from the hotel, drank a Calvados and smoked a final cigarette of the evening, said the hell with it, and went to bed.

The following day we drove to Versailles, which was so crowded Moira and Jim only saw the gardens. The car was clearly in trouble and on the road to Chartres the *rear* right tire almost blew out and the car began to drink water at an incredible rate making me think it should be taken to a vet or somewhere for an evaluation. Fortunately, a young mechanic at a gas station in a field just off the road said he'd change the tire and fill the radiator but after lunch. We picnicked on the grass beside the station until 14.00 hours when the mechanic reopened the garage and accomplished what he had promised.

One of the best restaurant meals ever to pass my lips we ate one night at The Inn of Little Washington, Virginia: American nouvelle cuisine and magnificent; also outrageously expensive. On the 9th of August 1983, coming from Chartres we drove the ailing motor car into the small town of Cloyes-sur-le-Loir, situated on a minor tributary of the great Loire River to stay overnight at the Hostellerie Saint-Jacques, about which we knew next to nothing except what LM had read in the Michelin red guide: a decent hotel with a restaurant. Actually we were very much looking forward to the following night in Valençay at the Hôtel d'Espagne because the Michelin gave its restaurant one of its coveted stars.

The Saint-Jacques sits on the main street of the town through which truck after even larger truck roared in a constant stream of noise and gaseous emissions to affront the nostril and ears. We tremulously thought: what by the wooden leg of the ancient vintner have we done? The following paragraphs, written for an unpublished narrative, tell the story of what we had done.

What makes a memorable meal? One that is clearly remembered years later, of course, but what makes the

309

meal memorable? The excellence and tastes of the food, yes, but the element of the unexpected, the smile evoking delight in surprise, the sudden appearance of Yves Montand on the terrace of the Colombe d'Or, and the ambience (a much abused word these days) of the environment also play an important role; this too is what is remembered. Does one even have to mention the behavior and attitude of the attendant serving personnel?

Coming upon a pile of old pocket notebooks evokes a variety of images and provides memories both vague and concrete, recalling times spent in various places with different friends and others. And how many of those noted events, in our lives at least, involve food and drink! One such small French notebook from the 1982-83 period recently emerged from such a pile as we cleaned out ancient things prior to moving into a new Key West house in November 2003, 20 years later and very much much water under the bridge and wine over the teeth. Perusing the yellowing pages of this quasi-journal, and noting how much my handwriting has changed over the years, I came upon a list of courses from what we have always considered one of the truly memorable meals. Memories fade, however, and while we remembered clearly that the meal *did* take place, we had long since forgotten exactly of what it consisted. The old, tattered, wine-stained notebook brought the meal's details back in a rush.

Except the Coca-Cola; *that* we remembered.

So, on that 9th of August the four weary travelers turned the old rattletrap Peugeot through the nondescript arched gateway into the courtyard of the Hostellerie

Saint-Jacques in Cloyes-sur-le-Loir, a smallish town just south of the Loire Valley.

We had been on the road since early that morning and were tired, hot, and somewhat short of temper, but happy to finally be where we would spend the night. LM had made the reservations some time earlier on the basis of the distance from Paris and the price of the rooms. We had no idea what to expect and actually did not expect very much other than an eatable meal and a reasonably comfortable bed.

The small courtyard did not provide sufficient space for parking so we unloaded the luggage and looked around: the gravel drive evolved into a grass covered terrace with lawn furniture beyond which lay a small park that ended at the banks of the narrow river called the Loir, not to be confused with its larger sibling, the Loire. Clean and glowing in the late afternoon sun this sight and the lack of street noise perked us up somewhat. After parking the car out on street we trooped into the typically waste-no-space reception area where a friendly and efficient young man gave us the keys to our rooms and informed us that we could have our dinner at 7:30 in the dining room if we wished to eat there. Having little energy to face the prospect of finding a restaurant on our own, we decided to accept the offer.

Accompanied by a young apprentice lackey, we carried the luggage to our rooms on the third and highest floor of this country style inn, leaving the doors open so we could freely communicate at what time we wished to have a drink on the terrace and walk down to the river. Now, in order to fully appreciate what happened next one must know that our good friend Jim had, at that time, a penchant for slaking his thirst with large quantities of Coca-Cola, a beverage in short supply in small town inns in the French countryside in those ancient days. In the final hours of our drive to Cloyes we had kept our eyes open to the possibility of espying a sign with the familiar logo announcing the presence and sale of the sweet bubbly; to no avail, a fact loudly and persistently lamented by Jim who soon began to mumble grave insinuations against the French policy of denying him the energy surge he required from this eminently American drink. The last word on the subject from him as we drove into town sounded suspiciously like, "The bloody hotel won't have any either."

So one can imagine the tone of voice in which he loudly proclaimed the presence of the soda pop in the room's minuscule refrigerator, the unexpected fulfillment of an oft-expressed wish and the silken bellow of satisfaction, "Gawd*damn!*" The young apprentice was a bit taken aback at this roar of pleasure emitted at the sight of such well-stocked ice-boxes. In fact, small inns in France did not normally provide this amenity; that is, a refrigerator in the rooms in which one might or might not discover cold soft or hard drinks. This one did, to everyone's satisfaction: Jim's joy could not but be shared by all of us; that is to say he enjoyed the Coke, we shared his joy, but we drank the cool beer from the mini-fridge. Indeed, the rooms themselves were well-stocked: the establishment also provided a large can of Raid and a screen for the window, the latter not in the window but leaning against the wall should it be needed. We needed neither of these mod-cons, but the Raid was a nice touch, very bourgeois, very part of the experience.

As a consequence, by the time we descended to the ground floor and walked out into the garden by the river we experienced no surprise at the wondrous sunset over the low plain flowing on from the other side of the waterway into the misty French distance. We had a glass of pastis (in honor of our destination in Provence, the ancient land of this anise-flavored schnapps) as we walked around the garden landscape, a far cry from the earlier experience with Jim's order of vodka and grapefruit juice in Paris. The maitre d' brought our drinks and a plate of phyllo-dough wrapped and baked cheese things on which to nibble whilst we perused the menu and asked him about the fish of the day and other menu items. The one reason we would have at that point entertained a niggling doubt about our choice of restaurants was the young man's inability to name the fish; in addition we needed a pair of heavy-duty pliers to pry much of any information about the menu from him. Polite, charming, handsome, yes, but much too ignorant about the menu.

All this is, of course, prelude to the meal itself. The scratchy handwritten words in the battered Heracles notebook (*cahiers scholaires*) give a bare but exact listing of what we ate and drank. Many literary critics deride the notion of lists in books; they view them as unnecessary filler, but those of us who appreciate idiosyncratic literature unburdened by critical theory feel deep emotions at coming across lists of oddments and other items of possible interest.

This particular text should excite the salivary glands as it satisfies the desire to read down an annotated list of what four people ate at one point in their (still) young lives in the home of great, if occasionally over-elaborate cuisine.

Seated formally at table by an attentive waiter in the high-ceilinged, darkwood paneled dining room with the tables set at a comfortable distance from one another, we finished looking through the menu and prepared to order. I can no longer remember whether English translations were appended to the items listed, but somehow I doubt it. Nonetheless we had little difficulty in comprehending the contents of the list, especially after we all agreed to order the 90 franc fixed price meal. With another round of drinks came another small plate covered with warm cheese wrapped in phylo-dough pastry and a second small platter containing a paté of fowl livers studded with raisins accompanied by rounds of toasted dark bread containing fragments of berries. On the house. We collectively began to feel, not think, *feel*, that this meal would be rather special.

And indeed of course it would be so.

The following in inverted commas are the phrases I wrote down in that old stained notebook. The rest is commentary composed for this fugitive piece of culinary memory.

"Salade de pintade aux choux verts tièdes (Jim and Moira)"

"Foie de pintade (LM and B) with julienned vegetables and a soy sauce vinaigrette," which we

314

watered well with a bottle of Cheverny sauvignon blanc, vintage 1982.

"Poitrine de pintade à la poire with small turnips and carrots (Jim and B)"

"Blanquette de poissons au fumet de moules (a leek mousse, white fish, and large sardines in a sauce (LM & Moira)"

The Cheverny having done so well with the first course, we decided to allow it to charm us during the second course as well.

"Fromage (extra charge for Jim's pear)." By the time we reached this point we had made a nice dent in the third bottle of the 1982 nectar and what a good year that was for this excellent wine! (I think I can speak for all of us, even after all these years, when I say that we've never tasted wine from this vineyard again. Alas. Ah, but what a memory!)

"Glace ou pâtisseries." Knowing the French we probably did not have coffee with these desserts, but no doubt finished the wine with them.

When the "café" did arrive, "chocolate truffles and swan pastries" sweetly, finely and fittingly accompanied it. On the house. We topped the two-and-a-half hour meal off with a round of cognac and needless to say slept soundly that night. The meal eclipsed that at the Inn in Little Washington without question, as excellent as that one had been.

The next day we drove on to Valençay where we had booked rooms in a hotel that housed a restaurant with a Michelin star where we intended to indulge ourselves that evening at what we had anticipated would be the culinary highlight of the trip. However, the meal the previous night had been so memorable that not even a starred restaurant could top it, especially one with no choice of food: the menu contained one first course, one second course and a dessert course, no choice and the meat was roasted chicken at 150 francs a piece. So we walked around the corner where we ate a typical French supper in a typical small French mom and pop bistro for 42 francs each, kidneys, snails, baked tomatoes, fish, mayonaisse and dessert, plus a couple of carafes of local wine and remained uplifted and happy.

Michelin awarded the Hostellerie St.-Jacques a star the following year, an act we unhesitatingly supported and roundly cheered.

We did not cheer when we looked into the 1996 edition of the guide to find no star next to the hotel's entry and felt saddened when the entry itself disappeared from the 2006 edition. Fortuna in the form of Bacchus or Dionysus had smiled upon us at the right moment. As one of the ancients has written,

> The wine of Dionysus,
> When the weary cares of men
> Leave every heart.
> We travel to a land that never was.
> The poor grow rich, the rich grow great
>   of heart.
> All-conquering are the shafts made
> from the Vine.

The following day rain fell heavily from Valençay to Orange, but not in Tavel which hadn't seen rain for two months. Valençay's castle sits amidst well kept grounds full of peacocks, ducks, parrots, goats, dogs, cats, and on that day, very few tourists. One can also visit the local automobile museum, which lack of time precluded our accomplishing, and the castle opened late that day so we only walked around the grounds. The inclement weather prevented a planned picnic. So outside Orange we stopped for a dry sandwich and glass of beer for lunch in a village café we shared with a silent figure who slumped in his chair, head face down on the table, a small glass half filled with what appeared to be red wine, of which the fellow clearly had imbibed too much. Just after we paid the bill the drunk (we thought of him as a mechanic, why and what kind remains a mystery) shoved himself up into a sitting position, jammed the last piece of baguette on the table into the glass of wine and ate it with a spoon. Memories differ on events in the past, but Jim insists the shabby fellow threw up on the table and we moved outside to finish our meal. The rest of us have no memory of this. We all agree we'd had more pleasant lunches.

The car began to cook despite the heavy rain, drinking a liter of water every 100 kilometers. In Orange we filled the radiator and that sufficed to get us to the house in Tavel where the sky remained light enough for our guests to appreciate the view from our terrace where we sat until 10 o'clock enjoying a glass of rosé and chatting as we smoked the Kent cigarettes they had kindly brought with them. (It must be stated that the very intelligent Moira did not smoke the nasty stuff.) They also provided us with a supply of Excedrin for headaches and hangovers, Cheese Whiz (!) and a half-dozen books: Christmas in August.

In the course of the following week we took them to the usual sites and restaurants, by now familiar excursions to us but not to them. No matter how often we visited these places the satisfaction of showing them to friends for the first time never diminished and we enjoyed the trips as much as they did: the marvelous vista of the Pont du Gard before the destructive renovation and development of the site, the Roman ruins and the institution at St.-Paul-de-Mausole where Van Gogh found refuge for his worst manic depressive stage outside Saint Rémy-de-Provence, and Maillane, the village where the poet Mistral lived for most of his adult life.

We had previously been to this small town of approximately 1700 inhabitants seven kilometers northwest of St.-Rémy and ten south of Avignon, to look into Mistral's house in which he lived from 1876 when he married until his death in 1914, now a museum, and to search for his grave in the local cemetery on the edge of the village. We had not found the latter and the former was always closed for some reason. Frédéric Mistral studied law for a year in Aix-en-Provence (1851) but found the Provençal language and culture far more fascinating than the dry provisions of the *Code Napoléon*, as a result of which he returned to Maillane and devoted the rest of his life to studying and writing epic poems and prose pieces in that language retelling in dramatic form the myths and legends of the region. He also composed a

Provençal-French dictionary and co-founded the organization called Les Félibriges intended to revitalize the language and culture. In this heart-felt attempt at reconstitution, the members, many of whom were fine poets, failed, and today their works are known if at all only in French translations. Some of Mistral's more popular poems have been translated into English with varying degrees of success.[49] Although he won the Nobel Prize for Literature in 1914 (shared with a today totally unknown and even then obscure Spanish novelist), the money from which he used to establish the Provençal Museum in Arles, the notion of his failure to resuscitate his Provençal heritage darkened his later years.

But as the English poet Roy Campbell wrote in his poem "Félibrige":

> To sit with Mistral under the green laurels
> From which his children gathered me my
>   crown,
> While the deep red wine that is the end of
>   quarrels
> Glows through me like the sunset going
>   down.

So one fine warm and sunny day we made our pilgrimage to Maillane to see if the door to the house would open for us this time, and it did and we wandered about the rooms that had been left as they had been the

---

[49] For a fine, readable overview of Mistral's life and work, as well as the history of the Félibrige movement, see Richard Aldington's *An Introduction to Mistral* (1956).

day the old man died at 83 years of age. Each hagiographic room resembled a religious shrine, as the estate managers intended, devoted to the memory and memorialization of the now legendary poet of the deep and lost past culture of Provence. The atmosphere could accurately be called stuffy, as if the windows overlooking the garden had not been opened in years, which may in fact have been the case. We did enjoy the well-kept garden around the house, though nothing spectacular jumped out at one; it rested the soul with its dense silence broken only by the occasional cock crowing and cicada snapping. And finally we located his tomb, which he had copied from Queen Jeanne's mausoleum near Les Baux.

Soon the time had come for Moira and Jim to move on to the next step of their European sojourn that summer.

Lashings of rain pummeled the Old Port in Marseille as we ate a hearty, well-watered bouillabaisse before going to a hotel for an hour or so sleep before we took our friends to the old railway station and their overcrowded train to Italy along the Mediterranean coast, where they would spend two weeks in Florence, Pisa and Rome.

A day later they called from Florence to allay our fears of a terrible disaster on the terribly overcrowded train full of loud backpackers and heat. After searching for their seats they discovered them occupied by unauthorized persons of dubious reputation and asked the conductor to eject them, which he did and they sat and dozed for the rest of the trip to the city on the Arno.

Chapter IX

The Writing Life

A writer must have the equipment with which to put the everlasting words of genius down on paper. Pen and pencil will do as they have since they were invented, but the typewriter had by the early years of the 20th century become the major means of word placement on paper, even Henry James dictated his late novels to a typist. This is not to say all writers typed their manuscripts, they did not; as the example of Hemingway shows some wrote the full first draft by hand, and Joyce never learned to typewrite until late in life and then decided he could not work with the machine, saying something along the line of "I need to feel the impulses flow through my arm and fist into the pen then onto the paper." Why we lugged a rather large electric typewriter from Washington to France (along with the necessary apparatus to transform the electricity from European current to the American, which for some obscure and no doubt unreasonable reason are different) will forever be a subject of skeptical speculation in our house.

Fortunately Mrs. Potter kept an old, battered but functioning Smith-Corona manual machine in the Apt house because the transformer at first refused to transform: too weak to power the electric machine, or so we thought. Consequently, the notes for various projects, letters and short pieces I wrote in Apt I did either by hand or on Mrs. Potter's machine.

In our baggage shipped from Washington lay a lengthy manuscript of a novel I'd written over the previous 18 months about Allied military government cultural affairs officers in 1945-46 Berlin, the politics of inter-allied rivalries in their work to control the revival of music, the theater, newspapers and the like, and the cultural life of the city the Nazis had violently and in many cases terminally repressed. Not to forget the sex in that desolate city at the crossroads of the postwar chaos that was Europe. Having been so closely involved with the written records of the American military government in Germany for five years I could have written another academic study of the period – and indeed had written several such essays and edited a book about cultural conditions in the city – but this no longer appealed to me. I wished to return to my original intent to be a writer of novels, poems, plays and film scripts – O yes – a desire repressed for various reasons for 15 years. So, using that archival material for background texture and ambience I began writing a novel and finished the first long draft in the summer of the year we moved to France. In the process I discovered that I had so much material in hand that one volume would not be enough into which to stuff it all: additional volumes would be needed. After all, I thought, why not? Had not Durrell achieved a grand success with both critics and book buyers with his *The Alexandria Quartet*? Had not Paul Scott done the same with his *Raj Quartet*? And what of Thomas Mann's

Joseph tetralogy? I'd need a trilogy to do justice to my material and story.

So, one of the reasons for coming to France was to write the second volume, and outline the third if time allowed before we ran out of funds. With the first draft of "Schade's Passage" finished at Bethany Beach in June of 1982; I'd now write the first draft of "Schadow's Meditations" in the south of France while we attempted to sell "Schade" (with revisions of course) to a mainstream New York publisher, who no doubt would offer a large enough advance on the books to allow us to remain in France to write the entire work, buy a small house with a garden, buy a motorcar that worked well, and settle in to the writing life. LM would surely find interesting employment teaching English and gardening and consulting at a distance with sufficiently interested organizations in the USA or London or Paris. (It should be kept in mind that those were the days of the typewriter, telegraph and telephone; personal computers, the Internet and email did not exist.) None of this happened, at the time, despite the valiant efforts of our friend Peggy Monahan in Washington who acted as my typist and part time agent. But other things certainly did.

The Reader will understand more easily what follows if given a few words about the nature of the two volumes in question here.

The title of the first refers to one of the prominent protagonists of the book, John Schade (pronounced "Schahduh", formerly Johannes Schadlerberg), a young man whose Social Democratic family the Nazis forced out of Germany in the mid-1930s, who returns there in the summer of 1945 as a cultural affairs control officer in the US Army's military government to participate in the denazification and reconstruction of Berlin cultural life. During his sojourn in the former German capital he is compelled to reconcile the experience of exile, leftist political leanings, and his precipitous affair with an intensely conflicted German actress (against the non-fraternization edict) with the political and moral necessity of both punishing and rebuilding Germany in cooperation with America's Allies.

On the most immediate level the book is the story of Schade's passage through various experiences to a stage of emotional and mental maturity by way of his complex relationships to his job, the city and its vital position in the immediate postwar world, the city's grasping for survival and renewal from a position of almost total prostration, and most importantly through his interaction with the people he meets, especially the actress, Gisela Albrecht, with whom he suffers a fractured love relationship.

The political disputes among the Allies, specifically between the Soviet Union and the United States, which came to dominate the city in the years following 1945, are expressed both directly and obliquely through the characters, e.g., Schade, his hawkish Minnesota-born colleague William Makepeace, their Russian, British, and French counterparts in cultural affairs, and the Germans whom they are to purge of their Nazi pasts. At the same time, everyone in Berlin is influenced to some degree by the policies and behavior of the Allies, and they react according to their circumstances and personalities. This is particularly true of the Berliners who require permissions and licenses from various Allied agencies in order to work (newspaper reporters and publishers; theater, film and music artists and administrators, and the like), several of whom are major characters in the novel, which is written in the third person.

A variety of other characters populate this and the succeeding volumes, including communist cultural functionaries; German academics, businessmen and politicians of different political leanings; Zionist organizers of the passage to Palestine (*Alliya*) in conflict with those Jews who argue for the recreation of European Jewish life and culture; and various historical personages who appear either as themselves or with altered personalities under different names (e.g., the poet W. H. Auden, the anti-fascist dramatist-activist Ernst Toller, General Lucius Clay and other ranking military government officers, and characters loosely based on the German Fauvist painter Oskar Moll and the American Ambassador in Moscow during the war, W. A. Harriman).

"Schadow's Meditations", as I thought of it then, would exist in four voices. The first is the old historian and former professor ordinarius Emil Schadow, a liberal democrat whom the Nazis dismissed from his position at the Berlin University in 1933 and who appears briefly in "Schade's Passage". He spends the last several years of his life (he dies in the summer of 1947) writing down fragments containing his thoughts about his life, the lives of his friends and enemies, and the recent history of his country, including his views on some of the characters and events in volume I.

Second, Schade has been demobbed and has returned to New York where he writes a novel about the fate of German exiles much like his own family and begins a second novel based on his experiences in Berlin. His friend and former colleague Makepeace (the third voice) sends him Schadow's manuscript along with his own comments on sections of it, to which Schade adds his own responses. Somewhat later Makepeace sends him a copy of the diary kept by Schadow's lover Helga Opladen (the fourth voice) from the period 1909-1919 presenting a different view of their affair from that described by Schadow. These are the four voices of "Schadow's Meditations".[50]

Throughout the year I admonished myself to work longer and harder, promising to smoke, eat and drink less, walk in the countryside more often, eternally planning to read more French with the help of the dictionary. I also occasionally jotted down comments on

---

[50] It might be of some interest, though not germane to this memoir, to know that many years later I reorganized the material in the second volume, creating two volumes by severely reducing the Schade and Makepeace comments on the Schadow and Helga material and shifting them to a third volume that is devoted to a much more detailed portrait of Schade, in the first person, and his life in Key West where he has gone to live cheaply and finish his second novel, introducing new characters and bringing back others from the previous two volumes. The fourth, and thus far final, volume returns to the third person and follows Schade back to Berlin during the Soviet blockade of the city and includes a bit about the foundation of Israel. Volume III is two-thirds finished; volume IV exists in scattered notes awaiting attention, which both will receive when this memoir is completed.

other writers' working methods thinking I might learn something useful from this exercise.

By mid-November in Tavel we finally got the clunky old American electric typewriter set up in the living and dining room *cum* studio: with some encouragement the transformer performed its mission, though on the coldest of winter days the machine had to be turned on 30 minutes before using it to warm it up to maximum efficiency. At the beginning of our time in Tavel we had a light problem, appropriately enough for that land of sun and light: as long as the sun blessed us with its brightness I could work at the table, but with the fall of darkness I could not see clearly enough to read or write. Well-lit rooms did not qualify as necessities in European houses at the time so that, except for a weak overhead light covered by an ancient dusty shade, no such other fixtures adorned the walls or tables. We soon fixed this problem with the purchase of several clip on lamps of various sizes; the largest of them with the long crane adjustable neck served perfectly well to light the table. Presumably these lamps also lie moldering in the garage with the rest of our goods.

In early December I wrote a synopsis of "Schade's Passage" to send to publishers as well as an outline of the story which did not make much sense and I didn't use it: the book has no traditional narrative development, thus it was difficult to outline it. (As isolated as I was from the literary centers of the civilized world, I could not have known whether or not such lack of traditional structure in a novel had become acceptable.) Work on "Schadow's

Meditations" moved ahead slowly and as early as mid-December I began to feel the pressure of time.

Journal entry, December 10, 1982:

Did a couple of water colors as Christmas presents – very primitive but perhaps will improve with practice and a better quality brush. Much more satisfactory than writing letters when the creative juices dry up and the novel does not move. Much more reading involved for vol. II than I anticipated and the structure is going to be difficult to deal with. Hard to say at the moment where it is going but time is running away from me. Would like to have it done in rough draft by the end of January.

A short time later, Andreas Meyer wrote from Hamburg asking for a 30 page sample of "Schade's Passage" which he thought he might be able to publish if a book club or a large newspaper bought the reprint rights. This raised my spirits for a moment or two until I realized that a translation into German would be required, and without a previous American or British publication what German publisher would fund both the translation and the publication costs? The question could only be answered in the negative and so it was.

Journal entry, December 21:

The days pile up like kindling and Schadow does not get any forrader except in small pieces. Too many

> interruptions and an odd lack of energy – nonetheless
> the notes pile up with the days and parts of it are taking
> shape. The problem is the thing as a whole has not
> come into focus, it remains as yet in parts.

The problem of the whole and its parts remained unresolved until many years later, but as time moved on in Tavel the parts themselves became clearer, which at a later time allowed their integration in a form that corresponded to Schadow's own mind as he wrote down his meditations on his life and times, not in a linear, chronological fashion, but spasmodically when something reminded him of a person or event in his past. I hoped that all these pieces would cohere at the end in a full-blown portrait of the man and the history he lived through.

For half the time in Tavel, the first priorities remained finding a publisher for Schade and writing Schadow; both proved to be recalcitrant and occasionally resistant to progress. What I had not considered seriously enough was the fact that writing the second volume would mean revisions in the first. I also admonished myself to be cautious when using historical figures as the basis for characters in the book. I thought I'd done well enough disguising (or deforming) real people in volume I. Only three persons appear briefly under their real names: General Clay, the head of the US occupation forces, the poet and bomb surveyor W. H. Auden, and Kenneth Faris, a deceased writer friend of mine from my time working for New York University at the end of the 1950s. All the others are fiction or fictionalized figures no one would think to connect to their real-life counterparts in any case.

While we still lived in Apt, Eugène Fidler suggested we write to his old friend Laurence Wylie, author of the seminal sociological study of a French village, *Village in the Vaucluse*, for advice on publishing "Schade's Passage", but I wanted to wait until we had a permanent address. And I never did write – what use would it have done? Wylie's expertise dealt with French rural life, not the shattered cities of the former Third Reich in 1945. In retrospect this was foolish and I've ever since regretted not writing to him. (Many years later we did have a drink in his house when the current owners, the French biographer and journalist Jean Lacouture and his lovely wife invited us for a post-luncheon sherry after a meal at the Fidlers. The view from the terrace is magnificent, balancing the fact that the front rooms of the house are practically unusable during the extremely noisy high tourist season.)

Journal entry, February 19:

Yasushi Inone, Japan's greatest living writer according to Donald Ritchie, did not begin writing in "earnest" until he was 40, but he'd written journalism for the years before that. (Seems to have had no trouble getting his stuff published.)

I began collecting examples of successful writers who started writing or publishing late in their lives and from time to time these exemplars reinforced my hope that I would join their august company. William Burroughs published his first novel just before he turned 40, Julio Gonzálas worked full time at the writing trade only after 50, Emily Dickinson's fame is of the posthumous variety but that was (and is) too late for me, Colette published *Chéri* at 47, Henry Miller *Tropic of Cancer* at 43, and Wallace Stevens published his first book of poems at 43. On the other hand, Stephen Crane died at 28, Rimbaud abandoned writing at 19 and turned to gun-running and other business ventures in Abyssinia, Raymond Radiguet died of typhoid at 20 in the same year as his *Le Diable au corps* was published (1923). I also reminded myself that I had been seriously if not full-time writing poems, stories and novels since the age of 18, but, except for a privately printed limited edition (*Hiatus 1959*), several individual poems and some college journalism, I had not published any of this.

Toward the end of January, in response to an inquiry supported by a letter from my old friend Peter Clark, a former employee of his publishing house, Roger Straus of Farrar, Straus and Giroux sent a note asking to see the full manuscript of "Schade's Passage". Fortunately Peggy had just sent the final corrected pages of the book, but unfortunately had not retained a copy herself, which meant the only copy existed in Tavel and that one I intended to send to a London agent. Making a photocopy of a 700 page manuscript in Avignon seemed to me to be prohibitively expensive. Why hadn't I written one or two short novels with a limited number of odd but curiously appealing characters and an uncomplicated story line that moved directly from point A to point B? I did not send the huge manuscript to Mr. Straus; perhaps this was a grave error; perhaps not. I did send it to London.

Through my friend and mentor at the University of Maryland's History Department, Professor George Kent, I contacted an editor at the London firm of George Allen and Unwin who recommended an agent who might handle the novel. The agent asked to see the complete manuscript; he returned it with a letter saying that he would not be able to place the novel at a publisher because of the negative economic situation in the United Kingdom: only already successful novelists were being published. I did not believe that then, nor do I now. The old saw about success lying in not what one knows but who one knows is weighted with ineluctable truth.

Doubts of varying size and intensity plagued me, as they do every writer of serious intent regardless of amount of talent and size of ego. One imagines even those mega-bestselling authors must have suffered the intrusion of a shiver of doubt from time to time. Well, perhaps not those such as Robert Ludlum and the author of *Princess Daisy*, but surely even John le Carré and Agatha Christie wrestled with some form of nagging doubt that the book would not achieve the desired level of competence and reader fascination.

I wondered, for example, if Schade the character was too uninteresting and the book not well enough structured as the narrative moved back and forth among times and spaces. Not then being able to obtain a professional opinion of it bothered me, yet I did not want it to be judged as a traditional narrative structure. I had tried to make it coherent and fragmented simultaneously to express the fractured nature of the city and its inhabitants as a result of the horrid tyranny of the Nazi regime and the war itself. The first volume also needed to be sufficiently well written to interest the reader in the second and subsequent volumes. Sometimes I despaired and began to doubt my talents and the rationality of the entire project, and that rendered me debilitated and lethargic. The fact that Andreas Meyer in Hamburg could not publish the book because of its length and cost of translation into German edged me further toward the abyss of the black hole called depression.

Journal entry, March 15:

Discussed the situation of the novel with LM last night. Main point is the possibility of having to do a major rewrite of vol. I if it is accepted which would seriously affect vol. II – thus it may be wiser to hold off completing II until the status of I is clear. In the meantime I would try to write a short popular, saleable novel – a thriller of sorts perhaps expanding the Radovic short story on the basis of a clear outline and considering public taste. The fly in the soup is that the status of vol. I may never become clear. But then vol. II would not have to be written in any case. Another point to consider is whether I can abandon vol. II at this time without feeling defeated. One thing is clear: I should not have begun such a grandiose project at this point but should have written a less complex, more straightforward novel as a start. Can I do it now? Should I?

I'll try to do an outline of the Radovic story and see what evolves while plugging away at vol. II with which I am having trouble anyway: too much atmosphere and too little story line. All this is very depressing. Still, I've got a few more ideas and notes for further additions to the "Med Sketches" which may work out well.

And Schadow did move forward; the decision to recast volume I affected certain sections of volume II, clarifying their substance and function and justifying the addition of new characters while adding detail to those who appear in volume I. And by early March I had begun to polish several short prose pieces and poems and write some new ones for a slender volume I would indeed call "Mediterranean Sketches", which I figured could be published at little cost because it would not be more than 90 or 100 pages in length. I wrote to Andreas Meyer in Hamburg floating the idea of Merlin-Verlag bringing out the volume in German and English, adding literary luster to the house and some francs to our bank account. I did not really expect this idea to go anywhere given the then economic situation in the German publishing industry, but the notion was not as outlandish as it might have seemed. After all, Merlin had just published Horst Janssen's fanciful essay in three languages. I also knew this was a form of sophistry because Janssen was a well-known art and literary figure in the Federal Republic – and what was I? True, I had edited a published book and written two published essays in Germany but these had enjoyed a very limited audience of professional historians, and despite an article in Der Spiegel (similar to *Time Magazine*) about the OMGUS Project with my photograph prominently featured, I fear my name remained unknown to the reading public in that country.

Journal entry, March 31:

Reading Camus' Lyrical Essays – more like prose poems of a budding philosopher – Myth of Sisyphus clearly outlined in ideas – translation in spots obviously defective. Problems of the non-linguist – no polymorph in languages: one misses so much. If nothing else these pieces reinforce my own recent attempts at combining personal experiences with idea structures and a bit of fiction when necessary to make a point. Began this before reading Camus' essays, thank god. The idea of working out an idea in a notebook prior to beginning it in earnest is very attractive but apparently I'm not yet capable of it, as this journal shows fairly clearly. One would have to be a Nietzsche to be able to simply (?) throw stuff on paper ready to print and satisfying. Instead of all the whining as evidenced in these pages I should've been able to make even obscure remarks useable later. Perhaps sometime I may find something in here to justify the time spent writing it down. Perhaps I should concentrate for a week on water colors and go back to writing with a cleansed mind.

Journal entry, April 11:

> Kafka wrote best in one continuous stint, despairing if
> any interruption to the point of losing the atmosphere
> and continuity of the piece. This is why his longer
> works have a chopped up quality about them. Sustained
> work evidently was not often possible for him.

Various matters occupied my mind and time, mainly the
attempt to publish the first volume of the Berlin novel
and the shorter pieces I wrote throughout the year. None
of these attempts succeeded which depressed me and
occasionally drove me to the thought that I was wasting
my time. The only piece I published during our stay in
Tavel was a translation into English from the German of
a short anti-war text by the well-known graphic artist,
Horst Janssen, which a Hamburg publisher, Merlin-
Verlag, brought out in German, English and Russian with
Janssen's illustrations.[51] I received the equivalent of
$150.00 for the work and was happy to get it, though it
was but a drop of water in the desert.

    Like many writers I used the journal not only as a
record of what we did and who we met, but also as a
notebook to try out prose and poetry drafts and compose
what might be called "warm-up exercises" (writing
letters can also serve this function) before moving on to
whatever manuscript awaited attention that day. These

---

[51] Horst Janssen, *Das Pfänderspiel. Ein Tagespolitischer Seitensprung*
(Hamburg, 1983). Janssen died in August 1995 of a stroke after blinding himself
in a studio accident five years earlier, a condition from which he extricated
himself with the help of his companion Heidrun Bobeth so that he could see
enough to continue to work.

exercises consisted of trial runs, first drafts written out quickly for future reference and possible use. Occasionally one of them achieved a level of successful completion and could stand as finished or almost finished pieces. Here is an example (March 8, 1983).

Wind almost gone, air chilly, sun bright. Much warmer in Avignon than the village. Beginning to feel the isolation somewhat. It's not a bother when the work is going forward but that isn't the case at the moment. Must work harder.

The chirping of spring birds grows in volume, a pleasing background sound complex (until broken by Finette who has returned to the fold, not much wiser for her sojourn in the v illage). We must begin to think of the garden, layout and content. Tomatoes, zucchini, some herbs, lettuce. Daylight is present until after 6:30. Thoughts of the grill return. At least my cooking goes forward. Little compensation for lack of increase in the number of MS pages, however.

The sun warms the room in a rectangular block of light formed by the window through which it passes. The door to the terrace stands half open; a soft breeze nudges the faded curtain. Motor sounds from the farm equipment in the lanes below the house commingle with similar sounds from the autoroute three kilometers to the east, somehow soothing to an urban habituated ear. The cock in the courtyard next door crows four times at regular intervals rising dully above the noise of the trucks. It is 3:30 in the afternoon. Birds in the garden do not sing but chirp their pleasure at the sun and mild gray-blue sky. In the distance, Mont Ventoux is hidden behind a haze of dark white. The giant pine trees of the middle distance stand unmoving, their tall green color bleached by the thinning haze. The mimosa in the garden gleams yellow and green as the season's first bees tentatively explore the ground, not yet buzzing or entering the house. On the table in the room with the open door lie books and pages of manuscript and letters, one explaining that the manuscript is not deemed strong enough to be published at the present time. The sun warms the small of the back dimming the minor shoots of pain; but the brown coffee in the nude white cup continues to cool. A restful pause in a day full of too much convoluted thought and tensed muscles. Knowing the deceptions of this cunning Midi weather I am not convinced that spring is here.

Late that winter I realized I had to create a detailed outline for "Schadow's Meditations" in order to see where the entire project was headed. This would be difficult given the structure I'd established for it: sections of Schadow's meditations would alternate with commentary by Schade and Makepeace, these latter intended to fill in gaps in Schadow's narrative, whether avoided deliberately or simply forgotten. The commentary would also give the reader some historical context for events Schadow described. This caused difficulties because of the previous working method of building a mosaic without knowing the final form in advance. I worried about the lack of connective tissue binding the fragments together, the lack of straight narrative drive. I began to dread hearing from Peggy that all the publishers and agents to whom she had sent "Schade's Passage" had turned it down. The dark thought that I should perhaps drop the entire project crept unbidden into my mind; perhaps I should leave it, consider it an exercise in the process of learning the writing trade, and write a straightforward thriller tied to a plot and a conventional structure. I was in fact surprised these doubts and hesitations had not begun earlier. I'd been so cocky about the matter, assuming the end result would be both good *and* saleable. If I'd started out close to the other end of the spectrum, that is, with skepticism … Perhaps I should not have started my new career with such an elaborate project.

Nonetheless toward the end of February I finished what I thought was the first third of the Schadow manuscript. At this point I believed a serious re-evaluation of the project would be in order. "Time is clumping inexorably into the future and I've got to make something that will bring in some money" (February 22). All well and good, but accomplishing six to eight pages a day mobbed the novel forward and increased my meager supply of optimism that I could actually complete the enterprise. If I could tighten the story line so it no longer would flap about like a spastic fish on the dock; if I could find that missing something at the core of the story that would hold it all together, some plot line – even if it did not become entirely clear until volume III – that would bind all the varied elements into a coherent whole. And make this missing piece such that would not require major re-writing of Schade's volume. I scribbled page after page of possibilities in the notebooks, grasping at even the most outlandish plot lines, to bring about clarity in my own mind. At the end of one such screed the sentence appears: "The possibility that this is all bullshit has occurred to me." It may have occurred, but that didn't mean the occurrence was helpful.

With all these thoughts squirming frantically about in my brain, buffeting each other like a swarm of children's bumper carts, I began in mid-April to restructure the first Berlin volume by creating a detailed outline of how I now thought it should be. This required a re-reading of the manuscript and this process restored some of my faith in the entire project. Though I knew it was weak in parts, it contained many strengths and some of the passages showed good, imaginative writing. So I felt more secure in continuing work on revising "Schade's Passage" and thinking about and making notes for inclusion in "Schadow's Meditations".

In addition to which our sightseeing trips around the region continued to give me ideas for stories, essays and poems. For example, at this point in April we walked down the rue des Teinturiers in Avignon, crossed the defunct canal and entered into the dark and chilled 16th century Chapel of the Gray Penitents (Chapelle des Pénitents Gris) smelling of mold and wax with a horrifying, blood-splattered realistic wood sculpture of the nailed Christ in his final agony hanging on the wall to the left of the front doors. What could be done with a tale of a minor thief running from a fumbled attempt at stealing something on the rue de la République chased by two policemen scrambling through those doors to be faced with that twisted, grotesque, silently screaming man on the cross? The story I called "No Refuge for a Sinner"; it is one of my best. By the end of March I had typed up six or seven of the texts that became many years later the bulk of the collection *Mediterranean Sketches* published in 2005 and the collection of my poems that appeared in 2007. I am particularly fond of "Refuge" and the lyrical essay, "The Olive and the Mistral", both inspired by the Midi and written there. Patience is often rewarded if not always a virtue.

Other projects rose to the table and fell to the floor with the regularity of the seasons because not every idea can be worked out, dramatized into as coherent, rounded and complete work. Perhaps in this age of post-modern fragmentation these considerations no longer apply with the same force as they did decades earlier. At one point I had an idea for a longish story, prompted by reading Amy Oakley's book on Provence, about an elderly Englishwoman murdered in an isolated village near Les Baux that would contain a savage mistral whipping through the canyons and around the sharp edges of the blocks of limestone, a doomed love paralleling some of the troubadour/court of love myths and legends from the eerie and forbidding great hulking shapes that dominated the Val d'Enfer. From time to time over a period of weeks I researched the background in the Médiathèque Ceccano, the public library in Avignon, and made a pile of notes, but nothing in the end came of the work. I suspect there was too much superstructure and the base could not carry it easily; I tried too hard to make an overly complex structure out of a relatively simple mood/milieu piece. The notes are no doubt moldering away in the Tavel garage. At the library I also researched a project on John Stuart Mill in Avignon and a piece I thought of writing about Van Gogh in Provence, neither of which advanced beyond a pile of photocopied documents and a pile of scrawled notes, also resting in a carton in the garage, if they've not been thrown away.

●

Radovic's Dilemma

As lack of real progress on Schadow continued to bedevil me, I began to think about writing a more saleable novel, but had little idea what it could be. By the end of February a London literary agent had rejected Schade as unsaleable under the then present difficult economic conditions, as did several New York publishers (Farrar, Straus & Giroux, Dutton, etc.) "In the mental chaos of Schade being turned down I started reading *Mistral's Daughter*; unbelievable trash but the research of the area is reasonably accurate. Drivel like this sells millions of copies." (February 19 entry). The concept of a limited amount of publishing space for novels and the imbalance of blockbusters and highly paid writers taking up an immense amount of that space some of which could be devoted to new and unknown scriveners occupied my mind. This is hardly surprising since I felt myself to be one of the excluded. Not only hastily and poorly written junk like *Mistral's Daughter* being published and selling millions gnawed at my brain, but the creators of high literature (if not all the time and with every book) crossed the sights of my anger and frustration. A screed at news of Norman Mailer's contractual arrangements with his then publisher appears in the entry for April 19.

> Lengthy article on N. Mailer and review of Ancient Evenings (marvelous title). Norman needs "slightly more" than $325,000 Yankee greenbacks a year to break even. Has a $4 million deal with his publisher who sends him a check for $30,000 every month. Well. If Norman can make that kind of money who's to begrudge him, eh? The answer is many people, for various reasons. My reason is that the situation is indicative of the perverse and harmful condition of the publishing system in the USA: superstars like Norman make millions – fine – but no one else makes anything near a living wage and in order to pay for the blockbusters publishers don't publish 20 novels by unknowns who might develop into, if not blockbusters, at least reasonable sales, and whose stuff might be good. These people are no longer being published. One Norman cancels ten others who are beginning in the trade. Of course, I take a personal interest in this.

The publishing situation has changed considerably since then, but the fundamental structure remains the same. And I think Norman Mailer is one of the great 20th century American writers whose books immediately following the publication of *The Naked and the Dead*, namely *Barbary Shore* and *The Deer Park*, are better than the critics have allowed. Having been impressed by Mailer's war novel read in the old double volume in one Signet paperback edition in the early 1950s, I followed his career until the end in 2008, not reading every book he published but enough to determine that his need for cash forced him to spend time and energy on books he should have left to others (those on Picasso and Marilyn Monroe, for example). Nonetheless with his death he joins the luminous list of those writers by-passed by the Nobel Prize Literature Committee which otherwise honored such lesser figures as John Steinbeck and Toni Morrison, to mention only Americans whose work did not reach the heights of Proust, Joyce, Durrell, et alia. In part to make up for this Swedish error I have put Norman Mailer into the Berlin novel as a former mailman driving a jeep for the American cultural control officers, a reckless but reliable partner in a tight situation.

On the other hand, how many new serious writers are cancelled by one Judith Kranz or Danielle Steele?

The notion of doing a comparison of French and German travel literature written before 1914 and between the wars (à la Fussell whose *Abroad: British Literary Traveling Between the Wars*, which I'd just read) I thought might be an interesting project. The differences in what they looked for, what and how they saw things (the same things), how they judged what they saw and did – all this might expose national characteristics in a new clarifying light. However, nothing came of the idea.

A telephone conversation with Karlheinz Schwaner the day before Christmas confirmed my low opinion of the mass reading public. Having been in and on the periphery of the business in Germany and France for about 30 years he knew whereof he spoke. Pessimistic about publishing anything "literary" in Germany, saying "the world is full of cultural illiterates," he noted that no one wanted to read these days except pieces with sex and exotic action, which was exactly what he wrote and sold, and which might more accurately be called soft-core porn. And it must be said that the Germans continued to buy if not read literary works by contemporary writers such as Ingeborg Bachmann, Günter Grass, Uwe Johnson, Arno Schmidt, Max Frisch, Bertolt Brecht, Martin Walser and Christa Wolf, as well as the older authors such as Thomas Mann, Elias Canetti, Kurt Tuckolsky and Rainer Maria Rilke in addition to the usual trash. Karlheinz's view of these things was at least in part conditioned by his general pessimism and view of the future as hopeless. Bread and circuses is all they want. The conversation did, however, set me thinking about writing something that would sell, like a thriller.

On Friday, January 14 in the New Year, I wrote four pages of a story about an aging professional assassin named Radovic who becomes conflictedly involved with two women and pays the price. I thought it might be called "Escape from Paradise" or "Another Side of Eden" and made several pages of notes for that story and the Schadow manuscript, in addition to drafting a poem about Avignon and listening to Rostropovich play Bach that evening. A good day. On January 21 I noted in the journal, "Finished story of professional killer and two women yesterday – 22 pages of unmitigated trash – perhaps four lines in the whole thing are any good. Still it was worth doing as an exercise: one learns about balance and proportion easier with a story than a novel. This story is wildly out of both; perhaps some day I'll go back to it." Some day, indeed.

Many other ideas for stories that might turn into books flitted across the screen of my mind like an erratic flight of blackbirds across the southern sky. Why not a story based on some of the sections of Ladurie's study of the Cathars, *Montaillou,* with all those priests sexually plundering the village women when they weren't doing heresy? Why not a novel based on Brecht's exile experience especially in Los Angeles, presented through the eyes of a critical but sympathetic American script writer to attain the appropriate Brechtian alienation effect, allow for the clash of American and European cultures at their most manipulative level (Hollywood and Brecht himself), and relieve me of the task of imagining and recreating a mind like Brecht's (which I thought I could not do)? He should have felt right at home in Hollywood, but he didn't. Those shallow, narrow-minded, bourgeois Americans did not take him *seriously* enough. And he couldn't make a steady income.

No consideration of themes while living in Provence would be complete without some thought of the ravaged and ravishing Vincent Van Gogh, and I contemplated on many occasions what to do with that striking scene where, seeking warmth and sunlight, he climbs down off the train at the Arles station in the middle of a snowstorm. I could not recall then, nor can I now, how Vincent Minnelli directed the scene with Kirk Douglas in one of his best *furioso* and desperate performances (and

346

Robert Altman would not make his *Vincent & Theo* until 1990 and Maurice Pialat did not make *Van Gogh* until 1992), but I thought about it a lot.

Notes:

> After description (lyrical in nature) of Vincent climbing off the train in the snow ending in the hotel, bring in the narrator: 'Almost a century later I walked from the RR station to the Hotel Terminus on the Place Lamartine. The only thing still the same is the name of the broad, open square the limits of which Vincent could not have seen that first night in the snow' ... Have almost decided to indulge in some poetic license re the Vincent piece – does it matter if he turned right or left at any given point? ... He left Provence the way he had come two years before, by train amidst total indifference, desperate in mind and heart.

Like so many ideas, this one never reached beyond a few notes scattered throughout the journal and the notebooks. This idea continues to roll around in my mind from time to time like a loose ball-bearing searching for a home.

Sometimes the notions for stories tumbled over each other as they found their ways into the notebooks. Some of them clearly not destined to advance beyond those notes, as for example this one.

It would be nice to write a short novel of character without worrying about action – development would be totally through the characters and their stories and interactions. Some ¾ through the book something radical happens and reactions to it put people in a different light, revealing aspects of character previously unseen. A series of vignettes tying the characters closer together as they confront each other and each other's pasts.

And the bats of self-doubt swept out of their caves to bedevil me from time to time, no different surely from any other man who came late to his trade.

What is striking about the early chapters of Penrose is not only the obvious precocity and genius of Picasso, but the massive amount of work he did to train himself, those thousands of pages of sketches he practiced until he'd mastered one form or technique. Such work one can only accomplish when young. Accordingly I should have spent my younger days writing thousands of "practice" poems. Not having done this will ensure I remain nothing more than an amateur at it. If the same necessity exists for writing novels, I'll not have mastered prose writing until the age of 80 or so if ever. The question at the moment is whether I can sell the "unmastered" pages already written to allow the freedom to work at the mastering process. If I can retain my health long enough I may yet do it and write a valuable book of some sort. What's valuable?

That journal entry is dated October 16, 1983. I am now ten years away from 80 and cannot tell how well or poorly I've mastered prose writing. I've enough books in print to allow the reader to make his own judgment about that. Nor did I sell enough writing to gain the liberty to practice until improvement became obvious.

●

As the year advanced toward spring, the notion of writing a straightforward thriller increased in size and intensity as I struggled with Schadow. By the end of May I had just about decided that I had to transform the assassin story into a saleable novel. If I could sell the novel and go back to teaching for the University of Maryland in Germany or Italy for the winter, we could return to Provence the following summer. This seemed to be a reasonable way to keep us off the streets in the USA looking for work and living a desperate life, which obviously neither of us wished to do.

The work did not always go easily.

My idea was to write a detailed outline of the plot which would be fairly straightforward and linear while I continued to work on Schadow and some of the short pieces for the "Mediterranean Sketches" collection. By creating a complete outline before beginning and sticking to it I could write the book with all due speed. In the notes I described the Radovic story as one of morality, honesty and sincerity – qualities which Radovic almost alone would possess. Then, I thought, the irony of his profession would stand out clearly: not a new idea but one that would work if the notion was dramatized, not "told." Keep the historical references to a minimum so the narrative plays out in a time of instability in which a place to stand is hard to find (I never forgot Ahab's cry about finding a place to hold on to in this slippery world of ours). In fact, I ordered myself to forget the philosophy and to write it straight as a pulp thriller.

This is how I described the as-yet not written manuscript: "A simple story, written simply (regardless of the complexities of the characters) to be read in one sitting with lots of sharp dialogue and pungent descriptive passages – the opposite of the convolutions of Le Carré (the best) and Ludlum (possibly the worst) and the length of such recent stuff. An easy Mediterranean story without introverted North European Calvinist involvement with the self." Rather good advice, but could I follow it? And should I bother? Terrible doubts about the project assailed me from time to time: was it worth it to spend my time creating trash? Not only that, but eventually even more important, could I do it well enough to make the result worth the time and effort spent on it? I could only tell if it was published and sold well. And this was an illusion because I had no real connections in the business. Would it not be better to attempt cutting the Gordian knot of Schadow and plunge on there? I put off starting the thriller because I'd little faith that I could do it any better than anything else. So I avoided the matter and found evasions that became mutually reinforcing leading me into a depression, a fact that finally forced me to get on with it. Thus, with such disturbing doubts and questions battering my mental equipoise I did plunge on, but with both Radovic and Schadow. A debilitating exercise given the condition of my health that spring, but I believed I had no choice. Throughout June and into July I wrote several pages at a stretch of the Radovic story, unfortunately not every day, but the pile of paper gradually increased in height as I battled the flies, the heat and the hangovers (caused in part by a slew of visitors who arrived and departed all summer). By mid-June the plot had fallen into place and I had a more or less coherent storyline and began to write it, constantly complaining to myself that it moved too slowly. I did not consider style at this point, only getting the narrative down following the outline; I knew the book would require major revisions and the stylistic matters could be dealt with then. This became one of my mantras: "Radovic going well: 10 pages done today. Will need much rewriting but it's moving!" This turned out to be a smart decision because my doubts about the entire enterprise diminished as the number of pages increased. I gave myself a deadline of mid-September to finish the first draft, and I tried all the little tricks writers use to spur themselves on: On Tuesday, July 26, I gave myself until Saturday to reach page 100, between two sets of visitors. My obsessive involvement in the project, perhaps to the detriment of rational thought about it, can be seen in the note I made the following day. "Twenty pages of Radovic done. It moves. The section on his meeting with the Colonel hopefully has some humor in it. Next stop Istanbul. If this bastard doesn't sell there's

351

ng miserably wrong with the publishing industry,
⸺ ⸺peak of the public."

But the story inevitably became more complex in plot twists and I cautioned myself to take care that the plot remained essentially believable and inevitable within its framework. Too many little things that did not mesh would lead to the reader not being willing to suspend disbelief even for the sake of a good read. And always in the back of my mind, despite the enjoyment of writing the thriller and its possible sale, the nagging thought that I should have been working on the Berlin novel, real literature. Or so I believed. Even so, even so ...

Any writer who takes on a project with more than one location usually has lived in or visited all of them; this lends verisimilitude to the narrative and makes the characters in those locales more believable. Radovic takes place in Paris, Marseille, Corsica, Istanbul, on a ship and in an entirely fictional area on the border of two small states on the eastern shore of the Mediterranean. With the exception of Corsica and the fictional places I'd been to all of the others with sufficient time and absorption to deal with them in the book. The fictional locales I made up; the action took place in a limited amount of space (a hotel room, an office, a prison cell) so the necessity to create detailed description of the society and people who lived in these places diminished to the point of zero. Corsica presented a problem. We could not afford to visit the island for research or any other purpose, but I could read several guidebooks in the Médiathèque Ceccano (the Internet and Wikipedia did not exist then) and took from them what I needed to fill out that part of the book with reasonable accuracy. I think I got it right.

"Action must move forward without too many pauses." "Ideally description forwards action." "As long as it flows and remains interesting background sections can be added if they are concise and short." Such are the notes I wrote to myself with some regularity. "But where should all those sorts of tennis fit it?" *Ouf!*

Further clarity came with discussions we had over dinners at home and in those inexpensive and shabby of décor restaurants on narrow streets inside the Avignon ramparts (*intra muros*) where the appointments were sparse, but the tables boasted white cloths and the knives in the hand held sufficient weight to count as sterling. Le Chien qui Fume, La Tâche d'Encre, Le Patio (finely chopped tripe rolled with onion, garlic, apple and celery in a sausage!), and a half-dozen others, placed before us a marvelous array of dishes to warm both the heart and the taste buds. (After the first visit to Henri le Kroner's hostellerie in Tavel we rarely returned there without guests, to save money but also because we learned to cook very well in the house of Mme Mourre. Mr. le Kroner accepted this absence with a Gallic shrug of the shoulders, a half-smile and the statement, "*Alors*, one does what one must, but tomorrow's *bourguignon à ma façon* will send you reeling through the streets intoxicated with flavors." What could we do but reserve a table and discover if his judgment of his own work reflected reality or not. Of course, it did, and I am convinced that the experience improved our solidarity with the Humanist tradition. Henri le Kroner possessed a genius for influencing the lives of his customers and proving the old saw that eating well brings peace to the soul and, by extrapolation, to the nations of the world. Too bad that narrow-minded husband shot him down in the Hostellerie's kitchen and deprived us of his talents and the peace that passeth understanding.)

Journal entry, July 20:

The style of the Radovic book appears to be one I associate with that of the Latin American writers now enjoying so much attention: ironic, detached, mildly sarcastic, humorous about essentially unhumorous subjects, lightly contemptuous of most characters, largely satiric in character construction and use of cliché to make points – on the whole unfelt as is much of literature today, esp. popular lit. This latter factor may be a mistake. The reader should care about R. and Hilary at least, possibly Canetti.

Hilary is Radovic's English lover and Canetti is his Marseille friend involved in legally dubious activities and who rescues him at the end from ... but why spoil the end for readers who have not yet read the book?

July 27:

Almost too hot to work today. O'Neill in Georgia sweating all over his pages. Blood in urine all morning put me off everything including 8:15 tennis. Too hot to type. When I think of the amount of work done by

DHL before 44 I cringe in embarrassment. Not all good, of course, but the volume is incredible. Much the same with others like LD, Joyce (legendarily working on Ulysses despite massive hangovers and bad teeth from falling in the gutters of Trieste), Faulkner (could I read him now?). My lethargy is the major obstacle to progress. Would it be any different in more stable circumstances? Thomas Mann doing four hours in the morning, no more, no less. Graham Greene doing minimally 250 words daily. Worked well yesterday from 5 to 10 PM on and off. Physical pain exhausts me and I can only read or make notes. Not a good sign. Later: another few pages of Radovic done but forced.

August 30:

With the assistance of Ferme Jamet rosé did 13 pages of Radovic finishing chapter 10 before dinner. If I could do twice as much each day! Still, if I do as much for the next ten days – 100 pp. – the thing should be finished. Must keep it below 300 MS pp. More or less.

September 8:

Finished chapter 14. 241 pp of MS thus far – needs rewriting but main thing is the end in sight. If it's no good in the end will the exercise have been worthwhile? It has shown me I need will power to overcome a profound lethargy and lack of discipline. I need long walks in the fresh air and improved health.

Mainly I must sit down in the mornings and work more, read less. My thoughts on the past year's isolation from other people, other writers, etc. are ambiguous. If I already had an agent, publisher, etc. it wouldn't be a negative factor, but without them there's no money coming in. Provence is not Paris where one can meet people in the business. We came to the Midi both too late and too early.

September 10:

Becoming more difficult to keep track of the days: everything is moving so fast now. We think too much of what to store here, to send by ship, how many boxes can we ask Tom to send through APO, disposition of the car ... I repeat that we don't have to do anything until October but our winter stuff should go off now. Ah, for a wealthy patron!

September 15: [Despite broken transformer for the American typewriter]

Finished first draft of Radovic before dinner. No special feeling of excitement or that something had ended. Revisions on a grand scale still to be done. Still, it's good to have it done ... Drank a bottle of Châteauneuf-du-Pape Cuvée Special 1979 to celebrate the end of R. Lighter than expected, but tasty on the tongue. Could drink that often if we could afford it.

Those revisions began the following day and continued as long as we remained in Tavel; indeed they continued after we moved back to Washington and LM typed the entire manuscript on a new electric machine, after which the work lay in desk drawers and boxes, untouched and unread, until 2008 when she decided it was time to take it out, dust it off (minor corrections and revisions because I had not the time to do more than that: too busy writing the third Berlin volume and this memoir) and place it in the hands of the same subsidy print-on-demand publisher which brought out my collected poems in 2007. Thus ends the story of *Radovic's Dilemma*, the moral of which might be, "don't give up on your work, someday ..."

•

Thinking about other writers and their works forms an inevitable but not entirely healthy part of a writer's life. One has one's favorites and pet peeves, of course, among the latter of which some food writers and D. H. Lawrence particularly annoyed me that summer. I seriously considered writing a response to restaurant critics like Patricia Wells and journalists like R. W. Apple, Jr. who are remunerated for blathering on about "inexpensive" or "reasonably priced" bistros and other eateries that charged 100 to 150 francs for lunch. Apple published an article in the IHT praising the *"quartier"* aspect of several places in Paris, by which he presumably meant the neighborhood ambience they exuded, but the prices were hardly those of a neighborhood café and they all appeared well recommended in the red Michelin. At those prices these joints were not bistros but brasseries or restaurants. My notes from mid-July give expression to the annoyance I felt at the time. "Who are these people writing for? What is their audience? Who can afford 100 francs for a quick lunch? And they get paid for publishing this elitist junk."

I promised myself that, if I ever did get to write the riposte, I'd end it with the story of New Year's Eve: Monsieur Boeuf and Le Petit Poulet on Place Clichy – 580 as against 80 francs (that's 80 francs for two!). Unfortunately I lost the Apple text and I doubted that a letter to the editor of the IHT would satisfy the matter, so I never did write the article. So much for an attempt to make some sorely needed cash by journalism.

I'd first experienced Lawrence in college when I read a pirated edition of *Lady Chatterley's Lover* (the book was still banned in the USA) and, at that young and impressionable age, responded enthusiastically and uncritically to what I viewed as a jab at the restrictive moral system that kept such things from being freely sold to people such as my literary friends and me. Other of the novels followed but I began to be increasingly uneasy about what seemed to be his primitive attitude toward sex and blood consciousness that seemed to me to border on the fascistic. Reading *Twilight in Italy* during the summer of 1983 reinforced the unease and pushed it over the edge into outright dislike. Reading the first chapter reinforced the notion that one can't invest inanimate objects or other people with cosmic meaning or attribute thoughts to peasants they couldn't possibly have. A mistake I'd made myself so I knew whereof I thought. And I thought that description is one thing, attribution of feeling or meaning is quite another. This can be accomplished sometimes with analogy or metaphor but doesn't work directly any longer.

In the end, one is left with the journal entry: "Bought copy of *Dubin's Lives* today for night reading. Should go well with the tiresome rantings of DHL in *Twilight in Italy*. What drivel when he gets on his blood sex hobby horse. Malamud should be an antidote." And, as I vaguely recall, it was indeed. In fact, I then thought, and still do, that if DHL were still alive it would be worthwhile to recommend he find a good editor. Perhaps no one edited his books. What utter tripe he published, "heavy blood", etc. Most of it seemed to be in the Italian crepuscule. On the other hand, there are certain books which editors would probably destroy: can one imagine an editor attempting to work on the chapters of *Tristram Shandy*? Maxwell Perkins had it easy with Thomas Wolfe in comparison.

In the spring Donald Hall wrote a review of a recent biography of the English writer Robert Graves in which the sentence appeared: "the self-imposed anguish of an aging nympholept." Graves simply lived too long – perhaps not wisely but well, certainly productively. How many of these aged writers, I wondered, Pound, Sartre, Borges, and the rest, like Graves lived so long beyond their ability to create, and became wistful, sad shells, remembering only what was long ago and forgetting to flush the toilet or worse. Reading a review of Sartre's recently published *Carnets de la drôle de guerre* and

359

Cahiers pour une morale brought uncomfortably to mind how *much* he wrote during his life and in what diverse genres: novels, plays, philosophy, literary criticism, journalism, memoirs, essays – it seemed unending. The energy he possessed is amazing, or should one say the energy that possessed him, in addition to the chemical derivatives that did possess him at the end. Perhaps the French write as they talk: at top speed with 50% more words than necessary. Still one is baffled by the quantity of stuff Sartre published, much of it of high quality, mostly interesting if wrong-headed. Whether he wrote anything "great" in any of those genres remains an open question and in his case might be beside the point.

When discussing other writers I cannot possibly evade the presence in my life of Lawrence Durrell and my relationship with his work is not easily described in a few words; nonetheless I will make the attempt. It began in 1960 in Greenwich Village when I ordered the boxed American edition of *The Alexandria Quartet* from the Reader's Subscription, a literary book club, which I devoured with the frantic enthusiasm of a 21-year old explorer discovering new and unusual territory. Vastly impressed by the exotic setting, fascinating characters and dense if not clotted prose, I tore through all four volumes and convinced one of my colleagues at the Bursar's Office of New York University's Washington Square College to read through the first volume, *Justine*, with me and talk about it at lunch in the park. Not everybody who read the books reacted as positively as Serge and I did: one critic complained that reading

Durrell's prose was akin to plodding through a field of oatmeal. I loved it.

As the years marched along toward the present I read Durrell's other prose and poetry and returned to the *Quartet* several times, once just before LM and I traveled to Alexandria to attend a conference sponsored by the International Lawrence Durrell Society and the University of Alexandria. (Curiously enough when LM and I first met I was living in Alexandria, Virginia, across the river from Washington.) As noted elsewhere just before we moved to Provence I corresponded briefly with Durrell about living in that part of France where he'd been since 1957. He abhorred the changes that had taken place since then under the names "progress" and "modernization", but allowed how there remained places where one could live the good life without being excessively wealthy. He probably did not have Tavel in mind but for us this became one of those places.

In 1974 Durrell published the first of a series of five related novels commonly known now as *The Avignon Quintet* after the place in and around which much of the narrative occurs. As noted in an earlier chapter, we purchased a copy of the third volume, *Constance*, during our holiday trip to Paris at the end of December 1982. In January I began to read the novel and while this in itself is hardly newsworthy it did have an effect on my own work, which is to say that I required an hour to read 20 pages because every other paragraph gave me an idea for "Schadow's Meditations" that had to be jotted down and expanded. So the pile of notes increased in size, new characters came to life and old ones gained biographical detail as I noted in the journal: as I sat "in the chilly room above the vineyards and the cemetery. The book *moves!*" By which I meant *my* book, and this caused my enthusiasm for the enterprise to rise again, continuing the roller-coaster tradition well-known to writers of lengthy manuscripts.

The danger with a writer like Durrell is that the work becomes too textured, too folded back upon itself, too artificial, becomes in fact artifact: so much a work of art that it is lifeless – it lies there before us: a gorgeously beautiful and complex corpse arousing our sense of admiration and wonder but not able to *move* us. If anything human saves Durrell from his tendency toward the baroque it is his humor and residual sense of the comedic grotesque (as in the character of Trash, a compilation of the most stereotypical clichés about American Negroes, especially when she confronts or is confronted by another character called Sutcliffe). Too often, however, his sense of humor is lost in the labyrinthine construction of his art.

I must admit I return again and again to some of Durrell's works, like returning to *Ulysses* to refresh my mind and reinforce the notion that true artists are eternal in their value and pleasure, and have even written a book about him,[52] thus he has accompanied me through my entire adult life. My only regret is that I only met him once, briefly, at a conference at Pennsylvania State University in 1987. On the other hand, it is perhaps better not to have met someone whose work one so admires;

---

[52] *A Chronology of the Life and Times of Lawrence Durrell* (Durrell School of Corfu, 2007)

how could the human being live up to the work of genius? Depends on how one defines "genius", I suppose.

•

Journal, March 23, 1983:

Reading Camus' Lyrical Essays from 1936- 39.
Themes of L'Étranger and Sisyphus all there along with the typical French talent for making non sequiturs seem to hang together: more style than sense. Must be in the language – the rolling beauty of the language overwhelms the writer to the point where he can no longer control the sense of what he is writing because the sound of the language is too beautiful to disturb with the rationality of real connections.

Chapter X

Autumn Finale

We wondered from time to time how we might earn sufficient incomes to remain in Tavel deep into the future. Would it be possible, for example, to make a living producing zucchini bread in France? Evidently people there had never heard of such a thing. What would one call it? *"Pain de courgette"* wouldn't do; sounds absurd to the French. A *gâteau* it wasn't, but perhaps could have been. Perhaps "Moiradonné" after the giver of the recipe? Mme Mourre was somewhat taken aback when LM offered her a piece. *"C'est un gâteau, alors?"* She did, however, allow that it tasted fine, different, but fine. We thought it tasted pretty damn good and ate a lot of it that summer. The zucchini patch overflowed and we gave much of it away.

During the cold days Mme Mourre spent most of her time in the two room apartment next to the wrought-iron bars of the green gate. She prepared her spare food (and that for the animals) in the small kitchen and used the unheated WC attached to the building only reached by leaving the apartment and walking two meters to the WC door. Not fun in the winter. Occasionally she walked into the village on her thick legs, moving very slowly to have her hair done or make some small purchase. Usually she walked in the garden a bit when the weather allowed. Except for an occasional trip with the Club du Troisième Âge (a senior citizen group) or meals at her daughter's house in Villeneuve-lès-Avignon, she didn't leave the village and most of the time remained on the grounds of her house. During that winter she occasionally asked me to pay a bill for her at the post office when I went there, which was fairly often because in those days one wrote letters to friends and for business purposes. Since she was 80ish and found it physically difficult to move, this is not surprising, but at my age then I found it sad.

Not to Mme Mourre, however. She read the daily local excuse for a newspaper (the *Midi Libre*), listened to the radio and spent hours in front of her large color TV, thoroughly enjoying shows such as *Dallas*, when not caring for the animals or talking at length and repetitively with LM about the village scandals and its history. It seemed to us that visits from her friends occurred rarely, but we weren't there all the time. Micheline came twice a week or so to clean the house and do some work in the garden and pass on any news from the village. On most Sundays her daughter and her family either came to Tavel or picked Mme Mourre up for the midday meal. We knew Mme Mourre did not use the telephone much because it rang in our apartment when she picked up the receiver, another Provençal mystery. She read in bed for a while each evening – classic French literature. LM gave her a Harold Robbins in French at her request but she later said she couldn't bring herself to read that trash and that she preferred Zola, Balzac, and the like. She grinned and murmured that perhaps she could read some of the trash during the day when she found the time, but not at night. We never knew if she found the daytime hour to do so, probably not.

One of her nephews who lived in the north somewhere enjoyed taking week-long hikes about the undeveloped countryside when on holidays and once during the depths of the hot summer he appeared at the gate for lunch, an arrangement clearly made earlier in the month because Mme Mourre had spent the hot morning cooking a massive cassoulet to feed the sweaty hiker, who immediately thereafter fell into a semi-stupor and napped for an hour before setting off once more on his appointed rounds. The cassoulet is not only one of the heaviest meals known to mankind, but when cooked properly one of the tastiest. It is not, however, in my opinion meant to be eaten on a hot summer afternoon but rather to warm the body and soul on cold winter evenings when the chill seems to penetrate one's very marrow. There is nothing elegant or graceful about a plump stew loaded with a variety of navy, fava and other beans, rendered goose fat, large chunks of sausage, duck or goose confit and large pieces of lamb and pork cooked for great lengths of time with red wine, tomatoes, onions, bay leaves, garlic and other herbs; it is a hearty peasant dish of great stature in some parts of the planet. Elizabeth David tells the story of the shoemaker in Castelnaudray who did not open his shop one day and posted a small note on the door reading *"Fermé pour cause de cassoulet"*. A heavy dish, indeed.

Also, like aïoli and the bouillabaisse, a controversial one in terms of ingredients and cooking methods. There are as many variations as there are claimants to the title of First Inventor. Len Deighton in his amusing *ABC of French Cooking* (1989), notes that the arguments about the dish are usually carried out among cookbook writers rather than between cooks. As the chef at the Hostellerie de Tavel, Henri le Kroner, once muttered, "A cassoulet is like a love affair: it can be elaborate and long term or simple, intense and of short duration. Both are pleasurable if not transcendent, but in today's hectic world the latter is more popular, *hélas!*" Monsieur le Kroner is obviously not an acolyte of the famous Escoffier whose advice to cooks was *"faites simple"*. Nonetheless the Tavel chef remains in the traditional groove of French professional cooks, which is to say a thoughtful man with many contradictory opinions. For example, he prefers the Provençal *daube* to the Languedocien cassoulet. "What could be simpler?" he told us one evening as we sat with a *pastis* before ordering one of his marvelous meals. "Anyone can make a fine *daube*, but you must ignore the instructions of that American fellow who lives near Toulon, what's his name … Olney, yes, that one. He wrote a book about simple French cooking, didn't he? Have you read his recipe for a 'simple' *daube à l'Avignonnaise*? Simple!? Good lord, two fat pages of explanation and instructions. *C'est trop, trop, n'est-ce pas?*" When M. le Kroner is upset about something related to his profession he begins to turn a sickly shade of pink as his agitation rises to a point just below explosion and he starts but cannot finish sentences, so great is his perturbation and anger.[53] Fortunately this does not happen too often, at least not in our presence, and his wife Gisèle easily competes with him in becoming briefly enraged at some perceived disparagement or perversion of their culinary traditions. Again fortunately they both are usually in agreement about what constitutes the disparagement or perversion. A good thing they hadn't read Elizabeth David's complex recipe in her otherwise admirable and well-written *French Provincial Cooking* (1960).

And when thinking about simplicity in cooking one can do much worse than heed the words of the lovely MFK Fisher.

> A stew ... is supposed to be the simplest of dishes, and probably in the fargone days it was, when you threw a piece of meat and some water into a pot, and let them boil together until they had blended into one edible thing. Now, a stew means something richer, and can be a fine tantalizing dish indeed, full of braised meat and many vegetables all bound together by a gravy heady with herbs and wine. We are proud to have raised it from its lowly place, and in doing so we have cheated ourselves of its first frugal goodness, for once having tasted the

---

[53] The book to which M. le Kroner referred is Richard Olney, *Simple French Food* (New York, 1974).

new kind, our palates are chilled by the starkness of the old.[54]

LM and I first met a *daube* in the L'Isle-sur-la-Sorgue Sunday market. In one of the narrow lanes a clean-shaven young man, whose name we never learned, stood behind a small collapsible table with a battery-powered small cooking ring on which sat a very small pot filled with a mildly bubbling aromatic mixture of well but slowly simmered beef meat and blood (or a heavy red wine), bay leaf, chopped onion and tomato and garlic, which had been marinating for several hours. The ring kept the stew warm so potential customers could taste tiny samples of the dish. If they decided to purchase the treat, the young man placed a rubber sealed jar of it in a paper sack with the advice to heat it slowly and not too long because he had already cooked it in a tightly lidded *daubière*.

"What is this?" LM asked the young man in French.

"*C'est une daube provençale, Madam, un miracle en cuisine*," the young man responded with a broad smile and the traditional seller-of-*daube* sparkle in his brown eyes.

"*Ah, bon*," said LM with laughter in her throat. "*L'odeur est délicieux*."

"*Oui, c'est vrai, et le goût ...*" The young man held out a small wooden spoon piled with the moist meat. "*Essayez-vous, s'il vous plaît*.

---

[54] From *How to Cook a Wolf* (1st ed. 1942; rev. ed. 1951) reprinted in *The Art of Eating* (1954).

"Bouf!" exclaimed LM. *"Vous avez raison. Trés bon, trés bon. Merci."*

"Et monsieur ...? He looked at me, but surely knew his question was superfluous.

"We'll take three," I said in English.

That evening this marvelously simple dish melted on our tongues and sent shivers of pleasure up and down the hills of our taste buds. We went back several times over the next months to replenish our supply. Regrettably, two years later when we returned to the Midi we could not find the young man, who apparently had taken on a different *métier* in a different locale. So with some hesitation we bought several cans of ready-made *daube* at the supermarket and tried one: eminently eatable, but not at all the same as our memories reminded us. The next night I added a can of *soupe au pistou* to the pot of canned *daube* and our faces lit up in pleasant surprise at the distinctly odd but savory taste that resulted. We served this version to several of our friends in the Midi and they all agreed this constituted a fine contribution to the national cuisine, even if made by a foreigner.

But this culinary excursion has taken us on a detour. To return to the proximate subject with a question: Was Mme Mourre lonely? Was there any reason to feel sad about her life? She certainly did not. And she did have a small circle of friends with whom to visit, chat and share the time. She did say she would much rather be alive then than in the past: she enjoyed all the mod cons, despite the outdoor WC. No sentimental nostalgia pulled her into memories of more youthful days, as far as we could tell. She received little or no personal mail; I knew this because I emptied the mailbox when I got there before she did. Crime seemed to bother her and at one point I thought she was a bit paranoid about it, but on the whole she presented to the world a placid, generally happy face which was quite lovely when she smiled.

●

As the summer inexorably began to edge its way into autumn, the daily events gained in intensity and color and the thought of departure became increasingly difficult to repress. The tenor of the time can be seen in the following journal entry dated August 20.

As I sit for a few moments on the terrace the guttural sounds of Micheline lecturing LM on the finer points of maintaining the garden drift upward accompanied by the distant hum of truck and caravan traffic on the *autoroute* to Spain two kilometers to the east and the raucous cawing of the confused cock in the yard next door behind the thick gray wall. The albino cat, which has slept on our bed all afternoon (tight against my leg for the hour I also lay there) rises shaking off whatever dream wakened him and gracefully jumps to the window sill, disappearing into the courtyard in search of food, no doubt. At the same time LM opens the great green iron gate, careful not to let the hysterical terrier out, and, with the green string bag, slips off to the village to buy another baguette. We have guests tonight for spaghetti and *courgettes farcies*. The odor of tomatoes and garlic drifts past my nose: the sauce has been bubbling gently for hours.

We know the summer is ebbing away when the darkness dominates the terrace at 8:30. Earlier it remained light until 9:45. Too much is coming to an end.

I hope Micheline sweeps Finette's shit piles out of the garage. It takes an effort of will to enter it to change the water switch every morning.

Leftover chicken last night with the lemon sauce. Excellent. Baudelaire and brother not here for breakfast. Mme Mourre thinks one of them may have sired her new kitten and one is surely Bambino's father.

Lovely pale blue sky in the east with three startlingly white cloud formations over the area where Mont Ventoux is reputed to be; we've seen it only once that I can remember this summer. The day has been bright with sunlight and cool with breezes. A form of perfection the leaving of which is painful to contemplate.

When the tomatoes ripen we will have 50-60 of them at the same time. With the new watering system suggested and demonstrated by Jim the fruit is much larger. We had been giving them too little water.

September 6:

The fact of having to leave intrudes increasingly into one's mind. It comes often in the form of dread — a strong word, perhaps, but appropriate. One dreads having to return to a place where one simply doesn't

372

want to live. On the other hand the idea of somehow staying here on the fringe of society holds no great allure at this age, though I'd do it if it were possible. To live poor in Paris as such is, of course, feasible. But it can't be done for one clear reason: the bureaucratization of life has made it impossible to live in Europe without the correct papers. Much easier in the USA, as all the wetbacks know. Illegal persons live in France by the 100,000s but we could not do it. We demand too much of life and that requires papers. How much easier it was in 1920 for Joyce to move to Paris with no financial resources simply by taking the train. The necessity for papers means having an income without which no papers are issued. We can hardly claim political asylum, although with Jack Lang's attitude we could probably claim cultural asylum! If there was such a thing and if we could show some income producing occupation. The bourgeoisie is trapped by paperwork and we certainly belong to it. In any case, it is not possible for us to live poor in France (which means Paris as the only place where there exists even the potential for either of us earning any money) without visas, *cartes de séjour*, etc., which one cannot have without income. This is distinctly detrimental to my mental balance.

As we came closer to leaving my general health deteriorated again, naturally. Exhaustion, blood in the urine, various pains in various body parts, in addition to the emotional and mental melancholy at leaving, all wore me down and led to the thought that the body is a prison which we all seek to meliorate but the attempt is only rarely successful, at least in this case. The distracting aches and pains caused sudden outbursts of irritation that cannot have been pleasant for LM and which I immediately regretted. Thoughts of death and dying occasionally intruded their ghastly disturbances making me morose and out of sorts. The physical pains I thought I could handle, but the psychological discomforts presented a different category of behavior. Why did I not seek out a physician? Afraid of the results? Too much time away from work? The lack of language? Human stupidity knows no limits except those of pain. Perhaps I'd not been frightened sufficiently? Fortunately there were compensations and I did my best to control any expression of frustration and anger. How successful I was, I cannot say. I only wished the mistral would clear my head and body the way it cleared the sky.

•

The wine harvest (*vendange*) began in mid-September. By 7:30 in the morning the village streets filled with small Spanish migrant workers of both sexes and all ages (though apparently mainly middle aged – 45ish – folk) waiting for the trucks to pick them up. They chattered a lot, smiled and nodded when one passed them in the street. After 6:00 p.m. the truck returned them to the village from the fields. They looked very tired but still spry. Micheline said the first day is fine, but after the second or third day at work the body, especially the back, aches unbearably. By the end of the month one is used to it. Not this one, however, since I would not volunteer for the experience (the pay was minimal in any case) just to regale friends in later life who ask how I broke my back. LM thought of trying it for the time when we might be marooned in the village with the car in the garage being repaired yet again. She knew, though, that Mme Mourre would not approve. Oh, la, la. Such labor might be okay for Spaniards, maybe Italians and Yugoslavs, but not Mme Leen, a lady with social standing in the village and Mme Mourre's mind. Our landlady was a very proper and socially conscious personage.

Throughout the day the oddly narrow tractors carrying small metal bins on wheels full of deep purple-red grapes moved noisily through the streets to the caves or the cooperative to be tromped on – not by human feet of course because such a time-consuming and inefficient activity could be found only in tourist-oriented establishments, not in any serious vineyard. The air became dense with the musty odor of grapes and their juices that shroud wine-making French villages in the autumn. "If it doesn't rain any more this month the harvest should be good," Monsieur le Kroner informed us one evening as we again sampled the wonders of his kitchen. "If it rains, which it threatens to do, the grapes will over ripen and, though still making drinkable wine, will not bring the prices desired by the vineyard owners. Nineteen eighty-three may not be a good year for Côtes du Rhône, Châteauneuf-du-Pape and Tavel rosé." As it turned out 1983 was an average good year for the wines of the region.

The village took note of our pending departure in various ways. The garage owner/mechanic and his family always showed an interest in how the writing was going: "*Et le livre? Ça va?*" What could I say in response but, "*Oui, oui, ça va bien, ça marche bien.*" And indeed Radovic did march well, but the Berlin volume remained in fragments and outlines, it did not march well. They expressed surprise that we would be leaving, saying that it was really too bad at that. It was typical of our superficial integration into some aspects of the life of the village that during one repair visit he had not had the time to write up the bill so waved his hands dismissively: "*Demain, demain.*" We remained outsiders, but as time moved on we became known outsiders, not quite of the village, but in it nonetheless.

I think we mystified the family, as perhaps we did many of the villagers, none of whom we really got to know well, except Mme Mourre. The garage owner finally recommended we invest no more money in repairing the car, but get rid of it and purchase another; putting so much money and labor into such a wreck made no sense to him. However, when we explained that we would be leaving the village during the first week of November he smiled sadly and nodded. *Tant pis, franchement.* We figured if we could sell the machine for a bit more than the repairs cost we wouldn't be too much out of pocket given the low price we paid the Benzes for it in Munich.

As summer neared its end and our departure crept forward, summing-up thoughts bubbled to the surface to demand some kind of attention, however unwelcome.

They were of course not all negative, despite the blanket of melancholy we had to throw off before it became too heavy.

Journal entry, August 22:

Wind blows dust over everything after such a lengthy dry spell. No real rain in months. This is an incredible place to live. And I have gotten a lot of work done. No telling about the quality of it yet. Still it is not enough. Radovic should be finished by now. Second volume of Schade should have been finished by March. Too many wasted hours. Not even counting the visitors and our travels. Just too much waste when alone and supposedly working. It's too easy to pick up a book or do a crossword puzzle or read a magazine article. Too easy and done too often. If we had more time it wouldn't have mattered but one knew a year was the limit. Will try for 21 pages of R tomorrow. Damn! This thriller cannot turn out to be a waste of time, too.

I was too pessimistic by far, but it took 25 years to get the thriller published. And the day after I made that entry the rains came, indeed they stormed through the landscape with a force not felt since the previous November. The winds lasted only for 30 minutes or so, but the rain continued and the electricity in the village went down. LM checked on Mme Mourre but she had gone peacefully to bed not allowing Nature's idiosyncrasies to bother her at this point in her life. The rains fell until the following afternoon when the sun appeared, pale as if recovering from a debilitating illness. Despite everything that had gone wrong with the weather it was very pretty there.

●

Journal entry, September 21:

Two chapters of Radovic revised. Two tomatoes picked and two snails thrown out, Mme Mourre appeared to be affected by our birthday present.

Terseness seemed to have been the result of the impending and unwanted departure, and raises a question: what did we give Mme Mourre for her birthday?

●

One result of a certain level of linguistic shyness on our part was not getting to know the village's resident painter, called Malo, who lived with his wife in a two story building on the main street next to the ladies hair salon and the village newspaper-magazine-stationery store where I bought the daily *Midi Libre* and the occasional *Paris Match* (the *International Herald Tribune*, our other source of news, had to be purchased in Avignon or by subscription through the mail which meant it arrived one or two days late). The ground floor housed his studio *cum* sales room and they lived on the two floors above. Toward the end of our time in Tavel one morning we spontaneously did what we should have done ten months earlier: we entered the dark interior of Malo's shop and introduced ourselves. Had we done so the previous winter, the conversation would have taken on quite a different quality, namely it would have been rather a disaster and gone nowhere. Now we spent more than an hour with the artist and his friendly wife Nora chatting and looking through his water colors of the village and environs. His oils were priced far above our budget limitations, but we did purchase a small watercolor depicting the back street on which I made my way to the bakery in the morning; the oils also seemed clumsier than the watercolors, less spontaneous, more strained or straining to achieve their effect. After a while he showed us his own collection including several Dalí lithographs (apparently Malo knew him many years ago in Paris), a Suzanne Valladon drawing of her mother and the 12-year old Maurice Utrillo, one of whose Paris street scenes hung on the wall along with a Picasso study drawing for an exhibition poster in Nice. Malo pulled a Léger drawing out from an obscure corner of the room and we duly admired it, though I have no memory of its content.

They gave us a brief tour of the rest of the building and back in the studio offered an aperitif, the consumption of which we shared with the wife of an architect who lived nearby who had come in to compare racing results with Monsieur Malo. In the course of the conversation he told us he had once many years ago lived in Max Jacob's room in the Bateau-Lavoir in Montmartre, which LM and I visited on the previous winter's trip to Paris. As we said "Adieu" he asked me where my Man Ray polo shirt was, but didn't seem to recognize the name Gustav Klimt. Altogether an interesting morning, of which perhaps there should have been many more. (The references are not as arcane as they may seem. In Washington the year before we moved to France I bought myself a bright red polo shirt with Man Ray's name emblazoned on the front with an image of his iconic metronome with an eye attached in black; LM got a mauve shirt with Gustav Klimt's signature scrawled across the front in white. We wore them quite often in France that year and, the village being so small, Malo had noticed.)

When we picked up our watercolor, which still hangs on our wall, we discovered that Malo was his *nom de peintre*; his real name being something long and complicated and unpronounceable. The waste of not having become more involved with the people in the village sooner became more painfully evident now that we could communicate easier. That is to say, LM could: At best I kibitz and throw in a few names of French figures, mostly artistic from the past (what else did I know?) that might have made me seem intelligent but still unable to hold a conversation except on a rather simple level; I had learned some, but not enough. It was sad and maddening that we had to leave just as things began to fall into place with the language.

The couple who worked at the *librairie* next door to Malo's shop, Nadine and Chook (presumably this was a French pronunciation of Chuck and the fellow's real name was Charles) could not quite figure out what we were doing in the village and why. Their goal in life was to get out as quickly as possible to the big city where things *happened*. The fly in this soup resulted from Chook's habit of driving their small delivery van too fast around the village's narrow lanes with his arm out the window holding a cigarette: the habit cost him his left arm when he took a corner too fast and scraped the side of the van and arm against a medieval stone wall, damaging the former and losing the latter. Thus condemned to remain in the village, barring some miracle in which they had long since ceased to believe, they did not ooze with friendliness and charm but took care of their customers with a sour smile and a murmured "bonjour". Chook taught himself to open a packet of cigarettes and light one with one hand, and continued to smoke, holding the lighted cancer stick in unholy deeply yellowed fingers. He also continued to drive the van, but probably did not smoke whilst doing so.

The village did not possess a laundromat per se; if one wished to do the wash and did not own a washing machine, one took the clothes and detergent to the public facility with running (cold) water and followed the timeless tradition of village life by soaping, rinsing and beating the textiles on the stone ledge of trough-like structure. Or one drove to the nearest pay for service laundromat, which for us stood on a back street (rue Paul Manivet) around the corner from the Place des Corps Saints, the square of the holy bodies mentioned in a previous chapter in reference to the episode of the liter-size beer mugs. As noted there, the immediate neighborhood housed several ladies of the night who washed their clothes in the same facility as we did. From time to time we exchanged a word or two about the weather and the increasing prices for soap and the coin-operated machines; they were no more or less friendly than any other French we met whilst living there. The bulk of the customers at this laundromat consisted of university students and those whose income did not allow them the luxury of an apartment complete with all the mod cons. In short, a cross section of the populace including the North Africans (Arabs) who lived in the neighborhood and kept to themselves. Washing clothes was always an adventure of one kind or another in Avignon. Once as I walked about doing errands in another part of town my path crossed that of one of the hookers who smiled politely and nodded with a murmured "*bonjour*". A first.

One of the village's residents with whom I never did say more than "*bonjour*" was the elderly man we called the Algerian, though it is entirely possible he had never been to Algeria in his 70 odd years on this earth. Nonetheless this is what we called him. He squinted when he saw someone he knew and always offered his hand with the smallest finger missing. His French was difficult to understand, but LM, much better than I able to converse in the language, stopped from time to time to chat with him about this and that. Apparently he viewed the passage of time somewhat differently than most of us; at least he could not remember how long he'd been in the village, though he did recall that he spent the years there working in the fields for various vineyards and he remembered being hungry during the war, but was not clear if this was the 1939-45 war or the Algerian war in the early 1960s the result of which was a huge influx of *pieds-noirs* (French who had lived for generations in Algeria which was a *département*, not a colony of the country).

A friendly fellow, always smiling and puffing away on a cigarette he rolled himself, always wearing the same clothes, a cap and overcoat even in mild weather, and was otherwise well dressed in rather soiled clothes from which a distinct odor emanated. He always had a warm *"bonjour"* for any one whose path he crossed during his strolls around the village. LM insisted he was a charming old man, though Mme Mourre thought he had a small leak in his attic, thus one could not hold a lengthy or complicated conversation with him. This of course was fine with us, at least with me, but I rarely spoke to him other than to say *"bonjour."* Like so much of what once was Tavel, the Algerian is no longer with us, but will be memorialized here.

●

Last Trips and Visitors

That September LM's long-time friend from St. Paul, Minnesota, Christine Watkins, flew into Marseille for a ten day visit, the last visitor of such length to our house. Part of those ten days we spent on a motor car trip along the Mediterranean shore. The aura of melancholy that hung over the last month of our sojourn increased in strength as we toured the shoreline towns in most of which the resorts, restaurants and casinos had already closed or would do so in a matter of days. The summer season had passed and businesses boarded up their establishments until the next April or May when life would return. In previous years along another shore on the other side of the ocean we had experienced a similar sense of closure and isolation when we spent a few days or a week in Bethany Beach, Delaware, or Ocean City, Maryland, during the Christmas/New Year holidays, where the city fathers even removed the parking meters from their now headless posts. The difference lay in the emotional response to the two situations: as the autumn began to seep into winter along the Mediterranean littoral we reacted to the chilled vistas of the sea and the shoreline streets empty of people with a sense of sadness and regret. When we left Bethany we had the comforting security blanket of knowing we would return before too long.

So with Christine we made our final long trip along the coast beginning in Menton where we stayed at the Hôtel Princess et Richmond facing the sea, a typical coastal tourist hotel with large rooms, a small balcony, filled with retirees on tour in loud clothes and voices. In future years we came back to Menton twice, once to celebrate my 50th birthday when we again stayed in that hotel. The weather along the coast that March of 1989 alternated between coolish and cooler with sunshine warming the air sufficiently to eat at midday outside watching the chattering women in fur coats strolling past somewhat younger women in bikini bottoms sunning themselves along the corniche. The third time we came to

Menton for lunch and ate sea urchins for the first time ever and wondered what the fuss was all about. The town is known for several things including the house (Isola Bella) in which Katherine Mansfield bravely fought the TB that would eventually kill her, the room in the town hall where marriages are performed which Jean Cocteau decorated and the Cocteau Museum in the old navy armory on the harbor. The latter is not very impressive consisting as it does of two badly lighted rooms full of pleasant things (tapestries, photographs, water colors, oils, drawings, etc.) related to the writer/film director and general cultural figure who flitted about the scene for much of the 20th century.

From Menton we drove in a gray drizzle through Monaco (and saw nothing to change our opinion of the place) and Nice (heavy traffic) to Antibes where we spent a couple of hours looking for a hotel still open with two rooms to rent. Many of the hotels and restaurants had already closed giving the region a provisional feeling, as if on the verge of something as yet undetermined, though that represented our impression, not the reality of the situation, like so many things then cyclical in nature: what closes will reopen in its time. After dinner we went to Juan-les-Pins, well-known in the interwar period as a resort populated by such figures as Picasso, Cole Porter, the Fitzgeralds, Robert Benchley, Sara and Gerald Murphy (though their home turf in the summers was Antibes), the Hemingways and thousands of French in search of thrills. On the terrace of the about to close for the season Hotel Juana an exhausted and indifferent waiter served us three glasses of cognac for 135 francs. It started to rain again so we moved into the spacious piano bar where we provided the only customers that night and I provided the piano music, competing with the screeching motor scooters driven by demented teenagers out past their bedtimes.

In Antibes we ate a late dinner one night at a nouvelle-nouvelle cuisine restaurant that should have known better and unfortunately tried the steak filet with raspberries, but the kidneys with bacon and mushrooms made up for the esoteric pairing. We did observe a couple of excellent crowded boules games played by locals with winter time on their hands in Juan-les-Pins on the informal court under the pines at the sea shore. Even the famous Juan-les-Pins casino crouched in the shadows, barely lit, ready to close the following day. The concierge shook his head and said, "Don't bother to go in. Only ten people there. Very boring. Try Cannes."

Antibes is the home of the former Grimaldi Palace which housed the Musée d'Antibes, better known today as (yet another) Picasso Museum because the Spanish artist and his French mistress, Françoise Gilot, spent the winter of 1946-47 at the nearby Golfe-Juan and used the second floor of the building as a studio. When he left to return to Paris he donated many of the works he'd done to the museum; indeed, to take several of them with him would have meant dismantling sections of the edifice itself because he painted directly on the walls. Over the years we have been there many times, drawn not only by the Picasso works and the gorgeous view of the harbor from the terrace but because, after an initial resistance, we became fascinated with the huge Nicolas de Staël mural-sized oil panting of a piano and bass with a startling mass of bright red background that hangs in the building's largest room. I am not entirely sure how the canvas ended up there but it fits, though at first sight it is like a punch in the eye. De Staël led a troubled life that he ended in Antibes not far from the museum along the corniche when he jumped from his studio's upstairs window to the stone road below at the age of 41 on March 16, 1955.

The road (Boulevard de Cimiez) up into the hills above Nice holds a fascination for art lovers in that the Chagall and the Matisse museums are located on its upward path toward the suburb of Cimiez. A series of light, brief rain falls made the day more interesting than it otherwise would have been and we spent hours in damp clothes, grateful it was still summer and not winter which required heavy clothing rather than shorts and suntops. Built in 1972, the Chagall museum may house the largest single collection of the artist's *oeuvre*, but the main attraction for me was the series of 17 canvases (and studies for them) depicting Biblical scenes. Their placement on the set-back walls illuminated by large windows that flood the spaces with that soft but firm Mediterranean light so diffused the paintings they seemed to glow and float with no connection to the mundane earth upon which the viewer stands. It is quite an experience; the famous southern light even continued to brighten the day throughout the rain shower, which did not disturb our lunch in the museum garden under an umbrella.

Further up the Boulevard de Cimiez lie the ruins of the Villa des Arènes built on the site of Cemenelum, an ancient Roman settlement within which sits the handsome 17th century building, now renovated into the Musée Matisse, the collections of which trace the course of the artist's development in painting, drawing, sculpture and tapestries. The curators have greatly improved the collection since our first visit that September, with the addition of several major works and the renovations have changed what was a shabby, dusty old building into an edifice appropriate for the art it houses. The adjacent archeological museum holds artifacts dug up from the site which is under permanent excavation efforts. The site itself is located near the cemetery where Matisse is buried and the massive pile which was the Hôtel Regina where the aging artist spent his last years.

We returned to the Fondation Maeght in St.-Paul de Vence to see the major Max Ernst retrospective. After spending an intense two hours in the exhibition, I finally "understood" Ernst's work, I "saw" it for the first time as the paintings unskinned my eyes. It came upon me as an epiphany as we stood on the terrace with the great Giacometti sculptures looking out over the valley toward the sea. This kind of sudden, non-verbal comprehension that briefly transcends the necessity to communicate what one has learned, a flash of deep, penetrating understanding of something or someone, occurs rarely in one's lifetime; it is a phenomenon to be cherished and nurtured. If the great goddess Fortuna deigns to smile upon one after such an experience the mind can continue to expand what the soul has learned through some perhaps atavistic intuitive epistemological process that one finds difficult to describe but not hard to embrace.

We ended the Riviera sojourn with a visit to the Léger museum in Biot, a building that sits atop a small hill surrounded by pine trees and landscaped grass upon which large blocks of mosaics representing some of his paintings are scattered. One massive ceramic sculpture dominates the lower front area and the wildly colorful frieze across the front of the building adds to the incongruity of the site. The building is a marvelous construction designed to use all the available natural light – and it is a shame it doesn't contain a more appealing collection of his work: Léger's things lose their attraction fairly quickly, especially his later works. Too much of it disorients and one rebels against the apparent simplicity in design, color and idea. The statement "work should be ennobling but is degrading" is arguable but provocative. The statement "work is ennobling and beautiful" is plainly naïve and reactionary. Léger painted the latter. The collection is heavily dominated by the later work, especially ceramics which all begin to blend together halfway through the barn-like room. At the time of our visit the collection contained only a scant handful of the wondrous Cubist works. The older he became the larger his works grew, and that is unfortunate. We judged the lunch in the museum's café to be eminently satisfactory.

Closer to home we ate a picnic lunch one day beside the château originally built in the 16th century by the barons of Castille along the road from Uzès to the Pont du Gard in Argilliers, unfortunately not open to the public. The eclectic older Italianate architectural styles (it was remodeled in the 18th century) stand in sharp contrast to the amazing collection of Cubist and other modernist art that once graced its walls when the English collector and art critic-historian Douglas Cooper owned and lived in the palatial but not extravagant residence from 1950 to 1974 when he left after the infamous theft of many of the smaller paintings and drawings from his collection, most in the styles of Cubism, which have never been located.[55]

In September of 1983 a small old man with one wooden leg hobbled over to the field where we sat on a blanket next to the residence, informed us his father had once owned the property (probably not so much true as wished), and regaled us for a while (with LM translating) with stories about Picasso, Braque, Cocteau, Nicholas de Staël and various personalities from the art world coming and going in large chauffeur-driven limousines, roaring with laughter and quaffing bottles of very expensive champagne. How many of the stories contained as much truth as the one about his father owning the château we'll never know, but those people did come and go at the place during Cooper's residence there; that much we do know.

Before she returned to the USA, we took Christine to all the usual points of interest near our house and enjoyed

---

[55] For a gracefully written and gossipy depiction of Cooper's sojourn in the Château de Castille, see the memoir by his then partner, John Richardson, *The Sorcerer's Apprentice. Picasso, Provence and Douglas Cooper* (New York, 1999), 84ff. Richardson is also the author (with Marilyn McCully) of the multi-volume biography of Picasso, three volumes of which have been published.

an unexpected memorable meal one evening in an old mansion transformed into an elegant restaurant, the Hostellerie de Varenne in Sauveterre's Château de Varenne, about ten kilometers north of Tavel. While I can no longer reconstruct the meal and its wines in the small yellow room in which we were the only guests, I vividly recall discussing the possibilities for dessert, during which I firmly stated that I avoided such sweet things as often as possible. Despite this avowal, LM and Christine ordered a platter of assorted meal-enders, which the waiter delivered in the middle of such an intense conversation about some obscure point of Samoan musical history that we barely registered the appearance of the sugary delicacies. A moment or so later after the question had been pummeled into a sort of answer we looked at the platter: LM and Christine had barely started but it was empty. We ordered a second helping for them and they have not allowed me to forget this exercise in sophistry.

We deemed it appropriate that one of our last visitors should have been one of our first, neatly closing the circle. Thus Andrea Anderson's flying visit in early September fit into the annual cycle of Nature's *recorso* so fitting for residents of a small village in the country where people are closer to the earth and its cycle of departure and return. We found it fitting to go with her to the various sites we'd gone to so often during our time in Tavel, including to Marseille for bouillabaisse and the purchase of wooden handled forks that we continue to use today.

The last of our visitors came in October for a brief but intense stay: Claudia Daly and Stanley Kusunoki breezed in from Paris for several days of sightseeing and conversation during which time we may not have solved the world's, or our own, problems, but spent considerable time and energy attempting to do so. Claudia who worked as a free-lance producer-writer of off-beat programs dealing with endangered cultures and the problems of children in the industrial and pre-industrial societies for public radio, then was manager of the KLSE public radio station in Rochester, Minnesota; at the time, Stan wrote reams of poetry, too little of it ever published, wrote an occasional arts article for the *Rochester Post-Bulletin* and managed the local coffee and tea shop; later he worked in and around the folky music world in Minnesota and West Virginia – we never lacked subjects with which to wrestle.

We took them to the market in the Places aux Herbes at Uzès and ate a pick-up lunch at the city wall overlooking the Alzon Valley. Afterward we walked around the center of the town absorbing its eclectic and well-preserved architecture along the narrow streets that suddenly open into larger and smaller squares. Years after this we came to know the town fairly well because we often visited our friends Nicole and Richard Stiel, whom we met through Denis Constancias, LM's former French teacher from CELA. One year in particular stands out in the memory because in a narrow, no longer extant bookstore I found several Signet paperback books from the late 1940s and early 1950s which I collect because they remind me of my youth when they cost 25 cents.

How these volumes found their way to this particular book shop deep in the Gard is a subject of speculation; too bad we did not ask the shopkeeper about it.

Uzès played an unusual role in the history of French literature. In 1661, the family of Jean Racine (1639-1699), horrified at the thought of their son becoming part of the theater world in Paris, sent the 22-year old to his uncle, the vicar-general of Uzès, to convince him to take holy orders and forget about his theatrical career and the shame to the family that would be the result. After more that a year with his uncle and his financial blandishments, Racine left the duchy to return to Paris: the Church lost a potentially great cleric, but the French nation gained its greatest classical dramatist. The 20th century writer and Nobel Literature prize winner, André Gide (1869-1951), faced no such problem, though he too struggled with the dichotomy between the desires of the flesh and the longings of the soul. His father, the eminent lawyer Paul Gide and his uncle, the famous economist Charles Gide, were both born in Uzès and André spent many holidays throughout his life in the town and surrounding countryside. We did not know this when Claudia and Stan ate lunch with us at the Uzès wall that warm October day in 1983.

After Christine returned to the USA, LM and I paid a last visit to the Stes.-Maries-de-la-Mer that month to witness the blessing of the sea and the celebration of the saints. We arrived around noon and rented a room in the same hotel we'd stayed in the previous October. The low temperature along the shore chilled the air and rain threatened as we walked around the grayish town to a restaurant for lunch of grilled sardines, roast chicken, *frites* and a salad with a Côte de Provence rosé. While we ate the threat of rain finally realized itself. There is a certain feeling of almost sanctimonious comfort in sitting behind a glass wall in a warm, dry place eating fine food, drinking a good wine and watching a chilly gray rain fall outside. The comfort leaves when one scurries through the streets in the rain to the café next to the fortified church where the saints are housed, but returns again, if in a milder form, when one imbibes a *marc du pays* and an *espresso fort* and one's clothes are not too damp. Three local Gypsy women came in for coffee and red wine, carefully counting their change to pay, shaking hands with some of the regulars.

Shortly after 3:00 p.m. we decided to look at the church's interior and remained for the service during which the relic box is lowered to the altar with much chanting in praise of the glories of the Maries. The light was dim and the smoke from the many cheap candles lit in honor of the saints filled the air making it difficult to breathe freely. We joined the queue to walk past the box and touch it for luck. We left the kissing of it to others in the crowd more intense about the spiritual significance of the event than we could bring ourselves to be. Many more tourists than the previous year jammed into the church, perhaps because they had not heard about the weather, and locals, many of whom dressed in the colorful and dark costumes of the region, added to the sardine can effect. The rain had stopped when we stumbled out of the church and breathed deeply of the chilled damp autumn air, grateful for the experience of course, but wondering how Manitas de Plata and his group could have whipped up so much energy in that enfeebling place when they recorded those wild and beautiful flamenco-blues songs many years before.

After a nap we went down to the Brûleur de Loups, less ignorant than the previous year so we avoided making the mistake with the over-priced lobster we'd made then. This time we ate the 102 franc menu of titillating nouvelle cuisine: the fish came with a surprisingly light lemon-cream sauce in which we reveled and thoroughly enjoyed the bottle of Cassis blanc de blanc and our own conversation. A small amount of Calvados before bed in the room did not result in the usual hangover the following morning, when a much welcomed bright sunlight greeted us.

We had time before the convocation and procession to the beach to visit the small Camargue museum opened by Baroncelli in 1942 when the region remained theoretically under the governance of the Vichy regime. Not a propitious time to open a museum. Formerly the *mairie*, the circular building sits in the middle of the old village; from the roof one can see the surrounding land and seascapes, except where the height of the church blocks the view. Most of the exhibits then consisted of stuffed birds of local origin, but there were also many copies of ancient and more recent documents, photographs, books, prints of the paintings and drawings Van Gogh made of the village and its beach. The museum did not neglect art works by local artists of lesser talent and genius, some of them pleasant enough to look at, such as the woodcuts by Hermann-Paul.

We marched in the procession with the *gardiens*, musicians, priests, local color, the tourists and the saints in their shabby little blue boat to the shore and the blessing of the sea. The ceremony is always the same and, as noted above, I've described it in detail elsewhere. At lunch in a noisy bistro one of the Gypsy women attempted to pin a medallion on my sweater and muttered grave imprecations when I refused. However, she had been muttering before she approached us so I thought I had a chance to escape whatever curse she had heaped upon my innocent head. Sometimes I wonder if I actually did.

The drive back to Tavel disturbed me for many days and nights because I did not at all expect what we saw. A drive through the Camargue is usually a pleasant enough experience: the cowboys herding the cattle, the thatched roof farm buildings (so different from the Provençal red-ochre tiles), the slightly rolling countryside into which at intervals are stuck resorts in the same style for tourists who desire to ride horses around the landscape. At one point however this ends and one finds oneself in the strange, lost region of Salin-de-Giraud, a town owned by Belgian and French desalinization companies in which everything is built on the principle of the square, the place is dominated by angles of sad ugliness. The rows and rows of workers' tenements, potted streets, monochrome clothing on the pale suspicious inhabitants reminded me of nothing so much as the polluted, gray industrial towns in East Germany. I recalled the same colorless drabness of the streets and buildings in Godard's dystopia, *Alphaville*; a twisted discomforting experience so out of place in "our" Provence where such nightmare visions have no space or being.

Sometimes it becomes impossible to escape the accoutrements of the late 20th century. After the disenchantment of this industrial intrusion into the bucolic landscape of the Camargue we boarded the Bac ferry across the Rhône to a main highway to Arles and drove along the west side of the river past the ill-formed giant Electricité de France (EDF) power plant that loomed over the village close to the shore. As we neared Tavel we attempted to drive up to the perched village of old Les Angles, but the road had been washed out. This and Fort Saint-André on the west side of the river are the two sites we had to leave until a future visit, something we seem to do with some frequency in places we love. Until today we have not been to either of them, always leaving something new to do for another trip.

●

The matter of the cats remained with us until the end. Occasionally we could not keep track of their identities: Baudelaire (sometimes known as Gray Cat) and Shy Cat (sometimes known as Verlaine, sometimes Rimbaud depending upon one's mood and disposition) closely resembled one another in their scruffy grayness. Mme Mourre and Micheline also cared for two or three cats other than the territorial albino Bébé. Finette attacked Baudelaire and Shy Cat whenever possible and the other two or three whenever, blinded with doggy aggression and rage, she failed to identify them correctly, a form of spoiled terrier "shoot first and ask questions later, if at all".

Much against our better judgment, we began to feed Baudelaire toward the end of July: he appeared suddenly on the terrace at the kitchen door, thin and scruffy and made mild noises that LM, a previous kitty owner, thought signified hunger. What the hell, one more animal could hardly matter in what we'd come to think of as a quasi-farm house environment, despite the distinct possibility that it served as a food supply for dozens if not hundreds of fleas which would add another force to the attacks upon the sorely tried flesh of the summer. Well, we thought, we'll see to it that it remains on the terrace where we'll lay down a water dish and dinner bowl. The thought that, as opposed to dogs, cats' digestive systems could not easily deal with human food probably determined that we added cat food to the weekly shopping list. This may not have been the smartest move we made in Tavel, but it had its happy as well as annoying consequences. Micheline thought former tenants had owned the cat, but couldn't locate it when they departed so left it to its own devices. Perhaps. We wondered where it had been all winter and spring, a question that shall forever remain a mystery.

About a fortnight after Baudelaire's first appearance on the terrace a second gray cat appeared with him begging to be fed, a desire we of course accommodated; in for a penny, in for a pound I always say. As we watched the two of them eat we mulled the matter of a name: Mallarmé? Valéry? Eluard? Georges? Almost identical to Baudelaire in physical appearance except rather larger (or, as LM suggested, smaller assuming the larger one was in fact Baudelaire, a matter we never resolved, but in the end it didn't matter): battered, bitten and nicked ears, suspicious yellow eyes, scruffy fur and chewed up tail, they bit themselves furiously – fleas, what else? Curious; perhaps they were siblings.

Slowly we learned to distinguish between the individual characteristics of the two: Baudelaire had a smaller head, un-nicked ears and was more aggressive than the other who we mundanely and unimaginatively named Shy Cat because of his passive, not to say lethargic behavior. He (or she) also ate at a slower pace than Baudelaire who inhaled his food and hung around for more. Mme Mourre claimed they ganged up on Bébé but we found this difficult to credit; we certainly never saw any such thing. True, sometimes in the night terrible noisy confrontations broke out in the courtyard or on the roof, but who could identify the participating belligerents? Perhaps Mme Mourre's other cats, including poor Mimi, whose jaw carbuncle seemed to increase in size every day, joined in the fray.

Excerpt from the journal entry on the last day of August: "Nothing to be done. Such is life in the countryside. Animal stories, crossword puzzles, obnoxious youths on stinking loud motorbikes, and split tomatoes." Only an urban cowboy could have written such phrases.

The gray cats came and went according to their own schedule, showing up for meals and disappearing into whatever cat neighborhood attracted them at any given time of day, or night for that matter since, we came to believe, they occasionally came into the house whilst we slept, though not as often as Bébé. From time to time we found a small puddle of cat pee on the floor in the kitchen or the living room. We thought this only happened on nights when Mme Mourre or Micheline locked the albino cat in some obscure corner of the garages so we couldn't blame him (or her) for that socially unacceptable act. In the morning the two cats slept peacefully on the terrace, one in a lounge chair, innocent as lambs.

Not that Bébé remained entirely innocent of similar transgressions, no indeed. The albino cat belonged to that species of feline that somehow retained the atavistic territory gene of its ancient ancestors in the wilds of Africa, whence much of animal life evolved. The cat took its time about staking out the borders, rather porous and moveable limits we thought, and did not begin to mark its territory until the later summer of that year. Which is to say, the kitty began pissing in various locations in the house including empty cartons, the space next to the newspapers on the floor, a picnic basket, and once, *horribile dictu*, the ungrateful wretch peed in a guest's hand bag. Sorry about that, Claudia. When the albino cat first began peeing in the house we chased him out whenever he attempted to gain access to our part of the building; after all, we didn't pee near or in his bedding. This did not last, alas, because the temperatures required that we keep the windows, unscreened, open for fresh air and a breeze; Bébé had no trouble slipping into the interior to do his stuff, and he was so cute with his pink eyes and bright red collar. And who, before going to bed, could throw the little ball of whiteness out of the living room chair where it slept so peacefully, even if one knew there'd be a puddle on the floor? *So it wasn't the gray cats at all.*

In contrast to Finette, who never seemed bereft of energy for very long, in late August Bébé appeared to have lost all his élan vital. He slept most of the day and half the night on our bed or on the cement terrace. A wild nocturnal existence, unimaginable to us, demanding much daytime rest? Another Provençal mystery. On an occasional night we did not have to imagine a wild existence: around 3:00 o'clock an intense battle of cats exploded outside our bedroom window. Spitting, hissing and howling for a full three minutes, until one side gave way and the combatants scampered away, away across the terrace and into the darkness. Naturally, the battle noises woke the hysterical mutt penned in below which yammered for a further 30 minutes, then flopped down exhausted to rest up for the morning's whirlwind of spastic, speedy, spontaneous sound and clamorous, catastrophic cacophony; in short, a normal Finette day. The note in the journal reads, "Ah, country life." And so it was.

Controlling Bébé became ever more difficult as we neared the end of our time in Provence. He began to come into the kitchen and yowl, we assumed for something to eat. At one point he absconded with a piece of Roswitha's apricot tart left over from the previous evening just as I entered the kitchen to make sure he was not up to some mischief. Later that day he gave LM a hard time whilst she washed the dishes. Perhaps he considered being fed as part of his territorial imperative vis-à-vis the gray cats, marking his space in a manner other than pissing in the corners. The gray cats hung around whining most of the following day and Bébé showed up at dinner time, headed directly for the garbage pail and yowled when we closed the door to the space under the sink where the bag was stored. After dinner he slunk back into the kitchen and loudly made his desire for entrance to the garbage known. Perhaps there was something under the sink we were unaware of? The cat was distinctly becoming a nuisance. LM once owned a cat but her behavior with these kitties did not indicate previous experience in the field of cat control. And I'd never owned a pet other than goldfish in my life.

The vicissitudes of the last days: October 13 journal excerpt:

> Lost the sun at the end of the day as we walked down (or up) the rue Freddy Mistral to find the secret office where one pays for garbage collection. Gray wind whooshed through the village, but the post mistress smiled on our small pile of packages and letters. Becoming accustomed to us. The hardware store owner asked, as I bought a last jug of gas for the stove, if we'd stay the winter. Seemed disappointed when I said we're leaving in three weeks. The woman in the *Librairie*, however, only wants to know the exact dimensions of the boxes we asked if she had to spare. The wind has begun to howl. AC [albino cat: Bébé] appears at the window and whines to be let in but we remain hard of

heart while Mme Mourre calls "Bambino!" into the wind. I wonder if the beast ever listens to her. Occasionally he wanders forlornly through our rooms, always ready to run away, fear eats his soul, alas. Mme Mourre says it's because she had him "fixed" – consequently she won't have Mimi done or have the poor creature's tumor on the chin removed. Might alter the cat's character. What's Shy Cat's excuse? Probably been shot at too often. The sound of guns is heard daily here now that hunting season has begun. What can possibly be left to shoot? A few small birds with no defense. Who of us has a defense against the gun? Morbid thoughts.

When the rains came and the temperature dropped that autumn we often wondered, where *do* cats go at night – especially when the lightning slashes the sky and the rains distorts the vision out of the glass windows? Cold and wet, tired no doubt, they must be convinced outdoor cats.

> But when hunger got the best of them
> they appeared as sure as your next beer,
> but it's alright now, because we're here.

The bit of doggerel comes from the journal; I wouldn't think of writing something so simple these days, but the final line does accurately express our feeling about the place. And, yes, after we had gone we did miss the cats, though not the dog.

•

Mme Mourre saw her first paper dollar bill on October 16. When LM said that French paper money was more colorful and attractive, Mme Mourre commented, *"Mais pas beaucoup de valeur."*

•

As the time neared our travels around the region took on a new intensity and length as we spent the last days attempting to cram as much of the experience into the remaining hours as possible. For example the 15th of October was a glorious day of the type one doesn't want to end but is happy when it's over because one is tired from all the gloriousness. Early that morning the fog crept across the vineyards and cemetery up to the terrace like an advancing army. Not since we'd arrived in Tavel had it been so thick and massed. On the road near Rochefort-du-Gard it began to dissipate and by the time we reached Nîmes the day turned blue and gold in its clarity. We visited the Jacqueline Picasso photography exhibition in the gallery under the great wall of the arena, some of them banal, some quite funny, after which we made some of our own photographs. Dropping the camera some weeks previously seemed to have damaged the focus mechanism, though LM claimed it worked fine when she used it. At the Centre Anglaise we bought an updated version of Roland Penrose's Picasso biography,

404

an example of why some biographies should not be written by people who knew the biographee.

For reasons no longer fathomable we drove to Les Baux, a fair distance of approximately 44 kilometers from Nîmes, to buy some gifts to take with us to Washington and eat lunch of white wine, *pommes frites* and chicken livers on a bed of lettuce drizzled with a warm vinaigrette in the October sun. That afternoon we finally saw the Pavillion de la Reine Jeanne (in the garden of the Gendarmarie station!) and the Val d'Enfer with its oddly shaped natural sculptured cliffs and abysses (reminiscent of some of Max Ernst's forms of fright and wonder). On a small road outside Paradou we stopped and walked among the olive trees along the ruins of an aqueduct and stone mill from Roman times, which opens in a cut through the hill to a vast panorama of the lush green-beige countryside.

From there we drove a short distance to Daudet's windmill up on a hillside overlooking a valley complete with a museum in the ground floor of the structure in which the poet evidently lived for a brief period. Later I mailed the curator one of my watercolors appropriately named "Daudet's Windmill" (though it did not matter since the piece was/is entirely abstract) to be added to the other artifacts stapled to the walls of the museum. On a visit several years later we found no evidence that it had ever been put up at all.

Obliquely across the road from the windmill rest the ruins of the Abbaye de Montmajour through which one can walk and climb wondering why local legend paints the monks that formerly inhabited the place in the 17th century as rather nasty fellows. Back across the road we enjoyed a cold drink in a scruffy garden apparently attached to the windmill. Thus we completed the trip in which the car and the weather performed admirably. Finette did not perform so: when we arrive back at the house the mutt was yipping hysterically at a cornered gray cat on the terrace. We rescued the cat and made chili for supper.

Journal, October 19:

Raymond Aron died yesterday and the nightly news devoted ten minues to his life. Can't imagine the equivalent happening in the USA. Who would be Aron there?

Journal entry, October 31:

Veritable mistral roaring across the terrace. Pale sun, cold air. Snow in the Pyrennees already. Hotel reservations for Paris confirmed. Meal at La Caleche nothing fantastic, but good, filling and tasty. Boudin (blood sausage) surprisingly bland but nice with cooked apples.
    The strength and intensity of the wind today is frightening. The radio flickers on and off as the wind batters the power lines. The living room overlooking the terrace and the vineyards is warm because the sun shines through the window. One begins to long for summer when winter hasn't yet started.

●

We also required heat in the cold winter weeks, something we had only erratically last winter, and in mid-October the electrician on one of many visits informed us that the furnace had not been turned on correctly all last winter, consequently we consumed a large amount of expensive heating oil for very little result. Had the bloody thing been turned on correctly we would have been warm as toast. *Tant pis*, I suppose.

●

We walked through panicky moments of indecision in the middle of packing up the last of the books to be stored there for our return. The grill had to be cleaned and put back into its original box. LM's tutor Sylvie would get the TV and buy the car (knowing about its history). And what of the cats? What will they do when we're gone? (This neatly avoids the question, "What will *we* do when we're gone?") We tried to organize everything so there'll be no last minute panic, but there would be, of course. Perhaps Paris wouldn't be too cold.

●

We rarely asked ourselves why we moved abroad to live, beyond answering the superficial questions occasionally asked by friends. Actually, very few people asked at all. They assumed they knew. After all, doesn't everyone want to live in some foreign spot, however briefly?

Well, no, they don't really, although most say they would if only they had the opportunity to do so without giving up anything important at home (car, job, house, regulated existence in a mastered language, and so on). A two-week holiday abroad is usually enough for most people. But they tend to "understand" why someone else would do it and accept this unquestioningly with unspoken envy. We, too, partook of this attitude and thus did not ask ourselves in any depth the question "why?" What would we have answered? These thoughts occurred as we neared the end of our sojourn in the Midi.

●

The journal entry for October 5 reflects the frustrating aura of sadness and our attempts to, if not repress it, at least squeeze some measure of enjoyment and satisfaction out of the last month in Tavel.

> Letter from Jim. We're more than welcome in "Tavel West". Not unexpected but nice to have confirmed in such a funny and hearty way. Sent off five boxes today via shipment office in Avignon. The usual formalities with customs papers, etc. Over 800 francs. Mounted a number of smaller water colors on variously hued paper. Reinforces my opinion that they look better, more "serious", when matted, if not framed. Am beginning to think seriously about trying to arrange a show in some gallery to make some money with the stuff. Not totally out of the question but surely improbable. Would like to know what the René Char

museum is doing with the painting. Waste basket more than likely. No revisions of R. today but thought about it. Attempting to do final correspondence with numerous folk. Takes time. Everything is begrudged at the moment that doesn't directly concern the two of us and my work. To say the situation is wrenching doesn't come near to describing the trauma of it. One is, of course, detached and accepting of the Fates' decisions in public, but one knows what melancholy is. Perhaps because there's time to consider it and, more importantly, this is where we wish to live. In the end it is that simple. But we've decided not to belabor the point in public. This is something the two of us must do; in silence and with as much cunning as we have: to arrange a return as soon as possible without blabbering like lost sheep about what we'd *like* to do whilst doing something else.

●

It was perhaps appropriate that the end turned into a rather unpleasant, uncomfortable dream-like experience. The last two days in Tavel I spent in bed with a horrible flu, forced to cancel a farewell lunch with the Fidlers in Roussillon. We would not see them again for two or three years. So the departure from Provence was something of a dying fall. We traveled by train to Paris, me in a mental fog from the medications, snuffling constantly with a runny nose, depressed with a clogged head and difficulty in breathing, making myself a burden to those unfortunate enough to be seated near me. Poor

LM. Too much nasal spray, I was convinced, rotted away the nose membranes, but I had to breathe, didn't I? We spent two foggy days in Paris before taking the train to Luxembourg whence we were to fly via Iceland to Baltimore-Washington International Airport on Icelandic Airlines, then one of the least expensive regularly scheduled airlines across the Atlantic. (We forgot a tube full of posters at the Grand Hôtel des Étrangers, but when LM telephoned later the manager said they would hold it for our return, though we had no idea at the time when that might be. In September of the following year when in Paris on business we stopped by to ask about it, not expecting a positive answer, the concierge pulled it from the back of a closet and handed it to us. We were saddened when a large corporate chain bought the place and "modernized" it into a price range above our means.)

From Luxembourg no planes flew out of the airport that day or night. Heavy fog forced us to be bussed to Köln on a three-hour journey down dark side roads whence the flight eventually took off. After one and a half hours at Reykjavik airport, two hours in Chicago where we were surprised at the swiftness with which we cleared customs, finally, ten hours late, exhausted and sad, we landed at Baltimore-Washington International after 30 hours on the move. Our life in Provence over, at least for the nonce (but for how long?), Moira and Jim drove us to Washington and a new set of experiences, as they had driven us to that airport 14 months earlier. *Le cercle refermé.*

Legacy 27 October 1983

Wind strewn leaves
Orange-brown and yellow
Patterns in the mind
Autumn of my years.

Envoi

The flu continued through the first weeks of our return to a chilled, rainy Washington. Organizing our lives in the new circumstances proved not impossible but for some time we felt disenchanted and out of sorts before the demands and pressures of living took us further and further away from Tavel and our life there.

Three months after we returned a not too skillful urologist surgeon dug into my left side and removed a large kidney stone, leaving a six inch scar but relieving me of considerable pain and discomfort. The headaches I still have with me.

What of the people we knew that year? Some have died: Mme Mourre, Eugène Fidler, Karlheinz Schwaner, Mme Barré, Raoul Lebel (died in 2006 at the age of 99 on Réunion) and Andreas Meyer; some have disappeared from our knowledge: Karin, Sylvie, Mary, Roswitha; and some we still see from time to time in Europe and in the States: Denis Constancias, now married to Dominique and the father or two teenagers; Edith and Natacha Fidler, Sylvette and Jean-Marie Berruyer (Mme Mourre's daughter and son-in-law) and their children; Wolfgang and Ute Benz whose children are now at university in Berlin; Michael Fichter and his daughter Sarah (and her mother Ilse) and his second wife Doris and her daughter Annika; Heiner Adamsen; Nancy Worssum and Bill Seach; my longest term friends Steve Goodell and Tom

Quigley; Jean and Blair Williams with whom this memoir has fortunately brought us together again after two decades; Claudia and Stanley; Christine Watkins; Andrea Anderson; Jim and Moira (and their daughter Nina, now in high school); Kate, Marty, Abigail (recently married to TC Maslin) and the youngest daughter Bethany, and Marty's niece Erin, now married to Jeff Sobecks, and the mother of three.

It is now 25 years later and we have arranged to return to Avignon and environs almost every year to recharge our memories and visit friends, adding new memories to the already bulging storeroom of our minds. Inevitably there remain the vivid images, sometimes fragmented, sometimes in a coherent narrative, of our time in Tavel, an erratic but crystal clear structure appropriately and inevitably reflected in this memoir.